Buried Indians

WISCONSIN LAND AND LIFE

ARNOLD ALANEN
Series Editor

Buried Indians

Digging Up the Past in a Midwestern Town

Laurie Hovell McMillin

The University of Wisconsin Press

The University of Wisconsin Press
1930 Monroe Street
Madison, Wisconsin 53711

www.wisc.edu/wisconsinpress/

3 Henrietta Street
London WC2E 8LU, England

1   3   5   4   2

Printed in the United States of America

Library of Congress Cataloging-in-Publication Data
McMillin, Laurie Hovell, 1962–
Buried Indians : digging up the past in a midwestern town /
Laurie Hovell McMillin.
p.   cm. — (Wisconsin land and life)
Includes bibliographical references and index.
ISBN-13: 978-0-299-21680-1 (cloth: alk. paper)
ISBN-13: 978-0-299-21684-9 (pbk.: alk. paper)
1. Mound-builders — Wisconsin — Trempealeau.
2. Indians of North America — Wisconsin — Trempealeau — Antiquities.
3. Excavations (Archaeology) — Wisconsin — Trempealeau.
4. Geographical perception — Wisconsin — Trempealeau.
5. Social perception — Wisconsin — Trempealeau.
6. Trempealeau (Wis.) — Antiquities.
7. Trempealeau (Wis.) — History — Sources.
I. Title.   II. Series.
E78.W6M35   2006
977.5′49 — dc22   2005032882

For my mother,
LAURENA VIOLA BOCKENHAUER HOVELL

In memory of my father,
ROBERT RAY HOVELL SR.

And once again for
TRACY SCOTT MCMILLIN

The intimate life of the community is best told in the personal stories of its citizens.

Eben Douglas Pierce, *History of Trempealeau County* (1917)

Contents

Contents

Illustrations

Acknowledgments

Many people have helped me pull this book together. John Ebersold inspired and helped me from start to finish. Rollie Rodell gave generously of his expertise and time. William Green offered his knowledge and enthusiasm. Anna R. Funmaker and the late Harold Wilber both kindly consented to be part of this book. Any errors that persist despite all the able help offered by others are mine.

Members of my extended family have been wonderful throughout the writing of this book, even when they didn't always agree with me: my mother, Laurena Viola Bockenhauer Hovell, provided comfort and transport, and undertook detective work; Robert Ray Hovell Jr. checked my facts, offered information, and kept me on my toes; Debra Sacia was always interested and ready to go exploring, and Pamela Grover helped make contacts, supported me in many ways, and fought the good fight. My late father, Robert Ray Hovell Sr., provided much of the inspiration for this book. I also want to thank Steve Grover, Ellen Hovell, Larry Sacia Sr., Larry Sacia Jr., and Lynn Sacia. I hope my family sees that this story is about process: you are all heroes by the end.

Kent and Donna Drugan lent me their photos of the McKern excavations of the 1920s and offered invaluable assistance; other family members who helped and encouraged me include Mike Drugan, Lu Ebersold, Russ Gilbertson, Roxanne and Ken Harris, Clyde and Barb Hovell, Kenny Hovell, Stan Hovell, and Tari Wood. A number of other relatives offered stories and insights.

I am extremely grateful to the members of my research group at Oberlin College—Kathie Linehan, Paula Richman, and Sandy Zagarell—for helping me to imagine and carry out this project.

Many people in the greater Trempealeau area gave of their knowledge and time: David Bratberg, Dale Ebersold, Arild Engelien, Chuck Forster, Evelyn Grover, Rev. Jerry Hanson, Tom Hunter, Karl Lettner, Phil Palzkill, Barney Stephan, Eugene Steffes, and the parishioners of Mount Calvary Lutheran Church. A couple of key people prefer to remain unnamed; I am grateful to them nonetheless.

Peter Fritzell planted the seed for this project long ago with his lectures on American literature; his genius and example continue to inspire me. James S. Duncan offered me the intellectual wherewithal to think about place. At Lawrence University, Mark Dintenfass and Jack Stanley also encouraged me in my efforts to write about home. For that I am still grateful.

Many others assisted me along the way. They include Robert Birmingham, Ernie Boszhardt, Lance Michael Foster, Jim Gallagher, Paul Gardner, Richard Grounds, Chloris Lowe, and Nancy Lurie. Jessica Grim and Joanne Dobson made valuable comments on the manuscript. Albert Borroni, Jan Cooper, Pat Day, Larry Dolan, Peter Dominguez, Peter Goldsmith, Linda Grimm, Kerry Langan, Steve List, Ed Miller, Jeff Pence, Len Podis, Skip Schuckmann, Eric Stewart, Anne Trubek, and Linda Weintraub provided ideas and encouragement. Judy Gautsch of the Galesville Public Library and the reference librarians at Oberlin College offered able assistance. Kevin Brown made the drawing of Nicholls Mound, and Linda Pardee created the mound graphics and the map of the area. I am grateful to Ellie Boyer, Gayle Boyer, Kirk Ormand, and Marilyn Ellingsworth for the back cover photo. Thanks also go to Raphael Kadushin, Sheila Moermond, the staff at the University of Wisconsin Press, and Polly Kummel for their acumen and support. A grant-in-aid and the James and Anne Ford Fellowship, both from Oberlin College, provided invaluable research support.

My deepest thanks go to my sons, Liam and Jack McMillin, for their patience and jubilance, and to my husband, Tracy Scott McMillin, for believing in the book from the start, for his unflagging support all through, for his sharp eye, and his love.

Introduction

The Mississippi river town of Trempealeau, Wisconsin, is home to a number of significant Native American earthworks: two-thousand-year-old Hopewell mounds, effigy mounds in the shape of birds and deer, burial mounds, and some 950-year-old platform mounds. While many of the predominantly white residents of the town think of the bluff remnant called Trempealeau Mountain (thought to be sacred to Indians) and some Indian burial mounds as important monuments, until recently most people were not even aware that the platform mounds existed. These three earthen mounds stand on brush-covered Little Bluff, just above Main Street; archaeologists say that they were used long ago for sun worship and other ceremonies by people they call the Middle Mississippians. (Their names for themselves seem to have been lost.) In the 1990s, when some archaeologists brought these mounds to the attention of residents, many did not want to believe the mounds were real. A local plumber said, "We used to play cowboys and Indians up there—there's nothing up there." When I asked my uncle Clyde about them, he smirked and replied, "Yeah, we heard about those mounds. Harold Wilber told us his dad and brother built them with a Cat"—a Caterpillar, an earth-mover. When I asked Wilber about the mounds, the local business-man and distant relative of mine did not actually claim such a thing; instead, he wanted to sink twenty auger holes into the mounds to look for proof of their authenticity. "I don't believe in the platform mounds," he told me. When I asked my farmer father about the mounds on Little Bluff, he said, "If there was anything up there, we would've known about it."

These men were eager to deny the possibility that a portion of local land at the center of town might be the home of something they knew nothing about and never dreamed of.

When I asked Anna Funmaker, a Ho-Chunk woman, what she thought about the mounds, she did not have much to say. She had done extensive research on the Ho-Chunk/Winnebago past, and she believed that the effigy and burial mounds in the area were all made by her people. But the platform mounds seemed to her to be the construction of some other native group, as they were unlike the other earthworks. Those things aside, she expressed a view of the land that differed markedly from that of the farmers and the plumber and other digging men who denied the mounds' existence. For her, the land was marked by the bones of her ancestors and bore proof of the violence of white settlement: "I have a theory about the state of Wisconsin: it's a huge burial grounds."

This book takes shape in the gap between those two views—the gap between the denial of Native American presence and the assertion of its long history and violent destruction. In this book I struggle to account for the histories, stories, memories, and amnesias that help to produce diverse views of the land around Trempealeau, particularly as these differences are manifested in controversies about preservation of the platform mounds but also as they are suggested in the culture of farming, the local use of Indian mascots, and residents' images of Indians.

One could write a story that detailed the platform mound controversy, and in some senses I do. But to me the controversy is not the whole story. As I see it, what people believe about the platform mounds and other archaeological sites in the area is connected to their sense of place even as it connects to their attitudes about Native Americans and Native American history. Further, what people—white, Indian, and those of mixed heritage—say and feel and believe about Indian histories is intimately connected to their sense of themselves, to their sense of their rights to the place, to how they remember and what they value. Not only is Trempealeau the site of these unique platform mounds, it is named for the mountain bluff sacred to several Native American groups; people still come across effigy and burial mounds; and Trempealeau's public schools are the home of the "Redmen." And Trempealeau is also just fifty miles from a sizeable Ho-Chunk community in Black River Falls, with a casino and powwow grounds and an old Indian mission. The land thus bears the marks of other histories; it bears the signs of other people who have passed through what is now a predominantly white, working-class region. Although the land offers many signs of the past, only some of these are acknowledged and fewer are actively remembered. White residents have memorialized certain histories, images, and ideas—which have become part of local mythology—while they have pushed others underground, so to speak. Yet this mythology is likely to crop up in unexpected ways, like the arrowheads and tools turned over in farmers' fields, like the bones of a dead Indian "princess" who was not laid peacefully to rest.

In short, I seek to understand the many ways that residents of this town in southwestern Wisconsin imagine their relationship to Native American images, histories, and archaeological sites.[1] As I see it, this imagining is part of a larger history of Euro-American remembering and forgetting, a complex of ideas and images that continues to shape and trouble the way white Americans understand themselves as owners of land, as the rightful occupants of this country. Furthermore, because I grew up in the region where the beliefs and attitudes of white residents prevailed, these ideas have formed part of my own and my family's consciousness; after I left home, however, and increasingly as I explored Native American images and histories, as well as local attitudes toward the place, I came to a different understanding of things. What follows is thus also the story of my coming to understand and unearth the death and violence of which Anna Funmaker spoke, the violence that the words of residents and town fathers deny but that is nonetheless at the base of many contemporary white attitudes, images, and beliefs.

Local archaeology is one of the subjects I deal with, but I also use archaeology as a metaphor to tell this story. I cannot understand the gap between Funmaker's perceptions of the land and that of many white residents' just by looking at the surface; if I use only the information that is presented to me, I will not have the tools to understand the gap between my father's denial of the mounds and Funmaker's assertion that all of Wisconsin is a burial ground. I have to go deeper—into memories, stories, histories. That I have to dig to get information, I believe, is also the result of particular and regional ways in which people in this area deal with controversy and relate to each other. In the family and community of northern European descent that I consider and in which I grew up, people place value on avoiding conflict, on the ability to suppress what they perceive as negative emotions and memories. I have to seek out what's been pushed under.

This process is not unlike Freud's descriptions of psychoanalysis, which he believed was similar to archaeology. The analyst's job, as Freud described it, was to find memories that had been preserved in the psyche—memories whose "burial," in a sense, prevented the analysand from coming to terms with her life, from creating a story that would let her live in the world. The process, he wrote, "was one of cleaning away the pathogenic psychical material layer by layer, and we like to compare it with the technique of excavating a buried city."[2] And, as he argues in *Totem and Taboo,* some of these buried memories have the power not only to affect individuals but to shape cultures, societies, and "civilized" human beings in general. In this project I dig not only for what bothers me personally but also for what has shaped my family and my town; I root around for a kind of primal scene that has shaped white American consciousness more generally.

What I describe, in effect, is a colonial situation and its aftermath. As Ashis Nandy asserts in a different context, colonialism does not affect only the colonized; it transforms colonizers as well, catching them "in the hinges of history [they] swear by."[3] In this mixed project of memoir, history, and story, I explore the impact of colonialism on the colonizers and their descendants because, as Nandy argues, "While the economic, political and moral results of colonialism have been discussed, its emotional and cognitive costs have been ignored. And as Freud has reminded us in this [the twentieth] century, what we choose to forget has a tendency to come back to haunt us in 'history.'"[4]

So I do archaeology in order to remember. Mine is an archaeology of a specific kind and of specific artifacts: I explore the relationships that local people—including my family and myself—have with this place, particularly as these relationships connect to Native American histories and images. I use the image of three burial mounds to represent these areas of investigation—self, family, and local attitudes.

I start at the surface of these mounds or, rather, at the surface of memory; thus part I introduces the issues that I will explore further in subsequent parts, including Native American earthworks, the platform mound controversy, the local Indian mascot issue, and local conceptions of land. In part II, I go deeper into each area/ mound to see what else I find, to discover how it relates to what I have already uncovered, and to gesture toward how it might connect to what I find deeper still. In part III, I try to go to the depths—the emotional, historical, and cultural bottom. What I find there is destruction, the violence of Native American removals, and a habit of forgetting. My discovery is, perhaps, nothing new: recent histories offer accounts of Indian removals, the devastation on the native population wrought by foreign-borne diseases, and the repression of Indian people in numerous ways. What I try to do, however, is to suggest that this violence is not simply part of the past; it connects to other and more recent forms of brutality. I see these different forms of violence—past and present—as partaking of each other, as animating and supporting each other. In the fourth part, while actively remembering aspects of the past, I try to put things back together, to consider how I might go on now that I've learned what I've learned. Remembering becomes something more than just recalling facts about the past; it becomes something active, a process of exploring relations between the present and the past.

The shape I give these figurative mounds is similar to that of a local Hopewell mound known as Nicholls Mound. Inside and at the bottom of this mound, which was excavated by professional archaeologists and local employees in 1928, were seven burials, some of which, at one time, were placed in a burial pit under a bark canopy of sorts. The archaeological evidence suggests that the people buried in Nicholls Mound were highly respected, as they were interred with elaborate and exotic artifacts that could have been acquired only at great expenditure of energy. In using this mound as a guiding image,

I suggest the way the burials were hidden and unknown until the moment of excavation—not that any violence was done to the individuals interred there. What I am pointing to is how excavation and knowledge of these burials can change our sense of what's on the surface, of what kind of place we live in; this knowledge might even give us alternative ways of occupying the region.

As I write now, of course, I know what I've found, but in telling this tale I present things in order to suggest to readers my feeling of discovery, my sense of dawning understanding. This comprehension came not just from seeing what was there and connecting it to my own past, however; I came to see things differently only because I am now also *outside* the place. As an outsider and an academic, I brought to the scene exotic tools and instruments to help me interpret what I found; I sought out archaeological knowledge; I spoke to local native informants; I researched local history.

A final note before I get down to work: In using the metaphor of archaeology, I am also suggesting something about the nature of my own investigation. Although there is much to be learned through archaeology, I nonetheless find something questionable and even grisly about the unearthing of human remains. It is often a desecration, a violation. My ambiguity about literal digging also haunts my own project; some will feel that I should not discuss topics at which I am not expert, that I should not disturb the dead, and there are certainly those who will feel that I have unearthed what I should not have, that I have desecrated something sacred about my family and my town. I can say only that I found it necessary to do so in order, finally, to begin to comprehend where I come from as well as to understand the remains of violence and denial that mark the psychic and emotional landscape of Euro-American consciousness. Instead of laying things to rest, then, I explore to remember—to know what I remember.

Part I

The Surface

1. Routes

First, the lay of the land. The Mississippi River dominates Trempealeau. The river runs through what is, in a sense, a wide gorge between lines of bluffs and ridges. As a character in Mark Twain's *Life on the Mississippi* notes, "You'll find scenery between here and St. Paul that can give the Hudson points"—places with "lovely prairies," water still as "a looking glass," and "ragged, rugged, dark-complected" bluffs.[1] Dammed in the 1930s, the river is a quarter-mile wide at Trempealeau; it is brown and deep, with a bottom of silt and sand. Carp, catfish, and muskrat ply its waters. From the banks you can see tree-covered islands and, farther across the water, the bluffs and highways of Minnesota. The main street of Trempealeau heads straight for the river, past Mount Calvary Lutheran Church, past the platform mounds, and halts at the river's edge.

The ground and waterfront from the platform mounds to Trempealeau Mountain—or from town center to Perrot State Park—are replete with structures and stories. Some stories gain prominence at the forgetting of others; some sites are covered over, renamed, displaced. The way from mounds to mountain can take different routes. Kids sometimes follow the bluffs that line the Mississippi for five miles north from the town center to Perrot State Park. They start at Little Bluff and go to First Peak (where the Boy Scouts solemnly fly an American flag), then pass along to Second Peak and Chicken's Breast, traipsing all the way to Brady's Bluff in Perrot Park and then on down to the bay. This walk takes them along the Mississippi, past Indian burial mounds, above the site of an old French trading post, and leads them near Trempealeau Mountain.

A hiker could also take an archaeological tour: this would take in the 950-year-old platform mounds at Little Bluff; the route would continue to the site of a French trading post from 1731 (this is Linctot's post; though most residents believe it to be Nicholas Perrot's post of 1685, that has not been supported by material evidence); the path would then skirt the reconstructed burial mounds in the park and lead to eagle, deer, and dog effigy mounds. Farther from the town center and in the other direction, the archaeologist's tour would extend to the largest burial mound in Wisconsin, the two-thousand-year-old Hopewell earthwork known as Nicholls Mound, which was excavated in 1928 and once was the resting place for the remains of seven people. Such a tour would take you through two thousand years of sporadic Native American occupation, through signs of Hopewell, Late Woodland, Middle Mississippian, Ho-Chunk, Dakota, and French occupation. And at Trempealeau Mountain you'd arrive at a landmark that, though variously defined, has oriented people for centuries.

Or you can go another way, the route prescribed by members of the historical society and seekers of family history. For them, Trempealeau's story is largely the story of white settlement. This journey takes you on an imaginary trip to the original settlement of Reed's Landing, which later became Montoville and, later still, Trempealeau. If you start at the old Hayter's IGA (which now houses a bank) and head toward the Mississippi, you end up near the river and the plots first settled in 1840 by James Reed and his succession of wives of native descent. There you'd be in the neighborhood of Napoleon Bonaparte Grover's general store of the 1860s, the site of the Trempealeau Hotel (founded in 1871 and today the home of the famous walnut burger) and now the heart of the effort to showcase the history of the town. Turn right to follow a route along the river and you also follow the railroad tracks, built here in 1871 and still running trains; the road will take you past the old Melchoir Brewery, where beer used to be stored in the cold of natural caves, and past Ed Sullivan's Supper Club to the historical marker for the old Perrot Post. Finally, you make your way to the campsites and headquarters of Perrot State Park, which date to 1916, season passes available.

Besides these journeys through space, there is also the route of personal memory. My uncle Clyde tells of the old grocery from the 1930s with wheels of cheese inside ("They didn't have no refrigeration"); he remembers his father and grandfather, who used horses to construct the road to the park in the 1920s, and the Civilian Conservation Corps guys and their work at the park in the thirties. Other stories include picnics and swimming at old Trempealeau Bay, the building of Lock and Dam No. 6 by the Army Corps of Engineers,

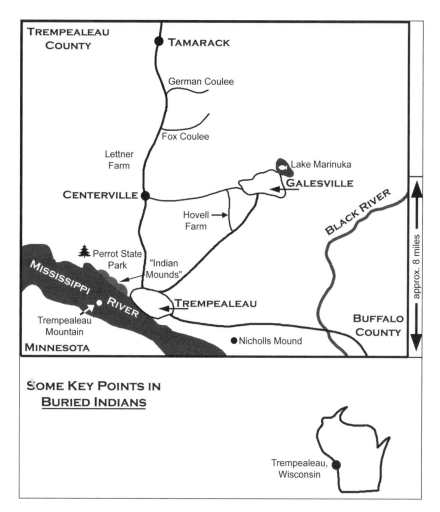

1.1. Key sites. Map by Linda Pardee.

and all the kids who drowned while swimming in that river: my uncle Glen, Troy Steffes, Peggy Dahl. I hear their names intoned between drumbeats, as in a solemn Memorial Day rite. For me, there is also the memory of being led to the river by my grade school teachers to see the old paddle-wheel boat known as the *Delta Queen* and to hear its happy calliope. Later, when my sixth-grade girlfriends and I ventured out alone to ride bikes all the way around the park for the first time, we marked a rite of passage. And there is the memory

5

of a 5K race I entered when I was thirty-six that followed much of the same road, from Main Street to the park and back; I ran it to mark the doubling of my years since I first did the race, to prove I could still do it after birthing two children. My husband and I started out together and he paced and encouraged me, but on the return journey I urged him to go ahead. As I pushed it on the home stretch, past the line of bluffside, river-facing houses to which my dad had wished to retire but never did, remembering my dad—dead four years by then—and our turbulent connection, I felt as if I was running more than a footrace, tears streaming down my face as the river ran next to me.

So there are many ways to get to Trempealeau. Many stories to be told.

◆

2. The Lay of the Land

For years the sign announcing the village of Trempealeau listed the population as 784. The 2000 census puts the figure at 1,306. Old-timers complained to me that they don't know their neighbors any more; the new people who are moving in pick Trempealeau for its picturesque location on the Mississippi, its small-town atmosphere. Many newcomers drive fifteen or twenty-five miles to work in Winona or La Crosse, and most people—no matter where they work—punch a clock. Trempealeau itself has very little industry. There's the lumber mill in town, and the lock and dam; they employ a few. Trempealeau is a depressed little town that lacks even a grocery store, though that doesn't keep away the cabin owners, boaters, and bikers (both kinds) who pass through the town in the summer, giving the economy a temporary boost.[2] Perhaps the most successful business in town is the refurbished Trempealeau Hotel, but—ask anyone—if you go there, you won't hardly see anybody you know. Just up the river is the old Ed Sullivan's restaurant, now under new management after Ed and Sally's retirement. The new golf course just outside town is the brainchild of the town's wealthiest resident, Harold Wilber.

Public works in the town depend a lot on the local Lion's Club, an all-men's organization. In theory the Lions are the movers and shakers in town, but in practice the membership includes almost anybody who can hold his head up high in town—guys who work on the dam, guys who get paid by the hour, as well as small business-men. The street signs all bear the Lions' insignia; the Duck Pond, the library, and the swimming pool were all constructed through its charity. The Lions' biggest fund-raiser is a summer event called Cat-fish Days, which until recently provided folks with an opportunity to stand in the middle of Main Street and drink beer in a large crowd. (The event has been shifted to a local park.) The celebration includes a parade; kiddy rides; dances; races for walkers, runners, and bike riders, as well as the crowning of the Catfish Queen.

My father grew up in Trempealeau, and our family stretches back to a line of Hovels/Hovells that started with the arrival of Thomas Hovel from England in 1858. The town was small and rural enough that when my dad was a kid, his family—like other families—farmed right in town, herding their cows onto bluffs and into fields all through the area. My dad's family moved a lot, changing houses and renting land, looking for a way to settle. By the time my dad married my mom in 1948, he and his family had been making pay-ments on their own farm for two years. They had abandoned Trem-pealeau for the prairies and coulees outside it,[3] where my dad, along with his father and brother, farmed their land, raising cattle and chickens, keeping horses, and often working other jobs as well.

Land, after all, was wealth; it was stability. Immigrants invented the village by claiming the land; the village grew by the carving out of plots, the labor of farmers, the construction of homes. All this effort gave the residents—former outsiders themselves—possession of the land. This orientation to land ownership worked for both farmers and the people who lived in town. When I spoke to one octogenarian in 2001—a man who claimed to be the oldest Trempealeau-born resident—he could not recall anything about his work with Milwaukee archaeologists in the 1930s, but he could tell me exact prices for the land on which his modest house was built, and he could describe in detail how he acquired the lots on either side. These property acquisitions were face-to-face transactions, between him on the one hand and widowed neighbor ladies and their sons on the other. The money for the land was hard earned, the deal was fair, and the land bespoke his attainment. Its size, its maintenance, reflected on him.

In Trempealeau who owns what land matters very much. My father's memory for land was prodigious: what he paid for it, how much acreage it was. It wasn't that he was especially greedy for land. It was how he was oriented; it was the basis for making a living. Although he worked a string of jobs all his life, farming the 160 acres he had first purchased in 1946 with his dad and brother was a constant. And possession of that land gave him both security and a kind of status.

In the 1980s my father, Robert Ray Hovell Sr., set out to document the events in his life. In a recollection from 1988 he describes the many places he lived as a young man in the late 1930s and 1940s.

> We left Trempealeau because the buildings and land were too small to make a living on. We lived the first year on a rented farm, outside of town. My dad worked on the Alcan [Alaskan-Canadian] Highway. They worked 11 hours a day, 7 days a week. . . . Anyway, S.J. [Stanley Joyce, my dad's father] saved his money and finished paying for the house behind the school. We had dug long ditches and driven pipe, all the way from Central Park, to have running water. Just got it working, then moved out to the H.E. Clark farm, now owned by Don Brenengen. Guess what? No water, no lights. [He describes the laborious process of laying pipe and putting up wire for electricity.] . . . The land on this farm was poor, the house and barn cold. Of course we had lights. After one year we heard of this farm [the one he was living on at the time of writing], the Harry

Marsh place, being for sale, looked at it and my dad decided to sell his house in town and put his money into the farm. So we all moved out there. My dad made the down payment, Clyde and I as partners, paid the taxes and interest, which by the way, was 4%, on a land contract. We also made the payments on the principal. . . . Guess what, this farm had no lights or water! So here we go again. It took us two years this time, to get electricity. Good ol' Ralph Ebersold helped us out again.[4]

For my father, the land was worked over, demarcated, and thus claimed. In his attitudes he was not unusual. The right to own land—and to keep others off it—is highly valued in the Trempealeau area. Landowners in the area are usually careful to mark off the boundaries of their possession; PRIVATE PROPERTY signs bearing the name of the landowner and often the owner's signature are common. From your car you can see these signs in the woods, along rivers, marking the edges of fields. The right to do what you want with your land is almost sacrosanct. If you want to dump garbage on your land—as my parents did when the town dump closed—that's okay. If you want to add on to your summer cottage on the Mississippi—as another relative did—you should be able to do so without the interference of the Department of Natural Resources (DNR). Indeed, "DNR" is practically a curse word around Trempealeau; although it is a government body created to defend laws that protect the land and water, many see the DNR as something that obstructs, an alien entity that always hinders you in your efforts to do what you want. People's feeling of entitlement about the land is not a new phenomenon. When the archaeologist S. A. Barrett appealed to the village to save the platform mounds in 1938, the response was a claim to landownership: we own it, and we will do what we want to with it. The close connection between the land and its owners is also suggested by the naming habits in the region. In the 1980s, when road signs were first posted in the township of Caledonia Prairie, the roads often took the names of the landowners who lived alongside them. Even archaeological sites were named for the farmers on whose land they stood: Schwert Mounds, Nicholls Mound. Out on the prairie, farm plots are known simply by the last names of their long-time owners: that's Carhart's, that's Meunier's, that's Bender's.

I learned my first lesson about private property when I was five. We were visiting my cousin Keri in town, and, along with another cousin, Tammi, we three preschoolers—our heads full of stories about good girls—decided to collect flowers for our mothers, all sisters. We got marigolds from this yard, petunias from that, a rose from another; we took them to our mothers and waited to be praised. Instead, we were punished, admonished by women who could hardly keep a straight face as they told us how you do not go onto other people's property, how you do not take flowers that do not belong to you.

These days I own a house in a small town in Ohio, and my dander still goes up when some college student takes a shortcut across my yard. It is my land, I think, and that is coming too close.

◇

3. Farmers

When we were kids, almost everybody we knew was a farmer. Boys would come to school smelling of cow manure and the work they had done that morning, the work that permeated their clothes no matter how much they washed. Both grandfathers and a good half of my uncles were farmers back then—dairy and cash crop farmers; some kept giant Holstein cows whose backs towered above my head. My grandfathers worked the hilly land on adjoining coulees named for the people who first settled them—Fox Coulee and German Valley, just south of Norway Valley. The Fox Coulee farm was the same one that Thomas Hovel had bought in 1866; a century later, after Grandpa Hovell had owned it for eight years, he sold it in 1961 to a big farming outfit that let him and Grandma work and live on the farm till he died. In the next valley Grandpa Earl Bockenhauer's land was especially hilly, and it was not unusual for a farmer to roll a tractor up in hills like those. Even today you hear about men who were pinned under their machines and killed. In these same coulees kids ran across arrowheads and flakes, the signs of old Indian camps. An old-timer from this area tells stories about some Indian kids who used to come around asking for sitting hens—old chickens— to stew; another recalls a ragged Indian family living on a hill and approaching the farmers for whatever food they could spare.

Out on Caledonia Prairie, my parents' 160 acres were laid out in fields with straight borders; only the occasional ancient oak inter- rupted a tractor's progress. My uncle Clyde recalls how they used to farm with horses and how hard the work was. Sometime in the 1950s the horses were fully replaced by second-hand tractors in frequent need of repair. By the 1970s, when Dad got ready to plant, some seeds came coated with bright pink chemicals; in late spring he sprayed on fertilizer, and in summer we girls went out with knives and hoes to chop down weeds. In the fall, when the soybeans were harvested and stored in the barn, we kids rolled around in them. It was like being dropped into a giant beanbag.

My parents kept cows only till I was four, though Dad continued to farm corn, soy, lima beans, and peas till he died. As my family did it, dairy farming was unsentimental work, and Wisconsin had not yet embraced the cow as a cute mascot. Farm animals were individu- alized but were not exactly pets; most of them had jobs to do. Cats killed mice, dogs herded cows and helped with hunting. And, more than that, cows were the center of a livelihood. They would be given names—Princess and Queenie, and even the names of my sisters, Pam and Debbie; they were milked and tended and sent to slaugh- ter without much remorse. Sick dogs would not have their lives prolonged by veterinarians' extraordinary measures; they would be allowed to weaken, and then my dad would take them out to the woods, shoot them, and bury them.

These animals taught a straightforward story about dying: death was present, it was possible. One morning before kindergarten I went out to the barn with my mother and father and saw there, lying in the hay, the ragged, bloody-ended head of a cow. Around the same time, a horse was caught in a barn fire on a nearby farm. Terrified, it ran all the way to our house and refused to be calmed. The children were secured inside while the spooked horse circled our house again and again, wheeling and racing.

Not long after, my father's mother, Grandma Hovell, called my grandfather in from the barn for supper. When he didn't come, she found him lying in the dirt driveway between the house and barn, dead from a stroke. At the funeral, no one lifted me up, but I must have seen him laid out in his best clothes. (When I imagine it now, though, I see him laid out in his usual jeans and chambray shirt, cigarettes and shiny Zippo lighter in the pocket.) My aunt Darlene and her three daughters were all crying in the crammed room of the funeral home. I didn't know why. Later, there was talk about a hatchet that needed to be buried. My grandma left the house in Fox Coulee not long after; the terms of the sale had been that they could live there only until Stanley died. I got cut on the barbed wire near her house and drank an orange soda while she was packing up her car with the bouncing-head dog on the dash. She was going back to Trempealeau, where she was born.

4. History

The standard history of the Trempealeau area is Eben Pierce's massive volume of 1917, *History of Trempealeau County.* The book, compiled by Franklyn Curtiss-Wedge, offers a comprehensive account of how the county came to be, with chapters on local history, geology, archaeology, explorers, historical papers, and local settlements, among other things. Reissued in 1978 during a boom in interest in genealogy, the book is a prized possession for many residents in the region. More than half of its nine hundred pages are dedicated to biography, for, as Pierce argues, "the intimate life of the community is best told in the personal stories of its citizens."[5] Pierce goes on to list the names and genealogies of prominent citizens (mostly male), from Anna (Knutson) Aaakre (*sic*) to John Zuza. (It's been a source of pique for my family that the Hovel/lls are left out of this account.) Not only do these accounts offer "valuable information," as Pierce sees it, they "also furnish inspiration for worthy emulation. In so new a county as Trempealeau there are few men who have not started as poor boys and attained success by their own efforts. The story of their equipment for the struggle by birth, training, environment and experience is of vital significance. So, too, is the story of the men of the younger generation, who with better preparation and under more favorable circumstances, have taken up the work which their fathers have laid down."[6] For Pierce the history of Trempealeau County is one propelled by men; women become part of the picture only tangentially, as wives and mothers. The story he tells is one of individual masculine perseverance, a tale of fathers and sons' succeeding to progress.

Naturally enough, the bulk of Pierce's book is devoted to aspects of white settlement of the county, for without Yankee occupation of the area there were no borders or incorporated villages; there were no tracts of land measured on the straight line.[7] Thus Pierce devotes a chapter to the dates of plotting out and incorporating each village in the county, and the book includes a list of land office records. As Pierce notes, even though "many people filed [homestead claims] on land which they had never seen and which they had never occupied," and thus the names and dates cannot give a true chronology of settlement, "the list gives the names of the first land claimants, resident and otherwise, of the various townships in Trempealeau County."⁸ In this way of seeing things one becomes a resident—one enters history—by claiming land.

As a kind of preface to white settlement, Pierce includes some details of the "prehistory" of the area. Sixteen pages on early Wisconsin cover the Indians, the French, the fur trade; he wrote another ten pages on Indian history, and he included nine pages on archaeology by the local scholar George Hull Squier, a decision that was unusual for a publication of this type. The tendency to separate data on Indians from that on whites suggests what seems clear enough to many citizens: history is the story of white settlement; what native peoples had was something different from history, lacking written documents and devoid of on-going progress. As this view suggests (and as archaeological discourses about prehistory suggest), Indians were among the "people without history."⁹ Discussion of Indian life in the chapter called "Reign of the Indians," with its prominent use of the past tense—"the Indians were peaceable and friendly"; "the men had guns and hunted and fished"; "they kept largely to themselves"—makes it clear enough: the significance of Indian life is all in days gone by.

Although a number of Ho-Chunk, Dakota, and other native peoples lived in Trempealeau County when the history was written, the families and genealogies included in the biography section of Pierce's book are only those of white settlers. (Norwegian Lutheran churches warrant their own chapter.) The recollections of Antoine Grignon, a noted resident and former fur trader of mixed French and Indian descent who died in 1913, are printed separate from the biography section; his progeny are listed separate from the offspring of later white settlers.¹⁰ Similarly, in one genealogy within the biography chapter proper, the Perkins line has been stripped of its Indian ancestry; although Mary Ann Farnham (who married into the Perkins line) had native blood (Potawatomi or Menominee), the listing declares simply that the Perkinses "were of French and English descent, Charles Perkins [Mary's son] being a farmer by occupation."¹¹

In Pierce's history Native Americans are pressed to the margins. Because native peoples had no surveys to establish property lines before European settlement and no visible legal procedures for establishing a settlement, their occupation of the area does not fully count for Pierce and other white settlers; the presence of Native Americans is not enough either to establish their entitlement to the land or to give them a claim to the history of the county. White settlers brought with them European conceptions about the nature of agriculture, private property, settlement, and civilization; they could imagine the American frontier as empty and ready for settlement. In this way of thinking about land, history, and settlement, native peoples effectively disappeared.

◈

5. Old Things

When I was five, Trempealeau celebrated its centennial. Though the village was first formed in 1852, it wasn't incorporated until 1867. The centennial celebration was a big deal. Many men grew whiskers and sideburns in their version of the fashions of one hundred years earlier. We girls got to dress up in long skirts and bonnets. I had my picture taken with my sisters and girl cousins for the "Historical Album" produced for the occasion; a photo of Trempealeau Mountain graced the cover of this publication. The centennial celebration sprawled over the ball fields by the school; it was like the county fair all over again—rides and treats and people milling around. I walked in the parade with my cousin Tim, pushing his little brother, David, in a pram, as if we were his old-time parents. My cousin Tammi's grandparents, Kenny and Elvira Drugan, lived right next to the ball field; we got to stay up late and wander the celebration grounds before our parents came to fetch us.

When I was in kindergarten, I rode the Carry-all bus to school with a girl named Susie Kramer. She was Indian, I knew, and her skin was dark as my grandma's oak dining table. Her parents were not Indian, and she lived just a few fields over from our farm. She was a big girl with round cheeks and shiny black hair and always looked ready to bust out of the pastel dresses she wore to school. I was a little in awe of her; she was tough on the playground but slow to pick up the alphabet. She disappeared in second grade.

On the road that my mom drove to work, just past where Hunter's Bridge crosses the Black River, were two shacks. They were near Powwow Campground. We knew them as Indian shacks. It seemed like you could look right through these little gray houses; there was no glass in the windows and in summer only a blanket over the door. Once in a while you could see an old Indian man sitting outside the house, his head bowed over some handiwork. That's how I remember it, anyway.

6. Mascots

My mother's 1948 class ring from Galesville High School—seven miles from Trempealeau—is gold and onyx. Set on the shiny black stone is a gold Indian head profile, with full headdress. My father had a simple gold class ring; he had graduated seven years earlier from Healy Memorial High School in Trempealeau in a class of thirteen. By the time I graduated from high school in 1980, the schools of three different towns—Galesville, Ettrick, and Trempealeau—had become one uneasily consolidated district. When the small Trempealeau district merged in 1972 with Gale-Ettrick—against many residents' wishes—the school was renamed Gale-Ettrick-Trempealeau High School—G-E-T High for short. If no one bothered to ponder the significance of that name—and, indeed, some class rings proclaim, without the hyphens, GET HIGH—there was also little debate about what mascot the school would use. Trempealeau lost its bear mascot, adding only the blue from its blue and gold school colors to Gale-Ettrick's red and white. With this red, white, and blue of the American flag as a backdrop, the choice was simple: we would be the Redmen.

My own class ring says simply GET arranged vertically, with an Indian head perched on top, as on a miniature totem pole. While growing up in the area in the 1960s and '70s, I was immersed in contemporary romanticism about Native Americans, but I don't recall ever pondering the mascot. As I read Hyehemost Storm's *Seven Arrows* and Frank Waters's *The Hopi Way of Life* and donned turquoise jewelry that my dad sold (another of his hobby businesses), I never wondered what it might mean for us high-schoolers to represent ourselves with images of warriors in Plains Indian headdresses, what it meant when our Redmen faced the Arcadia Raiders, a team whose emblem was a tomahawk-wielding savage. Everyone knew that the Holmen Vikings and the Whitehall Norsemen were named for the sizeable Norwegian populations that settled their towns. And everyone knew that the area we lived in had once been populated by Indians. Weren't there "Indian mounds" in the park? Wasn't this the home of Chief Decorah? Wasn't Lake Marinuka named for a princess? Weren't the names for Winona and Wabasha and for the very Mississippi itself Indian words?

That our school curriculum at the time contained almost nothing about Native Americans—no one questioned that. "The United States is the greatest country in the world," my sixth-grade teacher, Mrs. Grover, said adamantly, so we learned about Washington and Lincoln, took the Iowa Test of Basic Skills, and held a mock election between Nixon and McGovern. (Nixon won by a mile, despite my earnest campaigning.) Everyone knew that Nicolas Perrot had landed in Trempealeau a long time ago to trade with the Indians, but most people's sense of local history began with white settlement, with the arrival of the Yankee settlers, the English, the Scots, and later the Germans and Poles, with a little bit of old French thrown in. What role Native Americans played in this was not always clear. It was white settlement of the place that mattered. As one friend, an archaeologist, has described it, many people thought of history this way: first there were Indians and then there were farmers.

Within this view of history, then, there seemed to be a smooth transition between the Indians and whites, between past and present. The land itself, dotted by piles of earth said to entomb the bones of old Indian ancestors, reminded people of this other past, kicking up arrowheads, spear points, and flakes during plowing. And there were stories to go along with sites in the landscape: there was Trempealeau, of course, with its famous mountain bluff in the Mississippi, said to be a sacred site for Indians. During a local Indian war the Winnebago leader Chief Decorah was said to have hidden in the limestone peak that now bears his name. The lake at the center of the town of Galesville was named Marinuka, after Chief Decorah's granddaughter, an Indian princess. Ours was a tranquil kind of remembering; the few Ho-Chunk families or people of native descent who lived in the area tended to keep to themselves. Tom Thunder, a local Ho-Chunk man, was known as an honest fellow who scraped together a living for his family. During a recent debate about the Redmen mascot issue, one resident recalled Thunder in a letter to the editor, describing how "Chief" Tom Thunder used to "drop in to" her dad's store "to borrow a few bucks to pay hospital bills for his family or whatever crisis arose." She went on: "Chief Thunder was a friendly and affectionate man and as has been mentioned before, was proud of his large red nose."[12] When people speak of Thunder, they frequently mention this prodigious nose. A similarly prominent proboscis graces the profile of the school mascot.

◇

7. Casino

We were going to the Indian casino, Majestic Pines. We piled into my sister Pam's minivan—Mom; my sisters Deb and Pam; my husband, T.S.; and I—for the ride through the countryside to Black River Falls. The casino is a grand affair, a monstrous, expansive building with a giant sign and a southwestern motif running along the top. Although it was a weekday, the parking lot was full of late model cars and minivans, mostly with Wisconsin plates. Inside, the chairs were full of the butts of white-haired ladies and gents who stuck their nickels, quarters, and dollars into slot machines, hoping for a break. At the center tables white folks in T-shirts gathered around the mostly Ho-Chunk dealers in spiffy vests and ties. Although T.S. and I had never been to an Indian casino before, my relatives have gone quite often, and, interestingly, for a bunch of people who like to have a drink, they remain dry while at the casino and set their spending limit before they walk in the door. The place was dark and cool on a hot July day. T.S. and I exchanged a twenty-dollar bill for a cup of quarters and divided them. My family split up, and I found myself in front of a one-armed bandit. I won just often enough to keep me going, just often enough to spend every last quarter within forty-five minutes. We all ran out of money at the same time, gathered in the foyer, and headed back to the minivan. It was a simple transaction.

The casino works with a kind of beauty: retired folks and hard-working people make the drive to Black River Falls and hand over their money to the Ho-Chunk, one banknote, one coin at a time.

An entire vocabulary has grown up around this quite recent phenomenon of going to the casino and the exchanges between white patrons and Indian owners. My uncle Kenny told me how he spent his birthday: "Darlene and I went to Black River and gave our money to the Indians." When they are going to the casino, people say they "are going to buy the Indians moccasins." When people have had a bad day at the casino—which is often—they say "the Indians were on the warpath." Others say simply that they go to "feed the Indians."

There's no doubt that the casino has changed things for the Ho-Chunk, first and foremost by making the name Ho-Chunk widely known, replacing the term *Winnebago*.[13] The casinos have improved the standard of living of many Ho-Chunk people, and this has given them a voice in state and local affairs. The Ho-Chunks have their own cultural centers, human services, legal systems, historians, construction projects, and education projects. In Black River Falls, the site of one of four Ho-Chunk casinos in Wisconsin,[14] the Ho-Chunk Nation employs many local people, and the casino has brought money into the town and schools. Gus Vogel—a resident of Trempealeau who is half Ho-Chunk and half German American—works for the Ho-Chunk Nation. While many white residents in the area don't understand just why Native Americans should be allowed to run casinos when *they* can't, and others refer to the whole enterprise as a scam (one in which they participate nonetheless), Vogel maintains that "Indian gaming has done a lot for native groups."

My uncle Russ had told me that if I was going to the casino, I should also have a look at the powwow grounds just down the road. So on the day in July that we traveled to the casino, we also took in the powwow grounds, which stand near the historical marker for

Red Cloud, a Korean War hero. The grounds looked dusty and vacant that day, and we moved quickly on toward what a green-and-
white highway sign referred to as the "Indian Mission." We were a
bit nervous as we drove through the settlement, uncertain how wel-
come we were. We saw only a church set off from the main road, a
few modest houses, a ceramic figure of a black boy fishing. We
looked for the reservation that day, to no avail. Only later would I
learn that there is none at Black River and never has been. It's funny:
we'd always thought there was a reservation there; as far as we knew,
that's where Indians lived.

8. Memorials

I was born on Memorial Day. For years my birthday fell on the day
when we remembered the dead. Trempealeau always held a ceremony in the village park. Before consolidation of the G-E-T school
district, the Trempealeau High School band used to play. "The Star-
Spangled Banner." Patriotic songs. I was moved and astonished by
the playing of Taps by a lone trumpeter and how the song echoed
from afar. (Only later did I learn that it was another trumpeter, playing from someone's backyard.) My aunt Nancy was famous for her
lovely voice and would sing "Sleep in Peace, Soldier Boy" to the tune
of Taps. A veteran would call out the names of townsmen who had
served and who had since passed on, each name punctuated by a

bass drumbeat. Robert Arnold. Boom. Adam Little Bear. Boom. Clyde Jon Hovell. Boom. Then the veterans would blast their guns in honor of the war dead. My father teased that I thought this gathering was for my birthday.

After the service my dad's family would gather at my grandma Hovell's for a picnic, and then we'd all go out to look at the graves of our dead relatives. The Beardsleys in the public cemetery under towering pines. The Hovells out in Evergreen Cemetery on the prairie. We kids always wondered at the gravestone for a stillborn cousin, the rough graves for the Indians at the far edge of one cemetery, the tall headstones for town fathers.

In junior high I became one of those Taps-playing trumpeters. By then Trempealeau's school district had lost its autonomy and consolidated, and Memorial Day was no longer on May 30 but always on a Monday. In the summer of eighth grade I played Taps for the funerals of veterans for a small fee. I was chauffeured by my uncle Kenny—a Korean War army vet—and Carl Keefe—a spry eighty-year-old World War I Navy man in a sailor suit. Carl carried the flag and told jokes the whole way to the cemetery. There the jokes stopped as he stood at attention next to the mound of earth that covered the grave; my uncle Ken shot off his rifle, three shots, and I tried to keep my lips warm until it was time to play.

9. Church

I remember getting baptized. Although the usual route for Lutherans was infant baptism, my parents put it off until I was four and my infant double-cousin Stanley was ready to get baptized too. (His mother, Barb, is my mom's sister; his father, Clyde, my dad's brother.) So that our parents, who were not churchgoers, could avoid the embarrassment of a Sunday morning rite, Pastor Herfendahl met us on a Saturday afternoon, when we could have the cold church to ourselves. The A-frame Mount Calvary Lutheran Church was newly built with what seemed to me a majestically high peaked ceiling. I wore a red dress and Stanley wore a white one; we were wetted on the head and wiped with a handkerchief and the deed was done.

My brother, Bob, eleven years my senior, and my two sisters, Pam and Deb, seven and eight years older than I, respectively, went to church of their own volition; after my baptism I went with them. Debbie used to pass out sometimes when she stood up to sing, falling over the pew in front of her—not in religious ecstasy; it was probably low blood sugar. One day I was sick and vomiting in the church bathroom, my cries for "Pam! Pam!" echoing throughout the sacristy, punctuating the Gospel reading.

After Sunday school we would go to our grandma Hovell's, where she fed us sugar cookies and Jell-O, and my dad would come pick us up. Like my father, Grandma avoided church; neither could be stirred by pastors or the Sunday schooler missionaries who preached that missing church would lead to Dad's and Grandma's everlasting damnation. One Sunday while she waited for us, Grandma was visited by Bobby Elkins, the mayor's childlike adult son who was out wandering. He wanted to know if she had gone to church, but, he asked, trying out a phrase: "Mrs. Hovell, did you meet your Maker today?" She replied, "Bobby, I meet my Maker every day."

I was in eighth grade at G-E-T middle school, located in Trempealeau, and I forgot about confirmation class that Wednesday at the Lutheran church in the village. Normally after school I would take the bus for the five-mile ride home that took an hour, but on confirmation days I just stayed in town, goofing around until confirmation class at 5 o'clock. I called my mom and she said just stay, but the thing was, you were supposed to bring your supper. And I didn't have any. So I made a lot of noise about this at school; this little bit of deprivation would make me special. Maybe I would skip a meal, I thought, and just watch the others while they ate, a tragic though complacent look on my face. But I had a little money left over from lunch—a bottle of pop, a bag of chips, a candy bar from Eddie Gilberg's gas station—and, as soon as school got out, I headed straight to Hayter's IGA. There I bought a Hershey bar, pop, some Hot Tamales, and ate them before turning the corner below Little Bluff and heading up the hill. While the others ate, I would assume a deprived look—even though I was full of junk food—and draw attention to myself for the lack of a meal. But Pam Leavitt, a girl in my confirmation class who had been one of three kids in my Sunday school class since day one, spoiled it for me. We weren't good friends, really. In the sixth grade she wouldn't do what I wanted, so I poured Elmer's Glue on her head. Now I was in the cheerleader–basketball player–student council crowd, and she was in the smart but all-girl group. She would go on to be valedictorian, one place above me in our class of one hundred. Anyway, Pam had taken my supper dilemma seriously and told her mother. And dear Esther Leavitt had made supper for me. I remember it clearly: a thermos of chicken noodle soup, a sandwich, an apple. Lord knows I never ate food like that at home, having dived deeply into the joy of the packaged and processed. Though hardly hungry, I ate my meal, chastened.

One time, for a confirmation retreat, we teenagers climbed the bluff behind the church and Pastor Newman lit a fire. We didn't know it then, but on the same bluff ridge stood nearly one-thousand-year-old Mississippian platform mounds.

10. The Project

In 1991 Roland "Rollie" Rodell, an archaeologist at the Mississippi Valley Archaeology Center (MVAC), submitted a report to the Historic Preservation Division of the State Historical Society of Wisconsin. In it he summarized the archaeological evidence that pointed to the presence of Mississippian platform mounds on Little Bluff. This evidence includes Theodore S. Lewis's survey of the mounds from 1884, maps made by George Hull Squier in the same year, Squier's photos of the mounds from 1905, and extensive discussions of the mounds, as well as the results of more recent archaeological investigations, specifically, an excavation from a site below the mounds—known as "Squier's garden"—undertaken in the summer of 1991. This dig confirmed written descriptions of pottery finds made before the 1920s. In his report Rodell argues that "our efforts in this area have provided more detailed information that can be used to complete an application for listing the mound complex on the National Register of Historic Places."[15] In the same report Rodell notes that in the project the archaeologists had undertaken on the platform mounds "public interest and involvement . . . ranged from the individual level to community awareness. . . . The community of Trempealeau—specifically the Village Board—has taken an active interest in reconstructing and preserving the platform mound complex. As a first step in this endeavor Boy Scout Troop 101, under the direction of the author and their Scoutmaster Vernon Klingbeil, has begun clearing brush and trees from the mound complex."[16] Rodell describes plans to use one-hundred-year-old measurements of the mounds made by Lewis and Squier to determine how much the site had changed over the years, and writes of MVAC's desire to accurately reconstruct the mound complex. And he notes optimistically that "long term plans include public access to the mound and the borrow pit area, and an interpretive sign that . . . will explain the cultural significance of the site."[17] And why not be optimistic? In 1991 the village board was interested in the project. The people at Mount Calvary Lutheran Church—which owned the land—had been very receptive to the archaeologists, allowing them access to the site as well as the opportunity to dig in Squier's garden—or what is now the parsonage lawn. And several groups and personalities had already declared their excitement about the project. But there were details to be worked out.

Initially, the main problem revolved around the question of access to the mound site. The mounds rested on church land; the adventurous hiker could scramble up the face of Little Bluff to reach the mounds, but this would not work for tourists or vehicles. They depended on an old road up to the mounds. And just who owned the land and the road that provided access to the mounds was a matter of debate.[18] Village workers had been using the road for years to get to the water tower built on the northernmost platform, but two private citizens claimed to own parts of that road. The Boy Scouts were trying to clear the site of brush, but by June 1992, as noted in the minutes of the village planning committee, Scoutmaster Klingbeil "reported having problems with access to the Platform Mounds. They [reference unspecified] now have a logging chain [across the road]."[19]

Despite these obstructions, plans for preserving the mounds were proceeding. There was talk of building a walkway to the mounds with handrails to provide access to the disabled. And then the archaeologists from the Mississippi Valley Archaeology Center got a grant from the Wisconsin Department of Transportation. This grant provided $124, 590 "to develop the platform mounds as a cultural landmark."[20] More specifically, the grant would allow MVAC to preserve the platform mounds on Little Bluff, to make the site accessible to visitors through trails and a six-car parking lot, and to place interpretive signs near the site to help visitors understand what they were seeing. For those eager to preserve the mound site, it really looked like it was going to happen. The center's archaeologists hoped for additional funds from the Village of Trempealeau, Perrot State Park, and the University of Wisconsin–La Crosse, for a total project cost of $162,900. The *Winona (Minn.) Daily News,* just across the river, reported that James Gallagher, then a professor of archaeology at the University of Wisconsin–La Crosse and executive director of MVAC, had said that the project was "one of the most important archeological efforts he's worked on during his 15 years in the area."[21] As the archaeology center conceived it, the platform mound project was part of a larger enterprise to connect various archaeological attractions in Trempealeau via a bike path, which would run from Nicholls Mound to the platform mounds to several sites at Perrot Park.

Final receipt of the grant, however, required that the archaeology center and the village come to terms; "under the proposed agreement, the city of Trempealeau would be responsible for about $15,000 initially, and maintenance costs once the project was complete," the Winona paper reported.[22] The village board began considering the project and initially was quite favorably disposed toward it. But the issue of access remained. Then, during public meetings about the mound project, townspeople expressed other concerns. As the *Winona Daily News* described the situation in 1994: "About 25 Trempealeau residents voiced their opposition to the project at a two-hour special city council meeting in late June. . . . Some residents opposing the plan said they wanted more research done on how much maintenance costs were going to be before they could go along with the plan. Others, however, were concerned about the authenticity of the mounds, Village President Mary Kopp said."[23] Access to the land, the cost of the project, the authenticity of the mounds: these were the things that, ostensibly, hampered the project. But other obstacles, other logging chains, blocked it as well.

People in town were well aware of the Indian mounds out at Perrot Park. Located not far from the historical marker for Perrot Post, these burial mounds were a source of pride. As residents drove along the Park Road, many of us looked eagerly for the familiar conical shapes resting in the shade. We knew they had to be preserved. Most of us knew too that Trempealeau Mountain just up the road was a place sacred to Indians. But most of us were not prepared for platform mounds. We had never heard of them, and these archaeologists said they had been sitting smack dab in the middle of town for more than nine hundred years. There would have to be some hard proof.

11. How I Got Started

The platform mounds stand on a brush-covered bluff that ascends above the main street of Trempealeau. Archaeologists say they were used for ceremonial purposes; they overlook the river and face the rising sun. Though I grew up in the area, I first heard of the mounds at a family party in 1991, when I was visiting from graduate school in Syracuse, New York. I always put myself on the margins of these parties. As the only sibling to move out of the area, as one of the few cousins to leave town, as the only person in the extended family to seek a doctorate, I never felt very connected to the conversations at the center of these parties. While lingering on the margins, then, I started talking to my cousin Lu's husband, John, a self-described outlaw. In our town that might mean someone who likes to party a bit, someone who diverts from the straight and narrow. In John Ebersold's case, his reputation is also connected to his heritage, for around town John's nickname is "Indian." He is the great, great, great, great grandson of the third chief Wabasha and is thus part Dakota. (He uses the term *Sioux*. He is also of Swiss descent.) Growing up during the 1960s and 1970s and that era's romanticization of Native Americans, John was proud of his Indian heritage. In high school he ran the high hurdles with a black ponytail that reached to his waist. He was easily the coolest guy in his class, of the hood variety. When he married my cousin, the long ponytail fell across his black suit coat. The rumor still goes around about two streakers who disrupted a Catfish Days celebration in the 1970s. One of them, the story goes, was John.

So John never liked these parties much either and usually didn't come. He would prefer to go hunting, stay home to watch a Packers game, or tinker with something outside. But this time we ran into each other on the perimeter of the gathering. I think he remembered me as someone who was interested in Indians and archaeology; I had done a summer of contract archaeology with the University of North Dakota while in college, though more recently my interests had taken me to India and Tibet. He talked a bit about some of the artifacts he had found on his own archaeological surveys in the area, handmade tools and arrowheads that had worked their way to the surface of plowed fields and disturbed lands. We went to his car to look at his most recent find, and some relatives surely wondered what this unlikely pair was up to, since I was known as something of an outsider too. While we were talking, he told me about the platform mounds, how some archaeologists from the university in La Crosse were trying to get support to preserve them and make Little Bluff, on which the mounds stood, into an educational and tourist center. The mounds, the archaeologists said, were built before 1100 CE by Middle Mississippian people, an offshoot of a group that built an extensive and mounded city down in Cahokia, Illinois, near East St. Louis. But the archaeologists' plan was creating a controversy, John said. Some folks opposed the interference of these outsiders; some doubted the authenticity of the mounds. Indeed, when I later asked my dad, who had grown up in Trempealeau, if he knew about them, he said, "If there was anything up there, we would've known about it."

When I told John that I was interested in the project, he gathered all the materials he had—archaeologists' reports, news clippings, minutes of meetings—and gave them to me. They sat in a file while I was preoccupied with other things.

12. Playing Indian

The first time John told me about the platform mound project, I promised that I would come and study it. But as I also told him, I wasn't so much interested in the archaeology; what really interested me were people's reactions to the project, what they wanted to remember and believe. Before I could get back—physically, psychically, academically—to begin the study, I finished a dissertation, got married, worked four successive academic jobs, gave birth to two boys, and wrote a different book. By then the mound fiasco was over and the archaeology center's grant proposal was dead and gone. But I was ready to begin my project.

In the summer of 2000 I was visiting my mom, heard about a centennial celebration for Perrot Park, and drove over with my five-year-old son, Liam. The gathering included an assortment of archaeologists, naturalists, vendors, people dressed as settlers and natives, and observers in tank tops; this was a small version of a "rendez-vous," a reenactment, of sorts, of the gatherings of trappers, traders, and merchants that took place in the days of the fur trade. One fellow was dressed up as a Jesuit priest and wandered around carrying a staff with a cross on it. Others were dressed as settlers and voyageurs. Some practiced tomahawk throwing. And one white man was dressed up as a native of some sort, with buckskin breeches with fringe, feet in moccasins, shirtless and tanned, his long gray hair tumbling over his shoulders. Another big white man wore only a loincloth. Around the shelter house, the park's main public building, booths and exhibits were set up: a blacksmith's shop, a spinner's workshop, a table with archaeological information, a tepee, tents where people in costume sold furs, beads, dreamcatchers, home-made candy.

Every now and again someone would light a cannon, and the boom would resound over the bay.

Liam and I asked a white woman in settler's calico if we could look inside her tepee. Blankets and furs were the furniture, and everything inside was meant to be from the period. She said she and her family lived in it on the weekends, but now, as the summer wore on, she was getting tired of it. As I learned later, the people who attend rendezvous try to exist during the event's duration by using only technology from the period, that is, stuff from the late 1700s and early 1800s. They cook on open fires; they forgo coolers and sodas. They fetch water from pumps.

One settler turned out to be my former high school art teacher, Bruce Klubertanz. He wore leather breeches and vest, a bandanna knotted around his head; he carried a pewter stein. I asked him what the people gathered at such events did—did they reenact something? "No, we really just hang out."

My cousin Tim, whom I had bumped into there, expressed his interest in such an enterprise. "It's great," he said without irony. "It's a chance to get away from modern technology."

No Native Americans were among those gathered. The man dressed as some kind of native, Tom Hunter, passed by with a leather sack full of water. He reminded me of what it was like to be a kid and play Indian.[24] Indeed, much of the gathering felt like that— playing settler and Indian. Only in this case, grownups had the wherewithal to purchase more interesting toys and objects to go along with their fantasy.

Among the rendezvous goers, I bumped into John and Lu. I asked John what he thought of the people dressed up as Native Americans. "It's a joke, really," he said. He was wearing his usual tight white T-shirt and blue jeans. Just after this, John introduced me to Rollie Rodell, the archaeologist who had written the state report about the platform mounds and who had been involved in the controversy from the start. My project had begun.

So I started digging: reading, talking to people, taking notes, recording conversations, looking at old high school yearbooks, family photos, family trees, keepsakes, antique stores, jotting down memories. Although it seemed clear that the preservation project had failed in part because people wanted to believe and remember only certain things about their town, the story of the platform mounds, as I began to see it, was a story that included not only local history but family history, personal history. And if I was going to think about what these other people did, I'd also have to think about where I came from.

Later I remembered: When I was a kid we had an old green blanket with Indian-like designs on it in primary colors. The blanket had a big hole in it, just about in the middle, big enough for a girl to slip her head through. This was my poncho. In it I could creep into the woods behind the old farmhouse and be an Indian, rubbing sticks together, camping in the shade of the huge firs that towered next to the house. Blond hair tied in two pigtails, I sat in the fragrant pine needles or wandered among the oaks and pricker bushes, imagining myself one of those who had long ago walked this land, someone who could move silently in the forest, ride horses, and commune with nature. I was always a man in this fantasy, for Indian men were the ones who did things in the movies. I was not a hunter, though; I was on a vision quest. Silent and alone, I sat beneath the tall trees and waited for a sign.

There is a photo of me taken in a booth at Kmart when I was ten. In it, I face the camera head-on with all of my ten years, my blond hair in two strands on either side of my face. I had used a blue marker on the photos to draw a headband across my forehead and tuck a feather in behind. My father called me "the blond-headed Indian from Caledonia Prairie."

I realized that if I were going to explore layers of memory, I would have to consider this ground too.

13. Who Lived Here

So far I have described the surface of things—the surface of local memory, personal memory, the platform mound controversy. To more fully comprehend what these local views mean and what they omit, I had to seek out other ways of imagining the place and its past. I started by reading local archaeology and local history. (These were not subjects I was taught in school, and in college and graduate school I was interested in places farther afield.) In this chapter I try to show something of what I learned about this place from exploring the scholarly literature on it, seeking out Native American informants, and examining comparable situations outside the region. I want to provide some context for the earthworks and archaeological sites that I am writing about. I also am trying to bring some coherence to a long history of native habitation in the area. It takes a while to put even the briefest version of this story together. What I found offers a kind of counterweight to other versions of the past. In piecing this story together I worked through historical and archaeological accounts that are hardly unified in their presentation of the history. I used these tools, imperfect as they are, to pry at the first layer, to begin to uncover different stories.

While the knowledge produced by historians, archaeologists, anthropologists, or Native Americans cannot be read as offering the final truth about the history of the region, what I encountered in my readings, interviews, and travels gave me new ideas to work with, filled in some gaps in my understanding, and raised questions; it helped me scratch at the surface. And more than that, it changed my sense of the place I had grown up in, giving it a depth and a texture that extended beyond that of family and personal memory. Although the history that I present here is different from the benign narrative of progress that I grew up with, it too is a limited version. Of necessity it neglects other stories of human occupation of the region, as in Ho-Chunk, Ioway, and Dakota oral traditions. In depending on historical and archaeological accounts of human occupation of the area, I offer just one perspective of how we all came to be in this place.

In 1964 Robert Lettner, a dairy farmer, found some Indian artifacts in one of his fields. He picked up a fluted spear point chipped from stone. Looking around a bit more, he found another. This field—five miles from Trempealeau on the edge of the Driftless Area[25]—had been plowed many times; Lettner found the point on a clay knoll of Tamarack Valley, on a little rise that made Tamarack Creek bend just there.

Farmers had been finding Indian artifacts in their fields for years, so Lettner didn't think too much of it. Every once in a while he'd stop and look for more artifacts, and from time to time erosion on the knoll would reveal something more. Harland Stone, a teacher from nearby Arcadia, heard about Lettner's finds and asked if he could walk Lettner's fields after a rain and survey the surface. Stone found more points, end scrapers, chips, and flakes. But Stone recognized these artifacts as something other than the usual seven-hundred-year-old stuff: as potential Paleo-Indian finds, dating from ten thousand years ago.

The material that Lettner and Stone found takes us back to the earliest sign of human habitation in the Trempealeau region: to the mastodon and mammoth hunters who hunted and scavenged using weighted throwing sticks known as atlatls. These people tended to shift their settlements to search for food and probably lived in bands of twenty-five or so. This era of human settlement survived several thousand years in the area until the large mammals on which the people depended began to die out, perhaps as a result of overhunting.

The Paleo-Indians—and I am using archaeologists' terms for these people since their names for themselves do not survive—were succeeded by people in the Archaic period, starting about 8000 BCE. Fossils and the artifacts that these people produced indicate that they hunted bison and deer, along with other modern fauna; the artifacts also demonstrate that these folks, even at this early date, had developed networks of exchange with people far away. Copper came into the area from Lake Superior, as did marine shell from the Gulf of Mexico and exotic stone materials such as obsidian from the west. These people sometimes buried the dead with such objects in cemetery-like plots. They also adorned some individuals with red powder, a practice that suggests that death had a symbolic value for them.

Changes in the climate of the Upper Mississippi affected the cultures of the Late Archaic period, from about 3000 to 1000 BCE. People from this era settled into regional niches, shifting between winter rock shelters and summer camps along the river. Signs of their presence are still being found in "rock art" around the region that depict deer and other animals and, in one case, an image of a baby on a cradle board.[26] The tools these people created are found frequently on ridges, terraces, and sometimes on islands of the Upper Mississippi.

Archaeologists use the making of pottery to mark the advent of the next form of culture, that of the Woodland (500 BCE). Evidence of many Woodland warm season sites is also found on islands in the Upper Mississippi Valley in the form of shell middens; in these places people gathered clams and discarded the shells. People in the Woodland period constructed elaborate burial mound sites; they also used plants more intensively than their predecessors and extended the networks of trade developed in the Archaic period.[27] Hopewell culture, as represented by several mounds in the area, belongs to the Woodland period.

The distinctive and relatively lavish Hopewell culture flourished in southern Ohio and Illinois about two thousand years ago and made its way to the Trempealeau area not long after.[28] In Ohio, Hopewell culture connects an impressive array of mounds to circular, square, and octagonal embankments; these mound complexes were linked to each other in what seems to be a kind of pilgrim's circuit.[29] While not as extensive, present-day evidence of Hopewell culture in Trempealeau dates from 100 to 400 CE and takes the form of elaborate mortuary mounds in which a number of individuals were buried along with valuable artifacts. In the largest Hopewell mound in the Trempealeau area, Nicholls Mound, for example, human remains were buried in a deliberate manner, suggesting the high status of the deceased. Artifacts found inside it include copper ornaments and tools, elaborately chipped stone blades of Rocky Mountain obsidian, imported ceramic vessels, and drilled bear canine pendants.

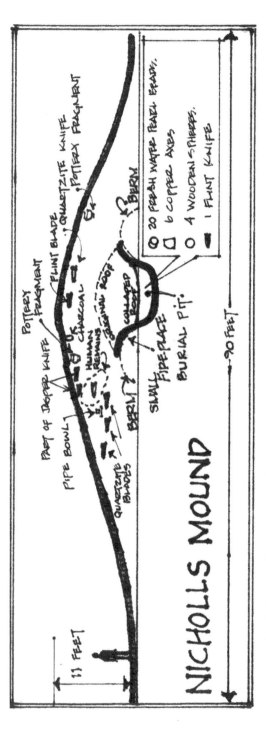

1.2. Drawing of Nicholls Mound by Kevin Brown, based on information from Wisconsin Department of Natural Resources. This is a large Hopewell burial mound (ca. 100–400 CE) located just outside Trempealeau. This mound was excavated by the W. C. McKern and others from the Milwaukee Public Museum; it contained several burials and a number of exotic artifacts from across the continent. Originally, there was a roof over one of the burials that collapsed as more earth was piled onto the mound. The skeletons and the artifacts recovered in 1928 were taken to the Milwaukee Public Museum.

Hopewell culture seems to have disappeared about sixteen hundred years ago, for reasons that are not clear. Local groups continued to hunt and gather in seasonal cycles, constructing smaller mounds that lacked the exotic artifacts of the earlier period.

Artifacts from the Late Woodland period suggest another shift. About twelve hundred years ago people in southwest Wisconsin began to construct mounds with distinct shapes—sometimes in linear form, sometimes in the shape of animals, such as wolves, deer, birds, and turtles. Although archaeologists debate who built these mounds, many Ho-Chunks believe that their ancestors were the architects. Some of these effigy mounds contain human burials, in extended, partial, and bundle burials.[30] Artifacts such as copper ornaments are also sometimes enclosed within them, and many mounds contain a dedicatory hearth, sometimes in a position that corresponds to the effigy animal's heart. Some archaeologists believe that the effigy mounds represent clan totems or territory markers, while others maintain that constructing the mounds was part of a process that helped integrate the society.[31] In any case, triangular chipped stone projectiles from this period indicate that the Late Woodland people had abandoned spear throwing for the bow and arrow. Hunting, fishing, gathering, and eventually corn cultivation—evidence of which is eleven hundred years old—formed the means of subsistence for these folk. Archaeologists use these changes to posit the beginnings of Effigy Mound Culture in southwestern Wisconsin. In 1914 evidence of this mound-builder culture in the Trempealeau area was still abundant; in a publication from that year George H. Squier notes the presence of a number of bird, bear, deer, and panther effigies in the vicinity, some of which had not yet been destroyed by cultivation.[32] These days deer and wolf effigies have been identified and are maintained near the Nature Center at Perrot State Park; linear and bird effigies remain unmarked and largely unknown on Trempealeau Mountain.[33]

About one thousand years ago the Mississippian culture of Cahokia developed in what today is southern Illinois. Mississippian culture maintained far-flung networks of exchange and produced a distinctive platform mound–building culture that reached its peak about 800 CE. Using architectural works typified by flat-topped platform mounds, the highly organized Mississippian culture relied on the cultivation of maize and beans in addition to hunting. About 1100 CE this culture extended its influence up the Mississippi, reaching what is now Wisconsin and Trempealeau.[34] The community at Cahokia began to collapse around 1300 CE, perhaps because of the pressures of sustaining a large, dense population. At Trempealeau evidence of Middle Mississippian culture takes the form of the three tiered platform mounds on Little Bluff.

Although Middle Mississippian culture did not remain long in Trempealeau, its proponents were probably contemporary with Late Woodland people. In any event, the local Late Woodland populations adapted some Mississippian technologies to produce a culture known as Oneota. *Oneota* is an archaeological term that was first used to identify the presence of shell-tempered pottery along the Upper Iowa River. In other situations the term has been used to refer to a group of people linguistically grouped as the Chiwere-Winnebago; this includes people later known as the Ioway, Oto, Missouri, and Ho-Chunk. (*Oneota* comes from the Oneida Iroquois, a tribe outside this group but that settled in northeast Iowa for a time. As the Ioway writer and artist Lance Michael Foster argues, the term *Hungeh,* or ancestors, might be a more appropriate name than Oneota, as it is a Chiwere-Winnebago term; he adds, "But we all know how hard-headed archaeologists can be, and Oneota is probably here to stay.")[35] Oneota material culture is typified by distinctive shell-tempered ceramic jars, triangular arrowheads, and abundant end scrapers (used as knives to cut wood and to prepare hides). Between 950 and 750 years ago the Oneota established several large village and mound complexes upriver in the Red Wing area. They hunted game such as bison, deer, and elk and relied on the Mississippi floodplain for fish, turtles, clams, and plant foods; they also cultivated corn, beans, and squash with hoes constructed from the shoulder blades of bison. In summer the Oneota lived in large villages on the main river terraces. In winter they may have shifted west to the fringe of the Great Plains in order to hunt bison. About 1300 CE the Oneota shifted downriver to La Crosse.[36] Remains from one Oneota village were uncovered in 1979 when the Valley View Mall was under construction. Archaeologists maintain that the Oneota eventually abandoned the region about 1625 CE, just before the arrival of the French. Although Oneota culture was contemporary with the arrival of Europeans on the continent, there is no evidence of contact in western Wisconsin. Robert Boszhardt notes that "to date no glass beads, kettle brass, iron, or other European goods have been found in direct association with La Crosse Oneota materials."[37] The Oneota probably moved to what is now Iowa and southern Minnesota and are historically identified as the Ioway Indians.

Although the La Crosse Oneota seem not to have been in contact with Europeans, the arrival of foreigners on the continent had a profound effect on native peoples throughout the Mississippi Valley and Great Lakes region. A host of foreign diseases was transported to America by conquistadors, mariners, and slaves in the early sixteenth century. Some scholars estimate that in the century after the first introduction of foreign microbes, thirty million Native Americans died; this population decimation was not confined to the eastern seaboard but pushed its way inland and west even before the foreigners themselves reached those places.[38] As Roger G. Kennedy describes it, "The Age of Discovery introduced Europeans and Africans to the Americas, and the Americans to those diseases which produced in the New World a Great Dying."[39] In the four hundred years after the arrival of Europeans, the native population continued to be decimated; disease, intertribal conflict, a bounty on Indians, poverty, starvation, war, killing, alcohol, and removal of native peoples to reserved lands all caused the numbers of the dead to mount. Some historians estimate that from a population of 15 million Native Americans in 1500, the numbers dropped to 265,000 by 1900. Others place the initial figure much higher, at 90 to 112 million.[40] Even if one uses a very conservative initial population estimate of 2 to 4 million, the numbers are devastating, and, as one scholar notes, "There is ample evidence for population declines of 80 percent or more—and occasionally of 95 percent—down to late-nineteenth century population nadirs."[41] In the case of the Ho-Chunk, Nicolas Perrot reports hearing of "maladies [that] wrought among them . . . devastation" before French traders even arrived in Wisconsin.[42] One scholar estimates that the Dakota Sioux population declined from an estimated 38,000 in 1650 to 25,000 in 1780.[43] While no exact figures can be produced for the Upper Mississippi region,[44] we can be certain that native peoples there were also among the casualties of foreign-borne diseases. Thus any discussion of human occupation of the Trempealeau area should be informed by this knowledge.

At the time of European contact a number of Indian nations lived and moved through Wisconsin—the Ho-Chunk, Ioway, Dakota, Menominee, Ojibwa, Potawatomi, Fox, and Sauk. (It is difficult to say just when these separate designations came into being or what they meant for native people. Contact with Europeans and their naming practices seemed to have helped cement tribal differences.) The French arrived in the Trempealeau area led by Nicolas Perrot, an explorer and fur trader in the employ of the French government; Perrot's exploration of the region of the western Great Lakes brought him into contact with representatives from most of the indigenous tribes there, though the claim of one of Perrot's editors that Perrot learned the languages of these tribes is probably a colonial exaggeration.[45] Ho-Chunk guides led Perrot as far as the Wisconsin River; from there many believe he made his way to Trempealeau Bay, where he wintered in 1685–86. Claude Charles Le Roy Bacqueville de la Potherie, evidently working from Perrot's notes, writes that Perrot and his associates "took up their quarters at the foot of a mountain, behind which was a great prairie, abounding in wild beasts."[46] Although Perrot did not stay long, his arrival in the area ushered in the fur trade; in 1730 the French military man René de Godefroy, sieur de Linctot, established a trading post near Trempealeau Mountain on the Mississippi, evidence for which seems clear.[47] The fur trade—extending from the late seventeenth to the early nineteenth century—invited the movement of a number of tribes into the area at the same time that French voyageurs and traders came to the region to bargain for and transport beaver pelts.

During the fur trade era representatives from a number of nations passed through the Trempealeau region; those with the most prominent presence historically include the Ioway, Ho-Chunk, and Dakota; the Ho-Chunk and Dakota maintain a presence in the area. All these people are speakers of Siouan languages. In what follows, I sketch in turn the history of the Ioway, Ho-Chunk, and Dakota and the shape of white settlement in the region. Most often I discuss these groups separately for the sake of clarity, but readers should understand that the lives of these peoples were often intertwined.

The Ioway

Tribal traditions and linguistic evidence suggest connections among the Ioway, Ho-Chunk, and Dakota; today the languages of the Ho-Chunk and Dakota are not mutually intelligible, which suggests that they have been separate for quite some time.[48] The languages of the Ioway and the Ho-Chunk, on the other hand, have much in common; their mutual intelligibility suggests a later point of separation. Writing in 1912, J. O. Dorsey and Cyrus Thomas describe the origins and the fate of the Ioway this way.

> Traditions of those tribes relate that at an early period they all came with the Winnebago [Ho-Chunk] from their common home north of the great lakes—the Winnebago stopping on the shore of Lake Michigan, attracted by the abundance of fish, while the others continued southward to the Mississippi River. Here the Iowa[y] separated from the main group, and received their name of Pahoja ("Gray Snow"); and near the mouth of Rock River seem to have halted for a time. Thence they moved, successively, up the Mississippi through Iowa to southwestern Minnesota; through Nebraska, Iowa, Missouri; and thence to Missouri River, opposite Fort Leavenworth, where they were living in 1848.[49]

Lance Michael Foster, himself an Ioway, maintains that the Ioway were—as part of the Oneota cultural complex—in contact with both Woodland peoples and Mississippian mound-building cultures.[50] Today the Ioway language is part of the Chiwere Siouan group, along with the Oto, Missouria, Omaha, Ponca, and Ho-Chunk languages. The anthropologist Nancy Lurie suggests that the Ioway, along with the Oto, Missouria, and Ho-Chunk, may be the descendants of the mound builders at Aztalan in south-central Wisconsin, the Oto and the Ioway having left that region first for the north and west.[51]

Traditions among the Ioway place them in what is now Iowa by 1600; several weeks after Perrot arrived in the Trempealeau area, he encountered some Ioway (Bacqueville de la Potherie calls them "Ayoës"[52]) at the fort he built along the Mississippi in 1685. At that time these Ioway invited him to their village, which was either along the Upper Iowa River or in the southeast corner of Minnesota. In an effort to acquire French goods these Ioway hunted beaver in the winter, going far inland to do so, returning to trade with Perrot at his fort.

The fur trade encouraged native groups to move and resettle, putting its own pressure on the tendencies of native groups to shift and relocate. Having moved into the area of what would become the states of Iowa and Missouri, the Ioway people trapped beaver and muskrat. The push of white settlers westward, however, changed that. In 1824 the Ioway gave up all their lands in Missouri; in 1836 they were placed on a reservation in northeastern Kansas. Some tribal members were moved to Oklahoma just after the Civil War. In 1890 another treaty shifted part of the tribe to yet another piece of land in central Oklahoma.[53] The Ioways' numbers were ravaged by disease, poverty, and resettlement in the nineteenth century. Today the tribe has two reservations, one in Kansas, the other in Oklahoma.

The Ho-Chunk

The Ho-Chunk maintain that they came from the Great Lakes region; some modern archaeological evidence suggests that the forerunners of the Ho-Chunk arrived in Wisconsin about 700 CE,[54] moving there from present-day Kentucky, though there is no consensus on this. The name Ho-Chunk means people of the first or "big" voice; tradition also translates Ho-Chunk, or Hochungra, as "big fish," "a reference to their traditional dependence on this source of food."[55]

Historical tradition has it that when Jean Nicolet first came to Green Bay in 1634 to broker peace between the Huron and Ho-Chunk, he wore a grand Chinese brocade robe, decorated with flowers and colorful birds, to greet the Ho-Chunk; he also hoped that the Ho-Chunk might help the French find a passage to the Orient. Nicolet was to be disappointed. At the time of European contact the Ho-Chunk relied on agriculture, hunting, fishing, and gathering for their subsistence. They built bark lodges and settled in semipermanent villages. While historically most Ho-Chunk lands were in eastern Wisconsin, near Lake Michigan, by the late seventeenth century they had moved as far west as the Mississippi and thus into the Trempealeau area.

The arrival of Europeans encouraged new alliances and antagonisms among native groups. The Ho-Chunk allied with the French in 1687 in a war against the Iroquois League. When the Iroquois pressed for peace, the Ho-Chunk shifted allegiance and banded with the Fox in two wars against the French. The tribe split for a time over whether they should make peace with the French.[56] These factions were reunited in 1755, when both the Green Bay and the Rock River Winnebago allied with the French against the British in the French and Indian War. When the British won the struggle for empire, the Ho-Chunks lost their European ally in the Great Lakes region.[57]

When war broke out between Britain and the colonies, the Ho-Chunk sided with the British. They did so again in the War of 1812, when 90 percent of the tribe left Wisconsin to fight with the Shawnee against the Americans. When the Americans won, the factional split of 1728 resurfaced and finally broke the tribe into the Rock River and Green Bay groups; the latter signed a peace treaty in 1816 with the Americans. When the tribe broke up, it also abandoned a political structure based on twelve patrilineal clans arranged in two parts, the Sky and Earth moieties. After 1816 the clan system retained only ceremonial function.[58]

More changes were in store for the Ho-Chunk. In the 1820s the fur trade—which had been based on barter and relations between whites and Indians—was displaced by a new society of miners of lead and galena who were hungry for land. Indians were mining and processing lead themselves, so they competed with white miners and their furnaces. From the point of view of white miners—many of them from Cornwall, England—Indians were an impediment, an obstacle in the road to progress. White settlers eager to farm also found Indians blocking their path when they moved to transform the Wisconsin frontier.[59] Immigrants and white Americans assumed that western lands were theirs for the taking, a fantasy suggested and reiterated by the title of a 1949 history of the upper Midwest by Theodore C. Blegen, *The Land Lies Open*. But people were already settled there; the whites would have to struggle for the land.

The Treaty of Prairie du Chien, signed in August 1825, fixed the boundaries of Indian territory in the area. Dakotas were assigned land along the Mississippi, and Ho-Chunk territory was fixed east of the Dakota lands. With these boundaries a part of what would become Trempealeau County was neutral territory between the Ho-Chunk and Dakota.[60]

This arrangement, however, did not last long; in a few years the U.S. government intervened again, reversing its position on Ho-Chunk lands.[61] The Ho-Chunk were required to sell their lands at a fraction of their worth, and the American government began implementing its policy of Indian removal in earnest. One architect of Indian removal, President Andrew Jackson, proposed that lands west of the Mississippi outside existing states "be guaranteed to the Indian tribes as long as they shall occupy it, each tribe having a distinct control over the portion designated for its use." Jackson initially called for a voluntary system of removal, "for it would be as cruel as unjust to compel the aborigines to abandon the graves of their fathers and seek a home in a distant land."[62]

In treaties made in 1832 and 1837 the Ho-Chunk lost all their land east of the Mississippi and were forced to move to Turkey River, Iowa. Through a treaty in 1846 the Ho-Chunk were again removed, this time to Long Prairie in central Minnesota. The tribe, which had numbered five thousand in 1820, was but half that size by 1848.[63]

The Ho-Chunk were subject to three more removals, next to Blue Earth, Minnesota, in 1855. Then in 1863 an act of Congress shifted them again, this time to Crow Creek, North Dakota; in 1865 they were moved to a tract bought from the Omaha in Nebraska. Throughout the 1830s to 1860s, however, a large number of Ho-Chunk attempted to return to Wisconsin. Initially, those who returned were opposed by white settlers, but in 1875 the federal government allowed the Ho-Chunk to come back and encouraged them to take up farming. A number of Indian missions and schools but no reservations were established for the Ho-Chunk. Today Wisconsin is home to more than forty-seven hundred Ho-Chunk tribal members with title to more than two thousand acres, all of which, according to the Ho-Chunk Nation website, they once owned and subsequently had to repurchase.[64] In 1963 the tribe elected its first officers of a reorganized tribe. Shortly thereafter the Wisconsin Winnebago Nation officially adopted a new constitution, changing its official name to the Ho-Chunk Sovereign Nation in the 1990s. Since then the Ho-Chunk Nation in Wisconsin has dramatically increased its wealth and power through tribal gaming.

The Dakota

Despite anthropologists' theories about how native peoples initially migrated from Asia and how the Sioux later migrated from the east, the Sioux maintain that they have always lived in the northern Great Plains. The only migration that they recognize was from the Black Hills into outlying regions.[65] Before European contact the Sioux Nation had seven major divisions, known as the Oceti Sakowin, and these groups occupied an area that stretched across the plains from the Mississippi River to the Rocky Mountains.[66] People of the Oceti Sakowin first encountered Europeans—the Spanish—in the Rockies and acquired horses from them.[67] By 1760 the central and western Sioux were fully equestrian cultures.[68] Farther east the Mdewakantonwan, or People of Spirit Lake band of Dakota, was an important division, with lands in northern Minnesota. This band subsisted on fishing and the harvesting of wild rice and herbs. Displaced by the Ojibwa, the Mdewakantonwan established seven villages along the Mississippi and Minnesota rivers.[69] These sites are near present-day Winona, Pepin, and Wabasha in Minnesota and thus not far from Trempealeau across the river.

The second Sioux encounter with Europeans was with French traders at the junction of the Mississippi and Missouri rivers. In the Upper Mississippi region with which I am concerned, French fur traders encountered the Dakota—whose name is a native term meaning "allies" or "league"—in 1650.[70] Initially, the Dakota were willing to engage and trade with whites; indeed, when the Dakota entered into the fur trade, white traders became assimilated into Dakota kinship patterns. As Gary Clayton Anderson notes, "A Dakota Indian did not have dealings with foreigners unless some sense of trust was established through real or fictive kinship bonds."[71] French and later English and American traders made "country marriages" with Dakota women, thus further establishing kinship ties,[72] and their metís offspring became interpreters and intermediaries between the two cultures. (This was not unique to white relations with the Dakota but occurred with other tribes as well.) In general, white people's relations with the Dakota were much more friendly than those with the western Sioux. (Perrot frequently interacted with "Scioux," or Dakota, in the vicinity of his Upper Mississippi fort.)[73]

The Dakota were a powerful presence along the Minnesota and Mississippi rivers, but they too lost sovereignty and control of their territory as the new Americans expanded westward. Soon governmental decree deprived the various nations within the Oceti Sakowin of their once vast lands. In the Trempealeau area the aforementioned Prairie du Chien treaty of 1825 declared that the eastern boundary of the Dakotas began on the Mississippi opposite the mouth of the Ioway River, continued several miles to the bluffs, followed the bluffs to the mouth of the Black River, and proceeded to a point just southwest of Eau Claire on the Chippewa River.[74] In this way Dakota lands were fixed on both sides of the Mississippi. Ten years later, however, a treaty signed in Washington, D.C., eliminated all Dakota claims to land east of the Mississippi. Writing in 1917, Eben Pierce describes this change: "In 1837, Trempealeau passed from the dominion of both the Winnebago and the Dakota, and into the possession of the whites."[75] In a subsequent treaty drawn up in 1851 and proclaimed in 1853, the Dakota relinquished their large landholdings in Minnesota and were placed on a reservation on the upper Minnesota River, in the western part of Minnesota.[76]

There the U.S. government continued to whittle away at Sioux territory. By 1862, for example, the Issati (or Santee) Sioux, one of the Mdewakantonwan, or Dakota, bands, were left with a strip of land ten miles wide and 150 miles along the Minnesota River, near New Ulm, Minnesota. In return for their land cessions these Dakota people were to receive payment in food, goods, and cash. Most of the money, however, went into the hands of traders to pay off debts for goods purchased on credit. In 1862 the situation for Dakotas in this area became desperate; the annuity was late and the buffalo hunts failed. A series of bloody encounters between the Dakota and white settlers eventually led to what is known as Little Crow's Uprising against the white settlers. (Opposing Little Crow, Chief Wabasha III called for peace.) The state militia was dispatched, and by the end of September the Dakota were defeated, leaving five hundred white settlers dead; thousands more settlers fled their homes, depopulating twenty-three Minnesota counties for many years. In the swift trials that followed, 306 Dakota were sentenced after being convicted of murder, rape, or taking part in a battle. The prisoners were taken to Mankato, where thirty-eight were hung. The remaining seventeen hundred Dakota—mostly women and children—were eventually removed to a reservation in Nebraska. (In reaction to the uprising and to calm fearful settlers, President Lincoln also removed all Ho-Chunk from Minnesota.) The Dakota population in Minnesota was devastated.[77] Today, however, Minnesota has four federally recognized Dakota communities, and a number of people in the regions of Trempealeau and southeast Minnesota claim Dakota heritage.

White Settlement

The first white man to reside in the area was Nicolas Perrot in 1685.[78] Linctot established a trading post there in 1731, and voyageurs, traders, and trappers passed through the region. A white settlement of any duration was not created until the midnineteenth century, however.

At the time of the uprising in New Ulm in 1862, Trempealeau was a new community and white settlers were in the early stages of parceling out the land and beginning to farm it. As I have noted, French traders had moved through the region for 150 years; in the early 1800s the trappers Augustin La Rocque and Louis Grignon built log cabins in the area, although they did not stay long. By the 1840s others came into the region not only to trade but to settle, though the area was still nominally Dakota territory under the third chief Wabasha, who at that time lived near Winona.[79] While local legend has it that James Reed was the first settler of the region, the settlement of Trempealeau seems to have been a gradual affair and an offshoot of alliances between Dakotas, French, and Americans that developed during the period of the fur trade. The historian Merle Curti describes the settlement of Trempealeau this way: "It may have been in the interest of Wabasha that about 1836 his cousin, François La Barth, the well-known agent of the American Fur Company at Prairie du Chien, sent two men to chop cordwood for passing steamers and, perhaps, to hold the strategic area in the interest of the fur trade with Wabasha's band. One of the two men, Jean Baptiste Douville, left the area for a while but in 1838 returned with a new wife. . . . Of Douville's background little is known. One tradition has him born in a cabin, near Trempealeau Mountain, of an Indian mother—a cousin of the famous Winnebago chief Decorah."[80] Douville's Indian and French heritage suggests what was often the case with these early settlers: numerous alliances between Americans, French, and native peoples—hardly pure categories, in any case—were built on trade, marriage, and parentage. Douville's new wife, as it turns out, was Elizabeth, the daughter of an acclaimed Kentucky-born scout, James Reed. Reed was an Indian fighter and diplomat and made a name for himself as a trapper and trader at Prairie du Chien.

By the time Douville returned to the area in 1838, the lands of Dakota, Ho-Chunk, and Ojibwa peoples had all been fixed east of the Mississippi, though people from those tribes still remained. The area was gradually settled by white people and their allies of mixed heritage. Thus, while the fur trade first brought new settlers to the area, it was actually wood that kept them there; the high banks of the Mississippi became a source of firewood for passing riverboats. James Reed arranged for Douville to cut wood for the steamboat men and look out for his animals, while Reed himself built a house and moved his family in 1840 to what would become Trempealeau.[81] Reed's domestic arrangements bear some consideration, as Curti notes that the Reed family included

> the children of [James Reed's] first wife (a well-connected Chippewa Indian whom he had married during his soldier year at Fort Crawford [Prairie du Chien] and who had died in 1830), and his second wife, Agatha, a Menominee of mixed blood, with her children by a former husband, the trader Russell Farnham. Then there were the children of Reed and Agatha. Agatha died soon after the brood was settled in the new log house. Reed then brought on a third wife and her progeny. She was Archange, sister of François La Barth, the prominent trader at Prairie du Chien, and widow of Amable Grignon. This new tie brought Reed closer into the orbit of Wabasha the Sioux [III], Archange's cousin, as his earlier marriages had allied him to the Potawatomi and the Menominee.[82]

Reed's settlement of the area arose out the networks of exchange developed during the fur trade; these family and commercial ties had welded Indians and Europeans into unique social and business relations that would be transformed later in the nineteenth century by changing governmental policies and attitudes toward race.[83] Nonetheless, Reed's own success depended on and was intertwined with the interests of native people and those of mixed descent.

For his part, after settling his family James Reed worked with the Dakota on a farm near Winona for a time, then moved for good to "Reed's Landing" in 1848; there he farmed a bit, kept livestock, trapped along the Trempealeau River, and oversaw his small wood-chopping business. The village soon began to be populated by newcomers of various backgrounds, a few of whom came to live there permanently.[84]

As river towns sprang up around Reed's Landing in nearby La Crosse and Winona, Reed and his neighbors, the French-Canadian brothers Michael and Leander Bibault, realized the value of the land itself; in 1849 they made legal claim on lands around the river settlement.[85] Soon others were speculating land in the area, including the enterprising pioneer Benjamin F. Heuston, a wealthy former railroad man named Benjamin Healy, and a businessman, lawyer, and later judge named George Gale.[86] In 1851 the township was named after a nearby bluff and became Montoville and part of La Crosse County.

Initially, land speculators focused on property in the village and on the fertile prairie near it, believing that the town's river location would make it an ideal site for trade in the future.[87] Because of this, good farmland went unclaimed and in the 1850s could be bought from the government for $1.25 an acre. Among those who took advantage of that price were three brothers from Devon, England, the Nicholses, who established their farm on the fertile prairie of the Black River Valley,[88] a site that Hopewell people had chosen two millennia earlier for construction of their elaborate burial mounds.

By 1853 a campaign to create the county of Trempealeau had been initiated by several key businessman, including Heuston, Healy, and especially George Gale, who has been called the father of Trempealeau County. Taking its name from the bluff island—*la montagne qui trempe à l'eau,* mountain that soaks in the water—the new county was eventually established in 1854; two years later Montoville became Trempealeau Township. In 1854, and also with Gale's initiative, the town of Galesville was established on the prairie northeast of Trempealeau. The state census of 1855 identified 453 people as residents of the newly organized county; they lived mostly in the south, in Galesville or Montoville. Five years later the population had risen to 2,559, a fivefold increase. The Village of Trempealeau was incorporated in 1867. Around the same time, five new townships were created, including Caledonia, the prairie on which my parents settled in 1948.[89] Today many residents of Trempealeau can connect their family tree to settlers of the 1850s and 1860s. Their names include Perkins, Grover, Uhl, Drugan, Dettinger, Wilber, Beardsley, and Hovel; some of these lines of heritage connect to my family.

Part II

What's under the Surface

1. Digging In

Archaeologists are no strangers to Trempealeau, and townspeople have been aware of archaeologists' interest in the place for a long time. Although the village with a mere 1,306 souls in 2000 barely enters the consciousness of most Wisconsin residents, when I looked into things, I found that Trempealeau has a national reputation among archaeologists for the number and variety of mounds located there. When I arranged meetings with archaeologists from La Crosse, twenty-five miles away, they expressed their admiration for the place. As we were deciding where to meet, one said: "I'd love to meet you in Trempealeau." And even after the mound debacle, another said, "I always like to come to Trempealeau." As William Green described it to me, "Trempealeau seems to affect people profoundly." Its physical distinctiveness has, over the centuries, encouraged people to respond in distinct ways—building earthworks, reshaping the land. These actions, in turn, have "fed back into the place's singularity," marking it with mounds and stories.[1]

Despite Trempealeau's archaeological fame, until recently few current Trempealeau residents were aware of the prominence of the place. Although it is the home of Wisconsin's largest Hopewell mound, many residents have never heard of Nicholls Mound, let alone visited it. And although Trempealeau Mountain is home to at least twenty-two Late Woodland burial mounds, most residents with whom I spoke claimed ignorance of them. "I've never heard of them," Barney Stephan, the oldest born-in-town resident, said. "I've been out there," Harold Wilber said, "and there's no twenty-two burial mounds out there." I had been out there many times myself as a teenager but had never seen them—or, rather, didn't know to look for them, didn't know what to look for. Hiking out there these days on the scrabbly bluffside, I can easily pick out the conical mounds; the center of each has been dug into and gouged out by a looter or curiosity seeker, probably before the 1920s. People are similarly unaware of the platform mounds. Until recently, this series of three terraced mounds, which dates to around 1100 CE and has been documented since the 1880s, has been largely forgotten and ignored.

Platform mounds are not usually burial sites; instead, they are more like stages or terraces on which successive leaders built structures. At Cahokia, downriver in Illinois, the largest mound, Monks Mound, tops out at one hundred feet; in Trempealeau the scale is much more modest. Today a visitor briefed on the dimensions and location of the mounds can make out three plateaulike levelings on the overgrown hill known as Little Bluff. But the platform mounds are not part of most people's conception of the place.

"I don't know anything about them," many people said.

"Never heard of them," others told me.

My uncle Clyde said that back in the 1940s, when he was in his teens, he drove a car up there and got in trouble for "parking" with a girl. "Someone saw my headlights and told S.J. [his dad]."

A local plumber told me: "We used to play cowboys and Indians up there when we were kids. There's nothing up there."

Many residents also claim not to know about the effigy mounds in the park, although a trail and interpretive signs now mark some of these earthworks. And, indeed, despite my own youthful interests in archaeology and Native Americans, I did not know of these places—Nicholls Mound, platform mounds, effigy mounds—when I was growing up in the region. At that time they were not part of the school curriculum; they were not part of local self-conception. What people *did* know about was Trempealeau Mountain, the bluff remnant that stands in the Mississippi within the bounds of the park and lent its name to the village. Said to be sacred to Indians—whose tribe was not specified in our folklore—the gentle rounded shape of the bluff was echoed in the nearby burial mounds—what we knew as "Indian Mounds." These burial mounds formed the other end of our sense of a significant Native American place. Integral to our self-conception, these mounds were the outer limit of our archaeological knowledge. Located along the road to nearby Perrot State Park, this series of seven little mounds of dirt—overgrown with grass and marked off by appropriate signage: "Indian Mounds"—were a source of pride. I imagined Indians laid out supine in them, as I had seen my own dead Grandpa Hovell arranged in a casket. We assumed a reverent aspect when we approached them: they were someone's final resting place.

2.1. Trempealeau Mountain. Photo by author. This view is from Brady's Bluff toward Winona, Minnesota, in winter 2004. In the foreground is Trempealeau Bay; railroad tracks run on the land in the lower left.

And because these mounds had been preserved in the park outside town, perhaps it didn't matter so much to people in the area that other mounds were destroyed. Farmers in the area had run across such structures since they started plowing up the land in the mid-nineteenth century. Mounds were also destroyed when Perrot Park was first constructed in 1928, when a private campground was built in Trempealeau Bay in the 1930s, and probably also when the campground became part of the state park in the 1960s and improvements were made. Although many people valued the Indian Mounds at the park as markers of the distant past, preserving other mounds—let alone recognizing their sanctity or integrity—was not a strong value. Mounds were destroyed when the outhouses were built near the park shelter house; mounds were leveled for beach access. As my aunt Barb said, "You used to be able to drive your car right down to the bay, have a picnic and swim, and put the kids to sleep in the car." Such convenience came at the expense of the mounds.

2.2. Indian Mounds at Perrot Park. Photo by author. The mounds have eroded; they are the small knolls in the middle ground, some of which have trees growing on them.

These two aspects, then—Trempealeau Mountain and the Indian mounds—have formed the two poles of most residents' local historical self-conception; they were the two physical structures in the land that we let remind us of the region's Native American past. (My sister Pam informs me, however, that until recently she thought of Trempealeau Mountain only in terms of French history.) We took pride in these things; they helped tell us who we were, we thought. And they didn't demand much from us, really, but rather allowed room for our sense of place to be filled instead with other, more personal mythologies and memories. Barney Stephan, an elderly man who as a teenager served as a cook for a state archaeological dig in 1930, had no memory of the sites he had worked on. But he could list the many jobs he had done in his long life and what he earned for them; he could tell me the story of how my great-uncle Kenny Beardsley gave him his nickname. (Offering a chunk of watermelon to young Byron, Ken said, "Here you go, Barney Google.") The site of the platform mounds was where kids took cattle to graze; they were where you played cowboys and Indians, but they were not where some long-lost, highly structured Native American group centered a life that we couldn't begin to imagine. Trempealeau Mountain may have been the site of significant mound-building activity, but for my family it was, in part, a place near where we used to water-ski. (My sister recalls that our brother instructed her to "lean back! lean back!" when she tried to skim across the water.) Even after one learns that the site around the shelter house at the park was once the location of thirty conical mounds and several effigy mounds, it is hard not to fix on it as the place where we used to play softball during family gatherings. Our memories have the advantage of being *ours*. Our childhood memories have a particular tendency to become imbued with nostalgia; we cling to them as we find ourselves becoming grown-ups, and perhaps we cling to them all the more as we fear that maybe we are not quite up to the role assigned to us, and as we bury our own dead.

Within this kind of remembering certain versions of Trempealeau Mountain and the parks' Indian Mounds became part of our personal mythology. We drew pictures of Trempealeau Mountain; we imagined Indians in breechcloths with canoes and bows and arrows on its banks. The mounds mattered too—the ones on the way to the park were a kind of remnant of those same Indians. Both structures were endowed with a kind of sanctity, if not sanctimoniousness. No wonder, then, that people were nearly unmoored by the revelation that the so-called Indian mounds were reconstructions, if not outright fakes.

At a meeting about the platform mounds in 1993, Harry Murray, who had worked at the park as a member of the Civilian Conservation Corps in the 1930s, revealed that there once *had* been three mounds but that those had been destroyed. He himself had brought in the dirt to remake them and added four more in the bargain. And later these too, it came to light, had been reinforced with plaster by an eager park manager, "enhanced" so that tourists might better see them from the comfort of their cars.

Harold Wilber, a leading businessman, taped Murray's confession and notified the state. The sign saying "Indian Mounds" came down, and the town lost a landmark, parting ways with one of its cherished memories along with it. For no longer could the sight of the mounds evoke simple reverence; the mounds reminded townspeople of their own foolishness, the way they had been duped into a false kind of homage, the way, in effect, they had worshipped their own childhood romances. The shame at having been fooled about the mounds seems to have been projected onto the proposal to preserve the platform mounds offered by archaeologists in the 1990s. If the Indian Mounds were fake, then maybe the platform mounds were too. If we were fooled, maybe archaeologists are fools too.

So the Indian Mounds became lost to many of us. But Trempealeau Mountain remains a sacred structure available to personal mythologizing. You can park your car and gaze at it from across the bay. You can see a massive painting of it in the Wildflower Café. You can even go over and hike on it, if you are willing to brave the railroad tracks to get there. There you can create your own memories of the place, making the mountain your own with hotdogs and beer and a forbidden campfire. So central does the island bluff remain to local self-conception that Harold Wilber named his public golf course after Trempealeau Mountain. You can see its stylized shape on the ball caps he sells in the clubhouse. After the Indian Mounds had been exposed as fake, he put tall, conical mounds of earth along the fairways; grassed and groomed, they are a kind of ironic reference to what we once cared about, what we once believed in.

In all this remembering and memorializing, our notions about Trempealeau Mountain or the Indian Mounds depended little on archaeological knowledge. If we saw our town as a nice little place on the Mississippi that had missed its chance to make a name for itself— set back by the greed of politicians and a fire that burned two blocks of the business district in 1888—archaeologists saw it differently. The degree of contempt for archaeological knowledge that would mar discussions about the platform mounds in the 1990s, however, was something fairly new. When the Wisconsin archaeologist W. C. McKern brought a team to excavate various mounds in and around Trempealeau for three summers from 1928 to 1930, there was no shame in being employed by the scientists. Instead, there was a kind of pride: this is how a bright kid might use his hands. My godfather's father, Kenneth Drugan, worked with McKern and company for several summers. A photograph taken of him in the late 1920s shows him grinning, clad in breeches and high World War I boots, his hands thrust in his pockets and his legs jauntily apart. In 1928 people used to come out to Nicholls Mound in their cars of a Sunday to check the progress of excavations of the Hopewell mounds. Photographs from the period show ladies in their best dresses looking

2.3. Kenny Drugan, ca. 1928. With permission from the Milwaukee Public Museum. This photo was taken of Drugan when he was a teenager and worked with McKern and other archaeologists with the Milwaukee Public Museum.

2.4. Excavation observers, Trempealeau, ca. 1928. With permission from the Milwaukee Public Museum.

down into the pits where McKern, Alton Fisher, Towne Miller, and others laboriously scraped dirt. If there was a distance between archaeologists and townspeople imposed by the archaeologists' education and their outsider status, I get the sense that they were not seen as intruders. Local people still tell stories about how the archaeologists cooked and ate with them. Photographs show the archaeologists in dungarees and work clothes, like other guys in town. And one photograph attests that despite McKern's university credentials, he had to shave his whiskers like every other guy.

In those days archaeologists dug trenches in order to excavate; it was not the noninvasive work it is today. So in a way, archaeologists were doing what some local folks had been doing all along: coming across artifacts, digging into mounds.[2] Even so, the archaeologists' work in the summer of 1930 on the Schwert group of two-thousand-year-old mounds (named for Leo Schwert, on whose farm they stood) near Second Lake uncovered artifacts bound to amaze the professional and the untutored alike: a finely wrought chalcedony dagger nine inches long, a knife chipped from yellow chert, copper

2.5. W. C. McKern, shaving, ca. 1928. With permission from the Milwaukee Public Museum.

implements and ornaments from a source near Lake Superior, sheet silver, freshwater pearls, and, as McKern writes, a "magnificent obsidian scraper knife nine inches in length, five inches in width and two inches in maximum thickness," whose source could only be Yellowstone in Wyoming.[3] There were bones and skeletons too, of course: one mound they dug into that year revealed "about seven extended individuals, buried in the flesh, and an indeterminate number of individuals represented by bundles of disarticulated bones."[4] One photograph from an excavation of the same period shows a collection of skulls and bones, arranged in a small heap here, tangled up in a pile with other bones there. While this funeral arrangement no doubt went against prevailing and local notions about Christian treatment of a corpse, another photograph shows a skeleton in a posture like that of the coffin-borne bodies of white settlers. Earth has settled between the ribs, worked its way into the cracked skull, found its way between the corpse's grinning teeth. Perhaps the tendency of many Trempealeau residents to think of all mounds as burial sites

2.6. W. C. McKern with Nicholls Mound artifacts excavated in 1928. From the collection of Kent and Donna Drugan.

originates from those summer excavations and the bones they exposed. The tools, artifacts, and remains that the archaeologists took out of those mounds in farmers' fields were important enough to be shipped to Milwaukee, where they were displayed and preserved in the Milwaukee Public Museum. Whether the townsfolk knew it or not, excavations in and around Trempealeau confirmed the extent of the Hopewell culture that stretched to Ohio; the mounds put Trempealeau on the archaeological map. But in a strange way the finds of those summers seem not to have become an integral part of local knowledge or local self-conception. The contact between locals and archaeologists became a kind of summer romance and involved just a few folks; Nicholls Mound resumed its conical shape in a farmer's field and was soon overgrown with prairie grass and poison sumac, another bump on the landscape.

2.7. Nicholls Mound, 2004. Photo by author.

Maybe it's not surprising that people would soon forget the Schwert, Shrake, and Nicholls mounds (like Schwert, all named after farmers).[5] People had other things on their minds in the 1920s and 1930s. Scraping together a living. Getting a bit of schooling (but not too much). There was marriage and family and kids. Sickness and madness. And the depression. And then the war. Progress was measured by new roads and houses, fertile fields, healthy livestock, and enough flour and sugar to make it through the week. My father's recollections of his childhood are full of stories about farms, horses, cars, and the many ways in which his family tried to make a living. In 1988, in his own attempt to come to terms with the past, he wrote that, as a child,

> for a time I drove Mr. Moore's cows to pasture in the summer. I still remember that they were named Molly, Maryjane, and Opal. The automobiles at that time, about 1930, were very few, in Trempealeau. The county snowplow would come through after a blizzard. . . . The frozen river was a sort of super-highway for the farmers. They used

it to haul cord wood to Winona and La Crosse. They also hauled hay and livestock to the [Twin] cities. Many of the people in cities were ex-farmers and kept a cow and/or horse. Occasionally, a team would go through the ice. The farmer that was experienced was prepared, he had choke-ropes on his horses, and he would tighten these—and his horses, being full of air, would float up well. A little hay or some brush on the edge and another team would pull them out.[6]

There was plenty of work to do in those days, Dad let us know in the pages of memories he recounted for posterity. For fun there were homemade music and picnics, card games, courtship, and dances. But archaeology? Hardly. People were still in the process of claiming the land, carving roads out of hillsides, making fields out of steep slopes and sandy prairies, making a go of a lumberyard, a stockyard, getting the railroad to run. Archaeology involved a kind of luxurious interest in a distant past, a past that no doubt seemed far away from these settlers of northern European descent. If the cathedrals of Europe had little to do with them, what could be the worth of these old Indian sites, especially now that the Indians were mostly gone?

Perhaps the general ignorance of the mounds was a question of education, of access to information, of being schooled in the value of mounds. In the old days the few citizens who were interested in archaeology tended to be educated men. The most prominent archaeological thinker in the area was George Hull Squier, who in the 1870s studied with Harvard's Frederick Ward Putnam, one of the most important archaeologists of his day; it is largely through Squier that we know anything of the platform mounds at all. More recently, local lovers of earthworks and archaeology have educated themselves on the topic. John Ebersold, who now maintains the streets and parks for the Village of Trempealeau, never went to college, yet he has read widely in local archaeology, has tramped the land extensively, and has become an asset to archaeologists at the Mississippi Valley Archaeology Center, who praise his knowledge of the area. Russ Stull, who grew up in Trempealeau and has since moved to Milwaukee, has also been involved in local archaeology; in his teens he drafted a fine map of the platform mounds and worked on mound excavations at Trempealeau Lakes with archaeologists from the State Historical Society.[7] My brother, a psych major at the University of Wisconsin–La Crosse and a voracious reader of history, has learned about the area's archaeology through his catholic consumption of accounts of local history as well as his daughter's recently instituted primary school curriculum. As for me, I only began to learn—only began to want to learn—about local history and local archaeology twenty years after I had left the place. Where there is interest in the past, the general trend in town has been to think of local history in terms of European settlement of the region; folks interested in periodic archaeological projects (like my dad) or pre-European history (like the rendezvousers) are largely on their own, dependent on books and websites, and have to make their own sense of things.

Indeed, the people of Trempealeau these days evidence a great suspicion of archaeologists in particular and academic knowledge more generally. In conversations with relatives and residents I hear disparaging remarks about academia. When one of my aunts asked me about my then-forthcoming book—a study of English-language texts on Tibet—she said flatly: "Oh, I guess about five people will read that." The stereotype of egg-headed academics who can't tie their shoes circulates widely among people who are not specialists, who in fact have learned to do a multitude of jobs and to do them well. My father, for example, could farm, plumb, fix machines, weld, sandblast, hunt, fish, build furniture, plow snow, tend factory boilers, work on boats, read, write, draw, paint, and play clarinet, tuba, bass, and electric guitar. My mother can sew, milk cows and garden, tend chickens, drive a tractor, chop wood, ride horses with skill, walk for miles, and dance; she is also a champion knitter. To many such folks, specializing in the excavation and interpretation of Indian bones and artifacts—or English literature or Tibetan culture—suggests a kind of myopia, a willful abandonment of common sense. And what are seen as the limits of specializing are exaggerated in conversation. For example, my aunt told me that one time when the archaeologists dug in the park, they had been dumbfounded by the discovery of blacktop on what they thought of as an ancient site. How could it have gotten there? In another story, about the excavation of the Perrot Post in 1996, the scientists are said to have discovered a big piece of old wood in the ground; as this person reported it, they'd thought they'd really found something until they dug a bit farther and got the strongest whiff of creosote. It was nothing but an old railroad tie.

But there are other instances when people don't quite see—or don't want to deal with—what's in front of them. I met a woman at the Rhino Bar who complained bitterly that some mother and her child sat in her dahlias during the annual summer Catfish Days parade. She does not seem to know that her garden is constructed on what is another platform mound, at the corner of Third and Jay. George Gale described the structure this way in 1867: "The mound at Trempealeau is about seven feet high, with a level surface at the top about twenty-five by fifty feet, with graded ways from each of the four sides about twenty-five feet long, with the full width of the sides."[8] Ernie Boszhardt has found Mississippian pottery in a utility trench at this site; Russ Stull also found pottery shards. Today yellow day lilies and a metal bench stand on the platform.

A friend told me that when the people who own land near this platform mound were building their house, they ran across lots of artifacts, tools, bones. Because they did not want their house building delayed, they worked fast, and at night, and simply covered up what they found. Their ranch house, in effect, is erected on a burial. We might say also that it is built on a denial, a refusal, the old digging-in that says, "I have a right to be here. This is my land."

2. Connections

It's not that people don't have an interest in the Native American past. It's that most see themselves as being disconnected from it—they don't recognize that what they think and believe now has anything to do with something that happened in the past, with something their ancestors did or believed.

While I was doing research on this project, I attended a twenty-fifth anniversary party one summer with my husband and sons for my sister Deb and her husband, Larry. We gathered around coolers of beer and pop, vats of barbequed hamburger, tubs of potato salad, and summer garden fare. When you live in a place where most of your dad's five siblings and your mother's six siblings have decided to settle and reproduce, no family party can ever be a small one. Sometimes I think these huge gatherings are designed so that you won't ever have to actually get into a deep and sustained conversation with somebody else; you acknowledge each other's presence but can quickly be distracted. Alcohol—cans of Bud, Miller Lite, City Lager and boxes of sweet wine—lubricate the conversation, provoking howls of laughter from the Bockenhauers, inducing lethargy in others. When some of my relatives hear what I am doing in town for the next two weeks—studying Native American history and archaeology—many have something to share, some story to tell. My widely read cop brother, Bob, tells me about a Ho-Chunk memorial wall established recently at the county courthouse; it was inaugurated with ceremonial drumming. My cousin Roxanne tells me about the Indian heritage of her husband, Ken; he is a descendant of James Reed's first wife, an Ojibwa. She says Ken's profile looks just like that of Chief Hole-in-the-Day, whose photo she's recently seen. My uncle Doug tells me about an "Indian camp" in German Coulee that his dad (my grandpa Earl) used to talk about—though, he adds, "You never knew when Dad was joking." Doug says, nonetheless, that near the trailer he rents out there's a place with a lot of stone chips and another such site down by the creek. And it strikes me that people do have a sense of local history—they do have a sense of past that includes Indians. What we have is fragments, shards of memory; these stories are not tied up to larger issues such as racism and removal. For many of the people who relate them, these are just stories that don't connect—to each other, to archaeology, to history, or to their tellers. It seems to me, then, that part of what I'm doing in this project is collecting these accounts, hearing them, and bringing them together to make a different kind of sense by including other stories, by setting these seemingly unrelated tales next to each other. They may not flow into one seamless narrative; they link up for a different kind of history, a story that suggests the layers and webs that connect people across time, that connect people to a place.

◇

3. Double Cousins

My family tells lots of stories. And then tells them again. And again. There is the story of how, as a baby, my uncle Clyde got his head caught between the slats on a potty chair. When my dad told the story, it was designed to assert Clyde's more mischievous nature, as opposed to the good-boy quality of my father, Clyde's older brother. There is the story of how my great grandmother Beardsley didn't like to be reminded of her grandmotherhood and thus her age. Everyone had to call her "Ma B." Once, when my dad was about seven, he saw Ma B at her back door and called out, "Hi, Grandma!" She jumped down from the top steps and, in fury, chased him around the house. Then there is the story of how she punished her young daughter

Merle by sticking her upside down in a full rain barrel. These stories were told over and over. They offered a kind of comfort to my dad and my grandma.

Two years after my parents got married, Clyde married my mom's sister Barb and set up a house across the country road. What followed was a succession of nearly matching kids: my brother, Bob, followed by Clyde and Barb's son, Clyde Jon (known as Jonny); my sister Deb, followed by my cousin LuAnn; my sister Pam, followed shortly afterward by my cousin Tari. Seven years later I arrived, and four years after that and somewhat out of sync, my cousin Stan was born. These double cousins were nearly as close as siblings, and for a while I had six to look up to and admire, six of them to push me around. (That's my memory, anyway.) My brother was the eldest of the extended brood and took on the role of big brother: obedient, good student, never a bother. And, just as in the story about Clyde as the mischievous younger brother, Jonny became the wild one, the one to test the limits. While Bob skipped third grade and hunkered down to read the *Encyclopedia Britannica,* Jonny taught me, the hard way, what a snuggy was, yanking my underwear up sharply from the back. While Bob tried his hand at wrestling and excelled at archery, Jonny taught the girl cousins how to spit greenies, hawking up snot and ejecting it purposefully. When the cousins set a section of the woods on fire, Jonny got blamed and my dad chased him around the house in rage.[9] Jonny got away. By fourteen he was smoking; by sixteen he had a motorcycle and had dropped out of school. He topped out at over six lanky feet, had long wavy hair, and was attractive in a dangerous kind of way. I'd be babysitting for Stan and we'd be hunkered in front of some cowboy-and-Indian movie, and if Jonny happened to drop by the house, we felt like we'd been blessed by a visitation from a prince or something. Of course, that kind of never-know-where-he-is behavior drove his parents nuts. Jonny was seventeen when he enlisted in the navy during the Vietnam War and was flown out to San Diego, where his head was shaved and he had to sleep, eat, run, and puke at someone else's command. He got some kind of infection and was discharged. At the same time Bob plugged away at college and withstood taunts about being a draft dodger. And while Bob lived at home to save money during his college years,

Jonny moved in and out of rentals, got, quit, and lost jobs, and was frequently in trouble for drinking too much, partying too hard, doing a few drugs. You'd see him and his friends on their loud motorcycles once in a while; he'd lean back on his long chopper, feet propped high in the air in tough-looking boots. No helmet, of course.

My family had kept horses on and off through the years, and when I was ten my dad bought two horses—pintos—one black and white, one white and red. Maybe Dad thought it would be a good thing for his adolescent daughter to learn how to ride and take care of big animals like that. As it turned out, only Dad could ride the black-and-white one—as wild as he was—while I learned to ride on the tame and somewhat lame white-and-red one My dad fenced off part of the woods behind the barn, and the horses had the run of the place, grazing beside the old oaks, walking the trails.

Jonny dropped by his folks' house one afternoon and decided to visit our horses. Dad wasn't home, so Jonny grabbed a bridle from the barn and headed out to the woods. He found the black-and-white one and was somehow able to slip the bridle over his head and neck, then ride him around the farm bareback. When my dad heard about this, he was ready to kill Jonny—all Dad's attempts at training the horse would go for nothing, he said, but his anger also held an element of rivalry of some sort, pique, I think, that this wild kid had been able to coax the horse that far.

The last time I saw Jonny was at a local fall festival; I was twelve and begging Dad for money to play tipboards and drink pop on the edge of the beer tent.[10] Jonny was deep inside the tent, but he'd been holding down a job for a while, and I can remember someone's saying that maybe this time he'd get his life straightened out. The next morning, a Monday, Tari's husband, Woody, came over, and when I answered the door, he didn't smile and he asked to talk to my dad. I sat on the stairway, hidden and eavesdropping. Jonny had been in an accident. He was coming home to Trempealeau at 2 o'clock in the morning and hit a train broadside. He was dragged a hundred feet; his body was discovered only after the train had gone to Winona and returned.

The family converged on Barb and Clyde's house. I remember Clyde's doing all right for a while—making conversation, smoking cigarettes—but there was a point when he just had to go out on the porch and cry by himself. The visitation was two nights later. The casket was closed, as Jonny's body was mangled beyond recognition. I could not stay in that dark funeral home where the inexplicable was so palpable; I went with three cousins to sit in someone's car and try to make sense of it all, telling stories about Jonny, shouting and crying. The funeral was at the Lutheran church—where Stan and I had been baptized, where Lu and John had married, and where I would be confirmed. Stan was only eight at the time, and someone had dressed him in a little suit. I remember that at the lunch afterward, Stan was dry eyed, lighthearted even, while it seemed that my heart had turned a corner out of childhood.

4. The Past

I complain about what has been forgotten. I take issue with what is remembered from the past. The past is not just there, of course, to be conjured and recalled. We make it, we seize on its objects. Like archaeologists, we make stories up from what is left over, what is left behind. Some things from the past we turn to because they are useful; some we turn to for pleasure. Some versions of the past we use to find our place in the world. Some things we remember because, bitter as they are, they are like medicine; they are good for us. And some things we remember because they help us to forget other things.

These days you can visit a number of antique stores in the Trempealeau area. Dressers, tables, chairs, pictures, china, clothes, lace, machinery, magazines: a jumble of old things retrieved from different eras. The past offered by the antique stores appeals to our eyes and our touch. The antique hunter seeks out objects that look a certain way but does not always use them for the purpose for which they were made. Few really want to have to use an old iron that has to be heated on a wood or coal stove; aside from the rendezvousers, few want to actually have to use a china basin to wash their faces. These shops have a whiff of mildew about them, and the joke is that antiques are simply somebody's old junk with a high price tag. But the joke soon gives way to something serious, for these stores evoke the depression and old settler days without their privations; we turn with reverence to an earlier time. As David Lowenthal writes, "Praise of the past is so conventional that almost anything old may be thought desirable."[11] We value these things because they remind us of the days of our youth, of our parents' youth, of the days of our grandparents and great grandparents.

Writing in 1913, Hamlin Garland, who once lived not far from the Trempealeau area in West Salem, offers a different view of part of the past commemorated by these objects. He describes his return to a former residence in Osage, Iowa:

> Every house I visited had its individual message of sordid struggle and half-hidden despair. . . . All the gilding of farm life melted away. The hard and bitter realities came back upon me in a flood. Nature was as beautiful as ever. . . . But no splendor of cloud, no grace of sunset could conceal the poverty of these people, on the contrary they brought out, with a more intolerable poignancy, the gracelessness of these homes, and the sordid quality of the mechanical daily routine of these lives. . . . I no longer looked upon these toiling women with the thoughtless eyes of youth. I saw no humor in the bent forms and graying hair of the men. I began to understand that my own mother had trod a similar slavish round with never a full day of leisure, with scarcely an hour of escape from the tugging hands of children, and the need of mending and washing clothes. I recalled her as she passed from the churn to the stove, from the stove to the bedchamber, and from the bedchamber back to the kitchen, day after day, year after year, rising at daylight or

before, and going to her bed only after the evening dishes were washed and the stockings and clothing mended for the night.[12]

The objects that helped to make up the life that Garland describes are part of what people collect and remember now.

Gathered as they are, plucked out of time, these old things soothe us somehow. They become trophies of what we have come through, what we have won. They help furnish stage sets for earlier versions of us.[13] The pasts we seek out need to be, as Oliver Jensen writes in another context, "far enough away to seem a strange country, yet close enough at times to bring a tear to the eye."[14] This is the past we turn to in nostalgia, because it pleases and touches us.

On one of the two main streets of Trempealeau, you can visit Montoville Antiques and Crafts, a shop named for the short-lived town that came after Reed's Landing and before Trempealeau; a block away you can buy wax candles made the old way at the Wildwood. When I was growing up, the Trempealeau Hotel was just another old man bar like Sportman's or Vet's. But since the 1980s it has been revived as a funky antique in its own right, its curvy wooden bar restored, old photographs from Trempealeau's past hung on the wall. These show the dam being built, the park road under construction, old shops and horses. T-shirts boast the antiquity of the place, displaying an old photo of the Trempealeau Hotel, which was built after 1871. The version of the past sold here is not the one of doilies, heavy curtains, and old lace but of wainscoting, curtainless windows, and wooden floors, of men and industry. The choices of the owners suggest a knowingness about the past; the hoteliers tip their hat to the old settler past and move on, marketing nouveau cuisine with locally brewed beers, inviting fading and rising rock and country bands to entertain their customers, many of whom make the drive from La Crosse and Winona to take a meal by the river.

One summer night when T.S. and I were dining at the hotel—for it offers a version of the past that I relish too—an old steamboat rolled by, calliope blasting, taking me back to my childhood memory of the *Delta Queen,* which even then was an antique that reminded us of an earlier time, that short-lived era of Mark Twain and paddle-wheels and gentlemen in hats, one we knew only through books and movies and through which we could imagine the past of our town. This nouveau steamboat—the *Julia Belle Swain*—makes a nostalgia trip from La Crosse, through the lock and dam, and for a moment it took me back to the nostalgia of my own childhood remembering.

There are other kinds of collecting as well—other relations to the past and its objects.

After my mother's father, Grandpa Earl Bockenhauer, died, my grandmother was left alone in a huge house, while her youngest living son, Doug, who still worked the farm, lived in a small trailer with his wife and baby. In a practical move they decided to trade houses. But there was hell to pay first. For in that tall farmhouse Grandma had amassed thousands of books, yards and yards of cloth, buttons, letters, dishes, magazines, clothes, plastic containers, and boxes and boxes of costume jewelry. She might use them some day. The house was stuffed to the roof with things she'd held onto, collections she might pass on. An inveterate shopper at rummage sales, Grandma Vi (short for Viola) purchased trinkets and toys as gifts for her many children and grandchildren. And each of these gifts was carefully thought out. She was famous for passing on broken items—a teapot with a ding in the china, a ceramic cat with three feet. One of the last gifts I received from her was a sewing box with little drawers marked NEEDLES, PINS, THREAD, and so on. Into each of these drawers she had tucked not only the signified but coins, candy, a slip of paper cut from a greeting card: *Happy Birthday*. She collected old things and passed them on to us; did she know these were the things we'd remember her by, that the secondhand things would be transformed by her intervention?

Although she was an expert at tucking things away, Grandma Vi was never able to put her car in the garage of the house she got in the swap, for its walls were lined with decades of *Life* magazines, *Family Circle,* old clothes-making patterns, and boxes of whatnot. After she died, her grown children had to wade through it all; burrowing into her deep freeze they unearthed twenty-year-old beef roasts. Only my mother, I think, was not surprised or appalled.

And Grandma often did find a use for these things that others called garbage. On my cousin Tammi's first wedding anniversary, Grandma sent the couple a plastic fork: three of its tines had been heated, softened, and then bent over, leaving one standing in the middle, like a hand flipping the bird. She included this message: "This is for everyone who didn't think you'd last a year." After she died, her kids also discovered, in addition to the ancient beef, my grandfather's teenage journal from the days of his courtship of Viola, then a fifteen-year-old farmhand; Iron Cross war medals that once belonged to some German ancestor; letters that intimated the ins and outs of Grandpa and Grandma's courtship; and a photograph of Grandma, shot at Perrot Park, playing Frisbee for the first time, during the summer before she died of a stroke at seventy-five. The Christmas after her death, the family opened the many boxes of costume jewelry amassed by this farm woman, and each of us in turn chose mementos. We went ten rounds of thirty easily, and still the supply of glittering jewels was not exhausted.

Genealogy is another way of collecting the past, of finding connections encoded in the names and dates of dead relatives. As a form of past seeking, genealogy helps to establish precedence. It offers a way to locate oneself in time and history. The genealogical fervor that has gripped Americans sporadically since the 1900s has not passed Trempealeau by. In the case of many local families that have lived in the area for years, tracing one's ancestry knits one into the history of the place and thus affirms a sense of ownership, property, power.

In our family my brother, Bob, has been the family historian, the collector of old photos, old names and dates, and old stories. Before my dad's mother died, Bob sat with her and recorded her recollections; in my father's later years Bob did the same. Using the Mormon archives and scattered renderings of the extended family tree, and while he and his wife began to produce progeny of their own, Bob reconstructed a genealogy of the Hovell clan that branches back to old Thomas Hovel, who crossed the Atlantic from northern England. Although Bob has done a lot of work on the various branches of the family tree, the past that he has found gives precedence to the power of fathers and patriarchs such as Grandpa Hovell and Great

Grandpa R.D. (Robert Damon). In this kind of family tree—this version of the past—men and men's names take precedence. Women occupy space as father's daughters and wives and mothers; they bear first their father's name and then their husband's. In this kind of family tree women who marry into the family appear as if out of nowhere; they don't exist until they become Hovells.

Images of the past are also circulated because, in some ways, they are supposed to be instructive. When I was in high school in the 1970s, my history teacher—like all history teachers through the ages—was fond of repeating the old saw that "those who forget the past are bound to repeat it." We were to remember because it was good for us. So we set about memorizing dates and names, uncomprehendingly collecting bits and pieces of "history." The incentive to remember the past also whispered of more terrible kinds of forgetting: we learned history so that the terror of the Holocaust would not happen again. We listened to tales told by World War II prisoners of war so we learned not to do that to others. (In this scheme of things *German* was almost a dirty word, though I knew myself to be German American.) In this way of looking at the past, history was only American and European. It was white. The days of the Indians, we learned, was a time of prehistory, a time without written records, a time skipped by the textbooks. We needed to forget what had happened; indeed, we didn't even see it, even though we knew that the earth in our town still bore signs of this prehistory. But historically white people had forgotten a lot about indigenous people; we didn't talk about that.

In the years since I was a kid, interest in local history has grown and become more formalized. The Trempealeau Historical Society offers versions of local history on its tours of the village, whose history, for society members, begins in earnest with James Reed in 1840. Innovations in school curricula also assure that kids get some introduction to the history of the place, with units on white settlement, on the Native American past of the Anasazi in the distant Southwest, as well as on the Indians from closer to home, of the Paleo-Indian, Oneota, and Mississippian cultures. While such additions to the curriculum certainly mark an improvement from my impoverished school days, the danger in such instruction is that children, like their teachers and parents, begin to think of Native American life as existing *only* in the past. A friend, for example, hesitated to take her daughter to a Ho-Chunk powwow with me because she didn't feel that the powwow would contribute to her daughter's education. "She wouldn't learn anything about the way they *were,*" this woman said, as if learning something about how Ho-Chunk and other native people live today would not be worthwhile. For my friend, the journey to the powwow grounds at Black River Falls was useful only if it were a journey into the past, a past commensurate with that purveyed by the schools, a past that could help her daughter achieve academically.

When as an adult I visited with my former sixth-grade teacher (who is now my sister Pam's mother-in-law and ninety years old), Mrs. Grover pulled out notebook upon notebook of family history that she had collected. With a bony finger she pointed out the names on the family tree that connect her late husband to Mary Ann Farnham, stepdaughter of James Reed and an early Trempealeau settler of Menominee or Potawatomi ancestry. Mrs. Grover went upstairs for her husband's high school yearbook, the *Arrowhead,* from 1916. And, trying to be helpful, she told me what she has encountered of archaeology in the region.

Some archaeologists—it's not clear who—were doing a dig near the house where she grew up, close by the Trempealeau River, so she went to see. "What were they looking for?" Pam asked.

"Garbage," she said matter-of-factly.

In presenting their work to lay people, archaeologists sometimes say that they study what people leave behind—their detritus, their refuse. In archaeological parlance, such findings are called *middens*. But how changed it sounded in my teacher's expression. What the archaeologists sought seemed recent and foul smelling, and in some ways these attributes still hovered over local Indians.

5. Hunting

When I was four, I set out to make a worm trap. I took a spoon and dug in the dirt driveway for what seemed like hours until I had carved out a shallow hole. I then took a piece of board, placed it over the hole, and drove nails into it. My siblings and cousins were busy with their own projects outside and teased me about mine: you'll never catch anything that way. I persisted, though I didn't so much finish the project as get tired. We were called in for supper. Afterward I ran outside to see if there had been any progress. Lifting up the board, I spotted a tangle of worms. The trap had worked: the wet worms miraculously appeared in the sandy soil.

Later I would learn that my cousin Jonny had placed them there.

The men in my extended family went deer hunting every year. Bob was especially keen and would head out as soon as bow season started. Sometimes he would go up in the hills near Fox Coulee, German Coulee, Norwegian Valley. Other times he would simply head into the woods on our own land. He told me one time that hunting was a way for him to spend time outdoors. I wondered why he couldn't just go for a walk; I was a vegetarian that year and was repulsed by the sight of deer carcasses draped in the beds of pickup trucks, tied on to car roofs. My dad was a less enthusiastic hunter but made an appearance in the woods almost every year, usually only in gun season. I think he liked the time in the tree stand, where, sitting in an old plastic chair, he could drink coffee from a thermos, his breath steaming, and munch on Snickers bars in the quiet of the woods. The first time he ever shot a deer he was nearly fifty, and it was on his own land. It was as if the buck—a six-pointer—had offered himself up to this reluctant hunter in a kind of sacrifice for letting him live on his land. Dad had to take a shot, and of course he hit it, the bullet searing the deer's side. Bob heard the shot, found my dad, and they tracked down the bleeding buck. They dragged the carcass back to the barnyard. I was probably eight or nine and watched with fascination as they proceeded to gut the deer in the driveway. After pulling out his organs, they used a garden hose to wash out his empty middle. I remember the water ran red for a long time. Later, they hung the hollowed-out body from a rope in the barn, to dry some. Later still, they cut off his horns for a trophy.

One year Bob decided he wanted to go bear hunting. For weeks he collected stale pastries and other sweet things to attract a bear. He came home with a black bear carcass, the skin of which he made into a rug. The meat, he said, was inedible. He did not hunt bear again.

6. Squier's Mounds

George Hull Squier had a view of Trempealeau and an interest in its earliest history and inhabitants that distinguished him from other residents. In many ways an outsider to the village, Squier was born on Long Island in 1849 and came to Trempealeau as a teenager in 1864, when his father became the new Baptist minister there.[15] Squier returned east to study geology, natural history, and archaeology. Although there is no evidence that Squier was actually enrolled at Harvard, he did spend two gentlemanly years studying with the distinguished archaeologist F. W. Putnam and conducting field geology before returning to work the family farm. In Trempealeau Squier continued his inquiries into archaeology, with the local landscape for his testing ground.

It seems astonishing, really, that Squier would be able to see the land around him as a potential site of scholarly interest. As I have noted, when I was in high school a hundred years after Squier, the places that mattered were always elsewhere. The schoolbooks noted England, of course, as well as France, Rome, and Greece. Within the United States it was all Washington, Philadelphia, New York, Virginia, the West. Those who rebelled against such versions of history simply dreamed of places farther afield: California, maybe, or, better yet (and as in my case), India, China, Tibet. If you gave a lick for Indians, you knew that most were out West somewhere—Arizona, New Mexico—toiling away on turquoise and sand paintings. Local Indians were too forbiddingly impoverished and had been too emotionally distanced from us to count as attractive or exotic. (My father, for example, subscribed to *Arizona Highways* and painted desert scenes of cacti, horses, and Indians; he traveled to the Southwest to buy Indian jewelry to resell at home. I read books about the Hopi and the Lakota.) In Squier's day the contempt for contemporary Indians was shaped by the brutal government policies against Native Americans and tempered by the not-so-distant memory of Indian removals. For much of the nineteenth century archaeologists shared this larger alienation from contemporary Indian cultures; what mattered to archaeologists were the histories that they could read in the land, shaped and buried there by people who seemed different, if not distinct, from the half-modernized Indians around them. But Squier was privy to the latest developments in archaeological knowledge and method, and he saw the land as connecting Native American habitation with European settlement. In 1919 he wrote that "the present political divisions of this county" corresponded "closely with the outlines of . . . older tribal domains or habitats"; for him, as interpreter of the land and its artifacts, this created a pleasing symmetry, "a peculiarly satisfactory theme for a writer."[16] Squier's taste for natural history distinguished him both from many of his contemporaries and from mine. So foreign did the intellectual interests of this one-time resident seem to one current citizen, Harold Wilber, that he referred to Squier simply as a "weird duck."[17]

As a young man Squier returned from Cambridge armed with the latest archaeological knowledge and methods, only to identify, on his father's own property, some unprecedented archaeological structures: the Middle Mississippian platform mounds that make up the terrace of Little Bluff. We might say that what he could not see before, he learned to see at Harvard. In July 1884 he described the mounds in a letter to Putnam, curator of the Peabody Museum of Archaeology and Ethnology:[18]

> There is, perhaps, no more interesting mound in the region, than the one . . . which occurs on a hill about two hundred feet high, over-looking the village of Trempealeau. The hill, a spur from a higher bluff, commands a very extensive and beautiful view to the eastward, although to the westward the view is entirely cut off by the higher bluff. . . . The extreme point of the hill . . . has been leveled by removing the earth from the top of the hill to one side. About one hundred feet back is a mound of rectangular outline . . . about forty by fifty feet on top, and about three feet higher than the top of the hill. Immediately against it, and rising about six feet higher, is [a] mound . . . also having the top rectangular in outline, and about fifty feet square. The angles, rather than the sides of the square, face the cardinal points.
>
> The earth of which these mounds were constructed, was obtained a little further back on the hill . . . where several holes were formed. As to the purpose of these mounds I am not prepared to advance an opinion, though sun worship is certainly suggested.[19]

Just who built them or what these mounds signified archaeologically, Squier was not yet prepared to say. That they were known by others in archaeological circles is supported by the survey and map made by Theodore Hayes Lewis in the same year (1884) as part of his larger collection of data on mounds for the Northwestern Archaeological Survey.[20] Nonetheless, most of what we know about the platform mounds depends on Squier's investigations of the site over many years. Squier also photographed the mounds; photographs taken from close range in 1905 distinctly show the humped terraces, while others, perhaps from the same year, show the mounds in profile. Because the site was disturbed later in the twentieth century, Squier's writings and photographs—along with his and Lewis's surveys— present the strongest evidence for the platform mounds, as documented by the archaeologists William Green and Roland Rodell.[21]

Squier mapped the mound complex several times, and though his results diverged from each other and from Lewis's survey, they have guided later researchers. As Squier reported in 1915, he also did

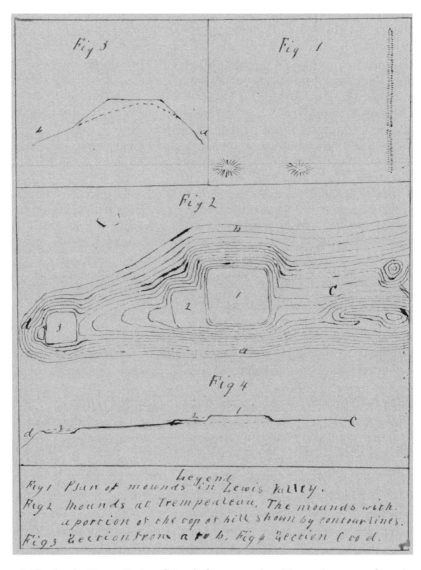

2.8. Sketches by George Squier of the platform mounds at Trempealeau, 1905, from the Charles E. Brown Papers (Image # WHi-23578). With permission from the Wisconsin Historical Society. Squier's figure 2 is a sketch of an aerial view of the three platform mounds; the width is marked a and b; length is marked c and d. His figure 3 is sketched from the side of a to b, figure 4 is from d to c; in both sketches Squier projects the extent of the mounds' erosion, with the 1905 contour signified by the dotted line. Figure 1 is of some effigy mounds in Lewis Valley, a site north of Arcadia in northern Trempealeau County, and is not directly connected to the platform mounds.

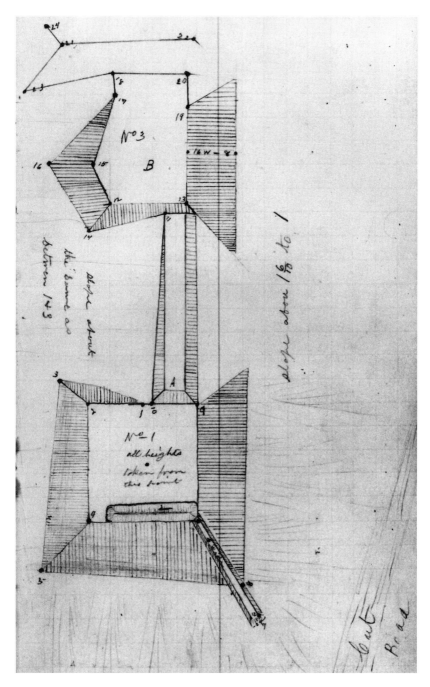

2.9. Theodore Lewis's sketch of the platform mounds, southern end, 1884, from Field Notebook #16 in the Minnesota Historical Society's Restricted Manuscript Collection. Used with permission. The shaded parts of the figures denote the sides of the platforms, while the unshaded parts (labeled No 1 and No 3 by Lewis) describe the tops of the mounds. The section between the two main figures is a sort of ramp. The structure at the lower right-hand corner extends toward the southeast and the Mississippi River.

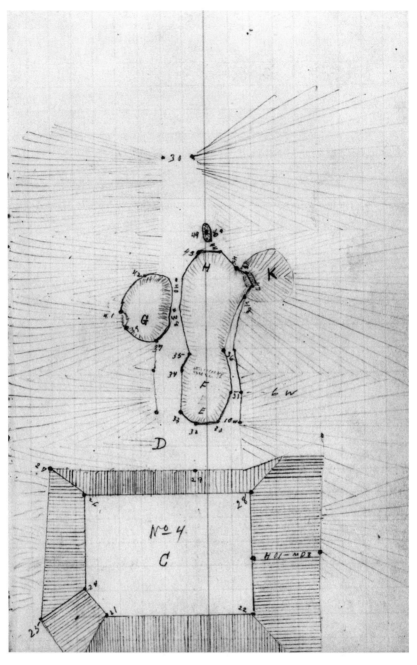

2.10. Theodore Lewis's sketch of the platform mounds, northern end, 1884, from Field Notebook #16 in the Minnesota Historical Society's Restricted Manuscript Collection. Used with permission. At the bottom of the sketch is the northernmost and largest platform (labeled No 4); the irregular shapes at the top of the drawing are borrow pits from which dirt was removed to make the mounds. Figures 2.9 and 2.10 can be joined to provide a sketch of the entire site by connecting the topmost line on figure 2.9 with the bottommost line in figure 2.10.

some soil coring with a 5 cm auger, though, as later archaeologists lament, "he did not record the number of corings or their locations."[22] Although these augerings revealed only plain fill, they confirmed for Squier that much of the soil for the platforms had come from another area of the bluff—from borrow pits. Taking it upon himself to investigate the site further, Squier dug into the northern platform down to the natural surface; this excavation suggested to him that the soil of the platforms did not occur naturally but had instead been imported: "Two occurrences of material [mound fill] from below [i.e., the river valley] evidently represented separate basket loads, which, though approaching within a few inches of each other did not join."[23] Further, Squier noted that when his father plowed the northern platform in the 1860s, he exposed black soil. Squier writes, "No such top soil occurs on the natural surfaces surrounding. I think we must regard it as the result of the use to which the platform was put; a perpetual fire being the most probable."[24] When archaeologists from the Mississippi Valley Archaeology Center (MVAC) had the northern mound augured in 1991, the bore confirmed Squier's descriptions. They found small fragments of mussel shell at 1.82 meters; just below this was a silt layer of "blocky structure." As Green and Rodell note, "Both appeared out of place in relation to the deposits immediately above and below them. The shell could only have been introduced during construction of the platform."[25]

Squier did not find any artifacts in or around the platform mounds. While some excavations of Mississippian mounds at Cahokia and elsewhere have revealed burials, pottery, copper, tools, and other artifacts, the mounds on Little Bluff appear to be empty, built as a foundation for another structure—such as a small building—rather than as a repository. While no archaeologist—including Squier—has found artifacts near the mounds, Squier did find pottery shards just below them, in his garden below Little Bluff. Using W. H. Holmes's classifications, he categorized these into Algonquin, Classes A, B, and C;[26] furthermore, Squier claimed that the pottery he found was almost exactly like a type found south of St. Louis.[27] Though Squier's collection is now lost, his descriptions remain, and in 1991 excavations in Squier's garden site confirmed that some of his finds were indeed Middle Mississippian. In this site

MVAC archaeologists found two shell-tempered pottery shards classified as Cahokia Red–Filmed and one limestone-tempered shard classified as Monks Mound Red.[28] Yet other pottery finds from the platform mound site at Third and Jay bear the red-slip coating of Middle Mississippian pottery.[29]

In the eighteenth and nineteenth centuries scholars across the country debated who, exactly, built the mounds that marked the continent—a lost tribe of Israel? Vikings? Hindus? In such arguments Euro-American scholars were frequently unwilling to imagine that native peoples—whose population had been decimated—could be mound builders. Unlike many of his predecessors, however, Squier believed that the mounds were built by native people. In his discussion of the mounds in *History of Trempealeau County,* Squier demonstrates his familiarity with archaeological debate and his considerable insight. For Squier, the question is *which* native peoples built the mounds and what their relationship is to other tribes as well as to contemporary Indians.

One theory in Squier's day was that the Aztecs had built the platform mounds found in the eastern half of the country. (Hence the name Aztalan—the legendary Aztec homeland—for another site in Wisconsin.) Squier rejects this notion in his 1917 chapter; noting that the pottery he found in Trempealeau was "almost identical to a type common south of St. Louis," Squier suggests, quite boldly, that "both the platforms and the pottery find their nearest counterparts in what we may broadly speak of as the Arkansas region."[30] To make this argument Squier notes that the placement of the Trempealeau mounds on a high bluff and their southeasterly orientation suggest a religious orientation to the sun; this orientation, Squier argues, is similar to the cultural patterns of the Natchez of the Lower Mississippi Valley. He writes: "Among the Natchez the chief was held as a superior being, a child of the sun, the religious as well as the civil head of the tribe. The sun was an object of worship involving a complicated ceremonial [*sic*] on the platform, on which a perpetual fire was kept burning. The chief, as a sacred being, also had his residence on the platform."[31] Squier is careful to note: "While we should not suppose that all tribes had identical customs, we should look for strong family resemblances, and such family resemblances [to the

2.11. Large Platform Mound, by George Squier, 1905, from the Wisconsin Archaeological Society–Charles E. Brown collection (Image #WHi-23598). Used with permission. This corresponds to Lewis's No 4 in figure 2.10 and No 1 in Squier's Fig 2 (see figure 2.8).

2.12. Mound and Barn, by George Squier, 1905, from the Wisconsin Archaeological Society–Charles E. Brown collection (Image #WHi-23603). Used with permission. This is a side view of the platform mounds that includes a barn on Squier's property; the numbers correspond to those in Squier's sketch of the mounds, his Fig 2 (see figure 2.8). Today the land pictured here belongs to Mount Calvary Lutheran Church and is near the parsonage.

Natchez] would seem to be indicated by the remains at Trempealeau and Aztalan [Wisconsin]."[32]

The theory that Squier outlines here anticipates later archaeological theories about the nature and expansion of Mississippian culture—its hierarchy, its sun worship, its ceremonies—as well as about the connections between the Natchez and the mound builders at Trempealeau, Aztalan, and Cahokia. In order to come up with such a point of view, Squier had to think considerably outside the box, as they say—outside the boxes of both archaeological knowledge and of hometown apathy and ignorance. In Squier's day archaeology, as a discipline, was in its infancy, and Squier's interest in and conception of Native American occupation of the region distinguished him from many of his peers in Trempealeau. To this day many local people maintain the sense of Indians as impoverished and backward, but Squier saw in local earthworks evidence of great cultural achievement. Similarly, the idea that native peoples could cover long distances without horses and by canoe sometimes defies the layperson's credulity; Squier, however, was aware of the many movements that native groups have undertaken. Indeed, the archaeological record attests repeatedly to the movements of goods and peoples over large expanses. (An example of this gap in comprehension is that one man who opposed the platform mound project in the 1990s had a difficult time recognizing the possibility of far-flung kinship ties among the various platform mound builders. Having apparently read [and partly misunderstood] Squier's chapter in *History of Trempealeau County,* Harold Wilber rejected what he saw as Squier's claim: "They [the platform mound builders] were supposed to have come from Arkansas?" he asked mockingly. "C'mon, Laurie."[33])

Wilber was not alone, of course. For many lay people, the whole archaeological enterprise stretches the limits of the believable: small pieces of pottery allow archaeologists to connect peoples who live at vast distances; little bits of bone and wood can be used to date objects thousands of years old. Goods and artifacts—the archaeological record—are used to show that indigenous people were able to paddle by canoe from St. Louis to Trempealeau—upstream all the way—and then that they moved dirt around Little Bluff basket by basket so they could worship the sun. And what requires the biggest stretch of the imagination for some Trempealeau residents is that Squier, a budding archaeologist, returned from college only to discover an unprecedented and significant archaeological site right on his father's land.

Squier's work on the platform mounds is arguably his most significant project, but he also surveyed and mapped effigy mounds wherever he saw them, excavated burial mounds near the park, searched for the original trading post of Nicholas Perrot,[34] and dug on Trempealeau Mountain. His vision of the land is one keyed to the presence of its previous inhabitants: in the area around the Trempealeau County Insane Asylum, near Whitehall, Squier sees "a favorite hunting ground of the Indians."[35] On the James McDonah farm he notes the presence of a circular mound, as well as effigies of bird, deer, and panther, and imagines that "there must originally have been many more mounds in the fields adjacent," now lost to cultivation.[36] Such an orientation to the land seems to have roots in his childhood. In a publication from 1914 Squier describes a group of mounds on the road between Arcadia and Independence in northern Trempealeau County "which I myself saw when as a boy I drove through this district with my father before the land was brought under cultivation. No trace of it now remains."[37] Squier attended to the signs of a history that predated white settlement of the region and sought out what the earth had preserved of that history.

7. Mississippian Culture and the Platform Mounds

Although many Americans today have never even heard of it, Monks Mound at Cahokia (opposite present-day St. Louis in southern Illinois) was the third-largest manmade structure in the Western Hemisphere when Europeans first arrived on this continent.[38] Within this massive construction the one-hundred-foot high mound is the largest earthwork in the world. But because of particular Euro-American habits of remembering the past, most Americans are more likely to know about the Egyptian pyramids and ancient Babylon than they are about the premier trading and cultural center of ancient North America. We tend, instead, to identify with the Old World and seek our roots there, and, as Maureen Korp writes, "We lack almost any comprehension at all about what it might-have-been-like-way-back-then for the traditional New World cultures of the very land we ourselves now inhabit."[39] A look at Middle Mississippian culture and the Cahokia mounds helps shed some light on these habits of forgetting and suggests the significance of the platform mounds at Trempealeau.

Platform mounds typify the earthworks of the Mississippian period (from about 700 CE to 1550, that is, to almost forty years after the arrival of Spanish expeditions). These mounds generally have a rectangular base and a series of flat tiers on top. Indigenous peoples began constructing them by 500 CE in what is now southwestern Georgia and central Florida, by 700 CE in the Mississippi Valley, and from 900 to 950 at Cahokia. Spanish accounts from the fifteenth century suggest that chiefs lived on top of these mounds in large and richly decorated wooden structures that some writers referred to as palaces and others as temples.[40] These accounts identify rulers known as Great Suns and suggest that in life as well as in death they were surrounded by Mississippian luxuries, which included fur cloaks and painted deerskins.[41]

At Cahokia the platform mound known as Monks Mound is the largest earthen structure; it measures 291 by 236 meters (about 970 by 787 feet) at its base, is 30 meters (or 100 feet) tall, and is made up of 615,000 cubic meters (22 million cubic feet) of earth. The mound was constructed by the highly organized and labor-intensive practice of piling up millions of basketloads of earth, one on top of the other. The mound was carefully engineered and its soil types carefully selected. In its final form the mound is actually a series of flat-topped pyramids that include three terraces and a fourth eroded terrace. A ramp connects the first terrace to the ground.[42] Monks Mound stands on a two-thousand-acre plaza. This plaza is diamond shaped, and each of its points marks a cardinal direction. At one time this plaza, which includes sixteen other mounds, may have been surrounded by a palisade, although only part of the wall has been excavated.[43] Standing atop Monks Mound during the peak of Cahokia civilization, one might have seen more than one hundred other mounds.[44]

Henry M. Brackenridge famously described the site in 1814: "When I reached the foot of the principal mound, I was struck with a degree of astonishment, not unlike that which is experienced in contemplating the Egyptian pyramids. What a stupendous pile of earth!"[45] These days Monks Mound is preserved, along with other mounds and artifacts, at the Cahokia Mounds State Historic Site, a twenty-two-hundred-acre tract just across the river from St. Louis, Missouri. The site is awe striking even now. From Monks Mound you can see the St. Louis arch across the river.

The indigenous population in the American Bottom (an area of the Mississippi Valley that includes Cahokia) was sustained by an

2.13. Monks Mound, Cahokia Mounds State Historic Site, Illinois. Photo by author.

agricultural base that included maize and beans; farming was supplemented by fishing and the hunting of wild animals. In other technological areas the Middle Mississippian people of Cahokia favored the bow and arrow[46] and were expert canoeists; they also built rafts, bridges, and causeways. Villages and towns proliferated during this period.

Just how many people lived at Cahokia at any one time is not clear. Archaeologists have differed widely in their views for the last hundred years. Some argue that the population at Cahokia reached 75,000;[47] others have settled for the much lower figure of 8,000.[48] George Milner, a prominent scholar of Cahokia, does not believe that the size and number of mounds necessarily indicates a large population. He maintains that at its height the population at Cahokia was in the low thousands, while the population of the greater American Bottom peaked at 50,000.[49]

Similarly, the sheer scale, number, and complexity of the earthworks at Cahokia suggest to some archaeologists that Middle Mississippian society there was centralized and highly organized. Basing their claims on the material evidence, many archaeologists maintain that Middle Mississippian societies were stratified into classes or ranks and that community activity centered on the temple shrine, which was an ancestor shrine and also the residence of a hereditary solar ruler. Rinita Dalan's description is typical of this view: "The communal construction and use of mounds, plazas, and other earthen features would have provided a means of creating and perpetuating social relations, and establishing and maintaining a labor force necessary for large-scale agricultural projects. . . . Monks Mound and the Grand Plaza were clearly critical in the definition and creation of a large integrated community. Their construction gave structure to this community, simultaneously emphasizing the importance of the ruling hierarchy and the masses."[50] But there is no unanimity on this issue. While some believe that Cahokia was the seat of an important chiefdom from 900 to 1300 CE, others argue for a more decentralized model. Milner asserts that "the Cahokia regional system was highly segmented socially, politically, and geographically" but plays down the centralized nature of that system. Instead, he envisions a number of "quasi-autonomous components," each of which focused on a local center and its chief.[51] Instead of a centralized chiefdom, then, Milner imagines a situation in which mound centers varied in importance over time in concert with the ascendance of particular groups and their leaders. Similarly, he argues that the number of mounds at any particular site depended on its longevity, the power of its chiefs, and the number of laborers they could enlist to build the mounds.[52]

In any case, Cahokia's position on the Mississippi River gave it access to north-south exchanges, while its location near the mouths of the Missouri and Ohio rivers facilitated east-west communication. Before 1050 exchanges tended to flow toward the south. After 1050 CE the people of Cahokia came into contact with goods from the Great Lakes and the Great Plains, as well as from the Ozarks and Appalachians.[53] At this time the distinctive Cahokia Mississippian tradition developed, extending its influence far beyond the American Bottom to a broad area to the north and west, an area that includes Trempealeau. The degree of uniformity in the constructions of the various mound-building centers suggests close networks of exchange over a large area. Indeed, mounds, plazas, and burials throughout the Mississippian mound-building region are strikingly similar.

Maureen Korp, a historian of religion who is interested in the way mound-building peoples constructed sacred space, notes that most Mississippian mounds were built near significant bodies of water; oriented toward the east, they face the rising sun. Of the fifty-seven Mississippian sites described in William Morgan's important work, *Prehistoric Architecture in the Eastern United States,* she discovered that "all but six have waterfronts shown on their site drawings . . . Of these 51, only three earthworks are not arranged in an easterly direction."[54] Connecting archaeological evidence to oral traditions, Korp observes that a similar emphasis on the rising sun as life giving is found in the myths of contemporary Native American communities, particularly the Creek, Choctaw, Cherokee, and Tuscarora.[55]

Cahokia was the largest of the Mississippian sites, but it was not the only one. North of the American Bottom, and important for this study, several Mississippian sites are well documented: Aztalan in southeastern Wisconsin, the Spoon River and Apple River sites in central and northwest Illinois, and the Red Wing sites in southeast

Minnesota and northwest Wisconsin, among others.[56] Although Cahokia—because of its concentration of materials and the higher number of elite burials—seems to have been an important center, we should not assume that every Mississippian site was simply its satellite. Indeed, we cannot know whether the presence of Middle Mississippian earthworks and material culture in the Upper Mississippi was the result of the settlement of Cahokian people in the north or whether Middle Mississippian cultural forms arrived in Wisconsin indirectly, through other societies.[57] Some groups could have moved into new territories but, at the same time, maintained a connection to central Mississippian society.[58] The people who constructed Mississippian sites in Minnesota, Illinois, Wisconsin, and Trempealeau itself may have arrived there after various groups splintered and relocated.

The Little Bluff mounds at Trempealeau consist of three linked platforms, a kind of miniature version of the earthworks at Cahokia and elsewhere. As I imagine it, instead of building a mound on a flat plain as at Cahokia, mound builders took advantage of an existing natural structure—the narrow outcropping at Little Bluff—and built on top of it. As Green and Rodell have documented, the surface area of the mounds at Trempealeau may have measured about 300, 150, and 125 square meters (about 359, 180, and 150 square yards, respectively) before they were damaged. The two largest platforms abutted each other and stood about one and two meters (or three and six feet) high, respectively.[59] Built on a small bluff, the mounds face southeast toward the expanse of the Mississippi River. The north platform adjoins the middle platform, which in turn is connected to the south platform by a narrow ramp that is 22 meters (more than 72 feet) long. Nearby are the borrow pits from which basketloads of soil were taken to make the mounds. Green and Rodell suggest that although the mounds at Trempealeau are much less grand in scale than Monks Mound, their multiterrace design might have been modeled after it, sometime around 1000 CE.[60] Unlike many of the mounds at Cahokia, the platform mounds at Trempealeau have never been excavated. They are thought not to be burial mounds but rather a site of symbolic significance that reflected a leader's power.

Although over the years most modern residents of Trempealeau have overlooked the platform mounds, archaeologists have kept their eye on the mounds for many years. Lewis and Squier surveyed the mounds on Little Bluff in 1884; Squier photographed, sketched, and studied them for years; McKern visited them in the 1930s, and Robert Hall described them in 1962. Most recently, the thorough study of the Little Bluff platform mounds undertaken by archaeologists connected with the Mississippi Valley Archaeology Center in nearby La Crosse combines historical and physical evidence. Much of the work of the center's archaeologists has been to assess Squier's reports and to connect the mounds to existing archaeological knowledge about Mississippian culture.

Writing in 1994 in the prominent archaeology journal *American Antiquity,* Green and Rodell maintain that Trempealeau was once a conduit for goods—for pipestone from the north and Hixton silicified sandstone headed south—as well as a source for information passing to and from Cahokia until about 1050 CE, when the focus of Mississippian involvement in the Upper Mississippi shifted to Red Wing, about seventy miles upriver.[61] For Green and Rodell, the significance of the mounds at Trempealeau lies in their early date of about 1000 CE. That makes Trempealeau one of the earliest Mississippian contacts in the area.[62]

In their interpretation of the Little Bluff mounds, Green and Rodell emphasize the ways in which the platform mound structure replicates and reaffirms aspects of social hierarchy. As they see it, the multiterrace platforms "might reflect actual social and political structure by both symbolizing and operationalizing ascent to the summit of power through a series of steps, placing rulers or other elite personages literally several levels above the rest of the population."[63] The selection of a building site on a natural landmark that was itself elevated emphasizes the connection between height and power, suggesting to these scholars that the mounds were established by Mississippian peoples who wished to impress their "power, prestige, and ideology" upon the local Late Woodland peoples in the area.[64]

Just what happened to the Mississippian platform mound builders at Trempealeau is not clear. After 1300 the Americas saw a tremendous population shift. As the historian Roger G. Kennedy notes, Chaco Canyon and Mesa Verde were abandoned for Hopi and Zuni villages in Arizona, and "soon Cahokia and the entire region at the juncture of the Ohio, the Missouri and the Mississippi were evacuated, leaving a profound desolation archaeologists call the 'Vacant Quarter.'"[65] The site at Little Bluff seems to have been occupied for a short time and then abandoned by 1100, the people moving on or becoming part of other cultures.

As far as I have been able to discover, no contemporary native group claims direct ancestry to the platform mound builders at Trempealeau; thus I know of no extant native stories about them. (The Choctaw and Cherokee, among other native groups from the Southeast, do claim a connection to the Mississippians at Cahokia, however.) When I asked Rodell in conversation what he thought happened to the platform mound builders, he reiterated the notion that the Middle Mississippian stimulus moved north to the Red Wing area, an area he has studied intensively.[66] He also suggested that local people involved in building the platform mounds became, in turn, part of what is known as Oneota culture, a designation that, he acknowledges, is much debated and hard to connect precisely to any living native community. When I asked him which native group he thought was most closely related to the platform mound builders, he said that in eastern Wisconsin, attribution to the Oneota means the sites are connected to the Ho-Chunk. But in the case of Trempealeau, he said, the evidence is less clear. "If backed into a corner," he said, "I'd say the Ioway have the best claim."[67] The anthropologist Nancy Lurie also suggests that the Ioway may be connected to the mounds; her evidence comes from archaeological work at Aztalan and elsewhere in Wisconsin, as well as from Perrot's account. When I followed up on this question with William Green, he replied, "I have to say that [the Ioway connection] would be a real stretch."[68] In pursuing this problem, I contacted Lance Michael Foster, an Ioway writer and artist, and asked whether he knew of any Ioway connection to the mounds; he replied this way: "Well, there are no surviving traditions that deal with this. [The] Trempealeau platform mounds are Mississippian in cultural association, and certainly the Oneota (ancestors of the Winnebago aka Hochunk, the Ioway, Otoe, and Missouria) were involved in the mound culture of the area. Archaeologists themselves cannot pin the correspondence down definitely for any one group; there are differing theories on this."[69] In any case, for the MVAC archaeologists the site at Trempealeau is immensely important and of national significance. The platform mounds—which are also known as Squier's mounds—contribute to archaeologists' knowledge of Mississippian culture, sharpening their sense of the highly developed and organized people who lived throughout the Mississippi region for a time. And although no native group that I know of claims to descend from the platform mound builders at Trempealeau, the mounds remain part of their general heritage. Foster writes of the people whom archaeologists call the Oneota: "According to tribal tradition, the ancestors of the Ioway Indians united as a people ages ago. The Clans had come together and agreed to become a People, the *Honga*, the Great Nation. Some clans had come from the Great Lakes. Others had come from the north, from a land remembered as very cold. Others had come from the western prairies or the eastern woodlands. Some of the ancestors had made great mounds in the shapes of animals and birds along the Great River. Others had traded down the River to the great southern mound cities, and came back with new ceremonies, new beliefs to add to older ones."[70] The mounds stand as a reminder of this history, but it is a history that cannot be fully accounted for in the stories left to us, whether they are told by archaeologists, townspeople, or native people.

8. Progress

Squier and Lewis documented the platform mounds in 1884; in 1905 Squier photographed the mounds and described them in an article for the *Wisconsin Archaeologist.* In 1917 he discussed them again in *History of Trempealeau County.* (Although this book continues to circulate widely among local people interested in their family tree and local history, most seem to have skipped his section on archaeology.) When W. C. McKern and other archaeologists from the Milwaukee Public Museum excavated Hopewell mounds in Trempealeau between 1928 and 1930, they visited the platform mounds.[71] Although these men, all outsiders of one variety or another, published articles that detailed the existence of the mounds to the world, few people in the village knew anything about them. So it was that in 1938, when the village board planned to place a water tower on Little Bluff, on the northern and largest platform, no resident saw a problem. S. A. Barrett, who as director of the Milwaukee Public Museum had overseen the Hopewell mound excavations a few years previously, was apprised of the plan and attempted to intercede, as evidenced by this letter to the mayor, E. M. Malles:

> I do not know whether you are aware of the fame of this particular spot or not, but it is considered to be one of the outstanding archaeological points of interest in Wisconsin and it seems unfortunate that any public work should destroy even a portion of this if the site of that public work might be relocated as it could, as I understand the matter in this case, only a very short distance away and just as advantageously with practically no more expense.
>
> We are very much interested in the matter of conservation of all our natural resources and points of interest and we are especially interested in the preservation of historic landmarks, whether they be prehistoric or historic in the sense of having been made after the coming of the white man.
>
> If this cannot be done, then may I suggest further that means be taken in the excavation of the spot to see that as much information is recovered as possible. I might say at the outset that it is obviously impossible to save any information if ordinary excavation methods are used. The workmen are in too much of a hurry and though you might have half a dozen well-trained archeologists on the spot, it

would be impossible for them to get much out of such hastily done excavating as will be necessary in connection with a project such as the building of a public work of this sort.

You can, however, at least arrange, it would seem to me, to cut a trench on the line where the pipe must be run and let this be done with a great deal of care before the actual excavating is undertaken. This will give us a cross section of this mound or platform and will enable us to tell something very definite about its construction and use. . . .

If you can do this [i.e., make such a cut] we will be glad to send someone up from here to look over this section of the mound as it is shown by this cut, simply make the ditch on the line prescribed by the engineers for your pipe line and we will be able to get the archeological evidence from the cross-section of the ditch after it is completed.

Be assured that we will be very glad to cooperate in any way we can in connection with this matter and I sincerely hope that you will be able to follow out one or another of the above suggestions.[72]

In his letter Barrett makes a case for the value of the mounds, suggesting that, even though they are not the work of "the white man" and thus historic, they still are a landmark worthy of preservation. Barrett's letter also draws a sharp distinction between the kind of digging done by workers and that done by archaeologists; he goes on to offer several ways in which the differing needs of the village and the archaeologists might be met. With each paragraph Barrett diminishes his requests: save it, please, but if you cannot, do this instead; and if you can't do that, try this. The reply from Trempealeau was short and swift. This from G. O. Leavitt, the village clerk: "We were not aware of any outstanding fame being connected to this particular spot when we bargained for this site, and there fore [*sic*] we have purchased same and it is included in our waterworks plans, all steps have been taken in the letting of the contract for the construction of a Reservoir on this site and work will commence within perhaps ten days."[73]

Diverging values inform the letters exchanged by Barrett and Leavitt. In his discussion of the site Leavitt asserts the primary importance of landownership—we bargained for the site, purchased it, and have contracted for construction on it; therefore our responsibility to the site is complete. The focus is on present needs; indeed,

Leavitt does not even mention the mounds as an entity. He refers to a spot, a site that has value only as part of his plans. Instead of disputing the mounds' existence, Leavitt picks up Barrett's assertion about the *fame* of the spot and uses that to argue for going ahead with the water tower: "We were not aware of any outstanding fame being connected to this particular spot." The water tower is built, one might say, on the town fathers' particular habits of remembering and forgetting the signs of prior inhabitants, on village residents' desires to think about their place in only very particular ways. And thus the platform mounds become for many townspeople—not an archaeological treasure, as Barrett might have hoped—but a place for personal memory—for cattle grazing, boys playing, perhaps some heavy petting, and an eighteen-thousand-gallon water reservoir. There the tower would stay until 1991, when it was no longer needed and torn down.

Like the platform mounds themselves, whose very height was supposed to underscore and reproduce social hierarchy, the archaeologists' claims to know more about the mounds than the local people seems an assertion of the academics' power and priority. But as the town fathers are the men who control the land through ownership, they get to say what happens to it: there will be a tower. In the controversy about the mounds in the 1990s, some townspeople bristled when they thought someone was going to tell them their business. Using populist terms, the town fathers cast the archaeologists—the outsiders—as the villains in this story and cast themselves as beleaguered and oppressed small-town folk—placed at the mercy of the citified, intellectual outsider. Sometimes, certainly, this interpretation of things fits the bill. Witness a recent controversy in nearby Rochester, Minnesota, that put the priorities of the multimillion-dollar corporation of the Mayo Clinic over and above those of small farmers and landowners: a railway line was to be diverted to the country so that train whistles would not disturb the Mayo's affluent patrons.[74] But sometimes it's too easy to fall into that old story—we are simple folk just trying to make a living. Sometimes the story that poses innocent insider against villainous outsider does not always do justice to the complexity of the situation.

9. Departures

There lay in him a strange sorrow that seemed not to go away even when he was thoughtless of it or asleep. And when he put his mind to it he knew what it was: it was the fear that in order to be what he might become he would have to cease to be what he had been, he would have to turn away from that place to which his flesh and his thoughts and his devotion belonged. For it was the assumption of much of his schooling, it was in the attitude of most of his teachers and schoolmates . . . that achievement, success, all worthy hope lay elsewhere, in cities, in places of economic growth and power; it was assumed that a man must put away his origin as a childish thing.

Wendell Berry, *The Memory of Old Jack*

My father loved to sing. He learned how to play guitar from his mother when he was a child, and his family used to get together and sing before TV came along. They would make records to send to my uncle Ken when he was soldiering in Korea. Andrews Sisters tunes. "Don't Fence Me In." The old songs. My aunts Darlene and Lorna recorded their own version of "Tumbling Tumble Weed."

Starting in the 1960s, and almost every Saturday night for thirty years, my dad played bass with one dance band or another. The Jim Bee Trio, the Jim Bee Quartet (when it added a sax), the Elmo Johnson Band, and the Kleinsmen, a band that specialized in Dixieland jazz. When he was in his sixties, my dad went with the Denny Martin Quartet to Jakarta, Indonesia, where the group was asked to dress in red-and-white striped vests, string ties, garters, and top hats and play "old-time" music in a five-star hotel. They lasted two weeks.

That was long after I had left home for India, Sri Lanka, China, and India again and again. When I was growing up, though, the routine was like this: all week long Dad worked—his job shifted from a lumber mill, to the Army Corps of Engineers, to the boiler room at a canning factory—and always he also farmed his own 160 acres. He'd get up before I went to school, fall asleep on the couch after supper, and wear the same clothes much of the week—plaid flannel shirt, blue jeans, boots. But on Saturday nights Dad would shower, put on a dress shirt, a tie, a jacket that matched the other players' sometimes, load up his amp and guitar, and drive to a night club or restaurant to do a gig. And then his band mates, those guys who were farmers or bus drivers in the other parts of their lives, became something else—the men who could make people remember, the guys who could get people to dance.

In the 1960s my dad was playing with the Jim Bee Quartet. The quartet played things like "Sweet Georgia Brown" and "Muskrat Ramble." Dad was assigned to electric bass. He had a boxy electric amplifier shaped like a big suitcase that was just the right size for a four-year-old to straddle like a horse, kicking her legs and shaking its thick black rubber cord like reins, the sound of which mimicked the squeak of a saddle. Though rumor has it that my dad was shy when he was a young man, when the band played he stood up front, singing lead or harmony. With a gig every Saturday sometimes the band would practice at our house, and there are stories about my dancing to their music, trying to get their attention. ("You're a ham," Jim Bee told me. "You mean ham—like bacon?" was my reply.)

When I was about five, Dad tried to teach me guitar; my first song was "Bye Bye Blues." We perched on the edge of my parents' bed, and he tried to show me how to strum and where to put my fingers, but I could not learn from him.

A few years later, when my dad and I drove somewhere in his pickup, we often sang together. Our special number was an old Mills Brothers' tune, "Cab Driver." He sang the verses—"Cab driver, drive by Mary's place"—and I would sing the doop-dooby-doops in between.

By the time I was twelve, we were no longer singing together. I recall one time he wanted to punish me for something and made the threat, "You're not too big to spank, you know." And I remember my reply: "If it makes you feel better, then go ahead." When he struck out then in fury, I pulled away.

I would continue to pull away. I hated the way his hammy hands felt if he tried to caress my shoulder. I had the sense that he was trying to hang on to me, hold me down, that he wouldn't let his little girl grow up.

When I was thirteen, I started singing in the chorus at school. By fourteen I was playing guitar and writing my own songs, many of which I sang with Ann Prochowitz. She soon became my singing

partner—she took the soprano part, I the alto—and we sang together through high school. Our senior year we won a slot in the
state music contest, and our voice teacher had us perform at the
school concert. As my dad pulled out of the school parking lot that
night, he told me, "I'm proud of you, Laur."

From my place in the back I replied coldly: "It has nothing to do
with you." I was already plotting my escape.

Sometimes reading helped me get away. When I was fifteen, the life
led by a Tibetan ascetic who walled himself into a mountain cave for
three years, three months, and three days seemed like a good alternative to what felt like the trap of home. So I read about Hinduism,
Buddhism, and Native American spirituality, wrote poetry, smoked
pot, drank, sobered up, dieted like crazy, ran long distances, pursued
ways to travel, and chose a college that would get me as far from
home as possible: first across the state to Appleton, Wisconsin, and
then across the world to India.

During my first year of college I applied to work for an archaeological dig overseen by the University of North Dakota. Without any
experience whatsoever I was hired. My parents drove me out to
North Dakota that summer in their Winnebago camper. We were
doing contract archaeology; it was the last chance to find something
before an oil pipeline came through. I was on an all-female crew led
by a male and female pair, and everyone else had plenty of experience.
We lived in an unfurnished farmhouse eleven miles from the tiny
town of New Salem, which boasted (on a high hill) the world's largest
(fiberglass) cow, a Holstein that, as it turned out, had been built near
my home, in La Crosse. We liked to think of the cow's coming out to
North Dakota in three different pieces, its body cut on the horizontal. Imagine driving along I-90 and seeing an enormous cow head filling up your rear view mirror, then passing you on the right.

I learned how to dig, small vertical cuts to outline our test pit,
shallow horizontal cuts to excavate layers. I learned how to push dirt
through screens, how to identify flakes, how to find energy for eight-
hour days of hard labor in the sun. After work we'd sometimes go to
drink bottled Budweiser in an air-conditioned bar near the super-
market, stomping around in our boots and work clothes. We were a

tough bunch: some of the women—big, husky Nebraska women—were stronger than many men. Others were tough in other ways: skinny Carla drank too much and listened exclusively to Bruce Springsteen's eerie album, *Nebraska*. Used to seeking the approval of men, I began to see women differently, even silently falling a bit in love with one woman, though I had a boyfriend in St. Paul. Our farmhouse was planted on an immense stretch of land where the weather could whip in and change without notice. One time I went running in the rain. It turned to hail, then a tornado.

On weekends I'd sometimes hitch a ride to a place I could hike and camp, tentless and alone in the North Dakota Badlands. I saw my travels as a kind of vision quest and imagined that I'd found my totem, the mule deer.

On other weekends we got together with other archaeology crews and drank. One Saturday night all of us women and the male boss we called Bwano ventured into town to go to a night spot. As sturdy women we were clearly the outsiders among the farmers and local white guys. Always on the lookout for the exotic, I took note of a young Indian guy in tight blue jeans swaying at the other end of the bar.

All in all, we did not find much that summer—nothing worth diverting the pipeline for, anyway. One of the last sites we worked on was a Mandan village site, punctuated by hearths.

And that was the end of my archaeological career. It was living culture that I wanted to think about, I decided, so that was the end of archaeology for me. I went to India the next year and got hooked on Tibetan culture, seeing in the turquoise and coral of Tibetan ornaments something Navajo, something native, and recognizing in the people folks who uncannily seemed like family. When I first visited Ladakh, a far western corner of Old Tibet, now part of India, I felt like I'd come home. "Hello, Auntie," I felt like calling out. "Hello, my uncle!"[75] It took me a long time before I was ready to come back to Trempealeau with something of that joy, something of that excitement. By the time I started this project on Trempealeau and the platform mounds, I had a family of my own.

10. Farmers Again

If you think crime doesn't pay, you ought to try farming.
Saying on a bumper sticker

Our route from Ohio to visit my birth family in Wisconsin is ritualized. It's about six hundred miles on I-90, and if you start in the morning, you can hit Ikea outside Chicago, have an early dinner in Rockford, Illinois, and get to Janesville, Wisconsin, in time for a swim in the hotel pool. The restaurant where we always eat is called the Machine Shed. Our boys love to sit on the genuine, old-time John Deere tractor parked outside; inside, waitresses bring toy tractors to the table for their amusement. The place is a tribute to the by-gone days of farming. You drink water out of jam jars, cover your lap with gingham napkins, and tuck into farm-style food. The wait staff wears bib overalls and kerchiefs, and the walls are lined with out-moded farm equipment—scythes, hoes, wagon wheels, washboards, straps for sharpening knives, bridles, horseshoes all neatly arranged on the walls—and signs: seed signs, machinery merchants' signs, ads for farm auctions, an ad for a wheeled scraper made in Aurora. The kids are encouraged to appreciate what's left of the farming life by coloring pages that say things like "Find the four types of pork in the picture" and "Farmers take good care of their animals and animals give us food in return." We eat thick-cut pork chops, half-chickens, and pot roast and share vegetables—overcooked, farm-style—from common bowls. In the foyer there's a shop that sells enamel cups, Machine Shed caps, and toy tractors—and a mechanical farmer that tells stories. He's lifesize and sits in faded denims, flannel shirt, and dusty cap and spins yarns in a droll but not very authentic accent, gesturing slowly, mechanically, from behind a wire fence as he relates his tale. The Farmer (capital F) has been memorialized.

In the 1980s, I probably don't need to tell you, a lot of farmers got out of the business. There was no way to make it on farming alone, and if they got a chance to sell out to some bigger outfit, many did.

Back home only one uncle is still milking cows: Doug is up on the farm in German Coulee that used to be his dad's. Only one other uncle is still raising crops: Earl Jr., who, in addition to his town job, leases farmland in order to earn a bit more. After my dad died, my brother-in-law Steve Grover started farming Dad's land in addition to his own, in addition to working his own plumbing business.

What Hamlin Garland wrote in 1914 still resonates: "Other writers are telling the truth about the city, . . . and it appears to me that the time has come to tell the truth about the barn-yard's daily grind. I have lived the life and I know that farming is not entirely made up of berrying, tossing the new-mown hay and singing *The Old Oaken Bucket* on the porch by moonlight."[76]

The machine shed on my parent's farm has not been touched in years. One summer day I peeked into it with my sons to see what was there. Thick and rusty metal chains, broken chairs, screws, nails, and nuts, rusty clamps, hammers, tires, weathered boards, and ancient furniture, all in a jumble.

An old house on my parents' property is called "the Bachelor's" for the old farmer who lived there long ago. When I was young, my dad rented the house out to Francis Hackett and her daughters; after they left, my grandma Hovell used it to store old papers and clothes. Nearly a mile from our house, for years it was a good place for high school kids to party in, a fun place for people to break glass, bust down walls. After looking into the farm buildings around Mom's house, I hiked out to the Bachelor's through the bean fields with my mother and my small sons, but we couldn't get near the house, so thick were the pricker bushes and nettles. All around the house and collapsed barn is cultivated land now, and we circled the lot, looking in at the weathered boards, broken floors, abandoned dishes. When we returned to my parents' house, my nearly three-year-old son told his dad, "I saw a broken farm today." Then, thinking better of it, he added: "*Two* broken farms."

11. Mother

My mother married my dad just after she graduated from high school. She was the first Bockenhauer to finish school. Grandpa Earl had quit after his freshman year, Grandma Vi after eighth grade. Mom's parents met when they were working on a farm in Minnesota; my grandma was fifteen when she eloped, sixteen when she had her first child, Laurena Viola, my mother. Seven more kids followed. One—Glen—was even born after my brother, so Bob could claim being older than his uncle. Glen drowned in the Mississippi when he was sixteen; my cousin Jonny and another friend were with him. The boys were trying to cross from the shore to a cement wall that was part of the dam; as it turned out, Glen, a farm kid who grew up in a valley far from the river, couldn't swim.

My mom was a beauty, as all our mothers were. But really, her high school photograph was so striking that the photographer colorized it, putting her in a coral blouse and painting in a matching carnation behind her ear; he displayed it in his shop window in Winona as an example of his best work. My father, seven years her senior, was clearly taken by her beauty; family photo albums are full of pictures he took of her in the first years of marriage. I don't think Laurena ever imagined anything other than getting married and having kids after high school; marrying my dad was, at least, a departure from helping to raise her own brothers and sisters. She was eighteen when she moved into the house on Caledonia Prairie, where my dad lived with his parents, sisters, and brothers. She was a shy person and not used to asking for much.

My mother—who also goes by "Laurie"—tells me that when my brother was born two years after she married my dad, no one had told her anything about "what to expect" about childbirth, though she had certainly seen animals born on the farm. She recalls how alone she felt in her husband's family's house, sitting up all night with her colicky baby, rocking him, rocking him. No one offered to help, and she didn't think to ask. My parents continued to live with my grandparents until Bobby was four, when my grandparents and the rest of their kids moved back to the farm in Fox Coulee.

My mother grew up to farm work. But in a sense the house was really her domain. It wasn't that she claimed it, as do some women who strive to make their house cheerful and tidy; it was that she inherited it, was expected to watch over it, just as she was expected to serve my father while he sat waiting at the end of the table. Much of what she did was connected to food: she milked cows, raised chickens, fed dogs and cats, tended a garden, and was expected to watch over most anything that had to do with feeding the family. And, of course, she tended us kids. When I think back to those days, I remember how active she was. She is still famous for being fast, and it's no wonder, with all she had to take care of. At seventy-five she is as likely to run out to the mailbox in her bare feet as she is to leave me in the dust in a shopping mall. This woman has things to do. When I turned five, she started working as a waitress, a job she did for thirty years. I think she liked it; it gave her a place and a role that did not revolve around Dad or the kids, even if it still meant serving food. Her work gave her friends and acquaintances she could joke with, especially if she had a drink; it made her more sociable and connected her to people out in the world, outside the house.

When I was growing up, my mother never spanked me or even yelled at me, even though those were common enough practices in that time and place. Sometimes it seems like my mother has discovered Buddhist detachment all on her own; she can maintain equanimity in trying times. More recently, though, my mother has expressed a little gruffness, as in one instance when she surprised herself by barking her irritation at my son: "Goddammit." Mostly, though, she is cheerful, and since my father died, Mom has adopted the philosophy of being upbeat. Her Germanic upbringing was one that involved lots of laughter and jokes but few announcements of affection or emotion. What she doesn't show—what she never has shown—is sorrow or melancholy (anger is displayed only by accident, in short bursts); by the same token, she does not seem to know how to respond to the complicated or less cheerful feelings of others. The whole time I was growing up as a sulky, moody teenager, I don't remember her asking, "What's wrong?" And while my own kids, for their own reasons, say "I love you" twenty times a day, it was not a phrase I heard growing up. (I do remember, however, one tearful conversation with my dad, after I was discovered drunk at a home-coming float meeting; he was at a loss as to what to do with me.) When my dad died at the age of seventy, my mother did not cry—at least not publicly—and this perplexed many of us. Didn't she love him? Had she already made peace with his passing? Or would she just not let herself feel this? On one visit she took me to see my father's headstone in Evergreen Cemetery, bringing along a Tupper-ware pitcher of water for the flowers planted there.

◆

12. Horses

When my brother, Bob, was a boy (and I was not even born yet), Dad bought a Shetland pony. These are small animals, just made for kids to ride, but this horse was stubborn. The pony would listen to my dad's directions but sensed in my brother a certain lack of au-thority. When Bobby stuck his foot in the stirrup and hoisted him-self up, the pony would spin around, leaving my brother hanging in midair. If Bobby managed to get into the saddle, the pony would sometimes take his revenge by running toward a barbed wire fence, sensing that he would not be hurt and knowing that my brother could not stop him and would have to bail off. One time this pony took off running before my brother could mount him. As Bob de-scribes it, his left foot was caught in the stirrup, while his right foot hit the ground every twenty feet or so. He could have been trampled.

He could have been dragged and killed. Dad was working in the barn and came running when he heard my brother yelling. When Dad caught up with that pony, he slugged him smack in his bony forehead. The pony fell to his knees. Bobby had to milk the cows alone that night and the next day because Dad's fist was so sore.

You know that we had horses during some of my adolescent years, pintos, a feisty black-and-white one and a large-hammed and gentler white-and-red one. Names never stuck to these horses. They made their home in the yard behind the barn where the cows used to be and were allowed to wander back into the woods sometimes. While I did not fall in love with them the way some girls of that age do, they did contribute to my fantasy of myself as an Indian. And in a way, my father wanted me to love them, wanted me to be a horse-woman the way my mother had been.

When I was twenty and in India, I played a game with college buddies called "Essences." The idea was to get to the heart of people through metaphors: If this person were a car, he'd be a Mustang. If this person were an animal, she'd be a basset hound. It seemed to me then that I was a deer, or aspired to be, and that my mother was a horse, one you had to approach gently. Reach your hand toward her and she might pull away.

13. The Dead

When my siblings were kids and the family still had a bevy of farm animals—cows, horses, chickens, cats, dogs, guinea hens—they had a pet duck, a baby one, that they fed and cuddled. As often happens, that duck soon got sick and died. The cousins got together and decided to bury it. They smoothed his feathers, then laid the duck out in a long donut box with a cellophane window so they could look in and see the corpse. They borrowed a shovel, buried it in shallow grave on the edge of the woods, and stood over it, repeating solemn words.

I was a good reader and an obedient grade-schooler, but in the fourth grade we had to read a novella in our reading book that I found utterly boring. It was all about pioneer people and olden times and log cabins and such—something about a candle. So I skipped it and relied for my understanding of the story on the conversations of my peers. In those grades we frequently found a way to get out of the teacher's oversight by making a play about whatever book we were reading. Although I had not read the story, I volunteered to dramatize it. I conceived of the play as a kind of satire whose final scene involved the main character's soliloquy about the death of his candle—the candle that he read by in those dark log cabin nights, the candle I had heard discussed ad nauseam in my reading group. This soliloquy, as I saw it, shed new light on the earlier scenes and turned the seriousness of the story on its head. When I turned my script in to the teacher, I noted only that there would be a final speech but, for some reason, left out its content. The teacher initially refused to let us put on my play. "It doesn't make sense," she said. When I explained the ending, she relented. In this scene I would place the all-important candle in a donut box, say a few solemn words, and put the story to rest.

As I was working on this book, the memory of that play kept returning to me: I saw myself standing in front of a class, donut box in hand. Although the memory kept tapping me on the shoulder, it took me some time to turn around and look at it. The memory echoed my fears about this book: that I was writing a story I really didn't know, that it wouldn't make sense until I got to the very end. And when I turned to the memory, I saw that, despite my initial intentions, I have been writing about corpses, dead bodies, putting stories to rest.

14. Platform Controversy Beginnings

Although I kept thinking about the dead while writing this book, the initial impetus for my exploration was the controversy about the platform mounds, involving archaeologists' efforts to preserve the earthworks and some townspeople's resistance to the project.

In the 1990s the project to preserve the platform mounds in Trempealeau hit several snags. One concerned the issue of access—who owned the land and thus the road that gave access to the mounds? Then there was the issue of cost: sure, the archaeologists had a bundle to start with, but the village was supposed to kick in a share. And, more than that, who would pay for maintenance once the outsiders had come and gone? A depressed little village like Trempealeau couldn't be expected to take that on. And, finally, there was the issue of authenticity: how do we know these mounds are real? No one had ever heard of them before, and several old fellows claimed to have piled dirt up there in the 1930s when they built the tower. Why should we believe the archaeologists?

It would be wrong to suggest that the whole town got involved in these issues. Instead, most people were indifferent to the project.

Living out on the prairie, for example, my parents stood clear of it, not because they actively chose to stay out of the controversy but because it seemed something far away, something that didn't really concern them. In 2001 the more I talked to people about their memories of the project, the more I realized that the controversy directly involved only a handful of people who were able to present a convincing story and sway others to their point of view. In effect, the blocking of the project had been led by a few prominent vocal men in town. Interestingly, two of the men who most distrusted the archaeologists were diggers themselves. One was a plumber, Jim Stull, who had to go into the earth to lay pipe and move water.[77] The other was Harold Wilber, who ran a lucrative quarry business; he had dug up many acres of local earth in his search for limestone. Because these men were so prominent, their doubts managed to turn many people's apathy into opposition.

Among the few who actively supported the project were educators—Scout leaders, park rangers, teachers—and those with an interest in local and Native American history: arrowhead collectors, rendezvousers, the liberal minded, the newly arrived. The identities and positions of many of those who supported the project were, unfortunately, the very things that minimized their ability to lead opinion in the town. Among the more prominent of the archaeologists' first contacts were the owners of the Trempealeau Hotel, the restaurant that had been funkily restored by newcomers to the area who sold specialty beer and went to Jamaica every winter. But when the village meetings turned into challenges to the archaeologists, "the hotel guys didn't step up to help," as one archaeologist noted. As businessmen, they crumbled in the face of the opposition. For what mattered finally—what came to rank highest—was the opinion of the town fathers. All others—outsiders, latecomers, intellectuals, teachers, outlaws, hippies, housewives—did not really count in this discussion about land, money, and authenticity.

The land on which the platform mounds stood has been owned by Mount Calvary Lutheran Church since the late 1950s. As Rodell describes it in his report of 1991, the church was generous in giving archaeologists access to the land. But unless they wanted to scale the steep and brambly face of Little Bluff to get to the mounds, visitors to the mounds had to walk the rough road long used by village workers. And who owned the road became an important question.

David Waraxa owned the Riverview Motel just below Little Bluff. His motel is a kind of apartment house as well as an overnight place. Its several buildings mount the hill below the mounds. Almost as soon as he moved to town, and after interest in the mounds was rekindled in 1991, Waraxa argued with the village about access to the mounds, claiming that the road to the mounds was actually on his land and opposing use of it to get to the mounds. In February 1994 the *Galesville Republican* noted that Waraxa's argument with the village was the result of "conflicting plat maps in the county Register of Deed's Office in Whitehall," the county seat. At issue was a fifty-foot-wide piece of land between the base of the hill and the hotel. Both Waraxa and the village claimed to own it, and both sides could point to a plat map to support their claim. The various owners of the hotel had been paying property taxes on the land since 1955; at the same time the village had been using the road for years to maintain the water tower. Those who wanted to restore the mounds needed this very same road for access to them. And this road, Waraxa claimed to the reporter, "runs just a few feet outside the front doors of Rooms 7, 8, and 9,"[78] which was why he was against allowing the archaeologists to use it. Waraxa posed for a photo of himself near the steep snow-covered approach to the mounds and offered his perspective: "I'm not saying they're authentic, but if this (project) goes through—if they insist on it—this (route) [which went straight up the bluff face and avoided the road] makes more sense because it eliminates the problems with the property owners down there."[79] In effect, Waraxa hoped to cut all access to the road to the mounds and pressure both the village and the archaeologists to find another way.

Waraxa was something of an outsider to the area, having moved up from Fort Atkinson, Wisconsin, a few years earlier; thus, while local people could sympathize with his insistence on his rights as a landowner, his latecomer status ensured that residents would not fully embrace his cause. His protest was too noisy, too public, perhaps. Waraxa's resistance, however, gave the project its first whiff of controversy and thus added to the general climate of opposition.

Although the *Republican* framed Waraxa's opposition as a story about private property, two informants described his issues with the project differently. James Gallagher, the archaeologist who led the project, told me that instead of seeing the mounds as something that might actually draw visitors and thus motel guests to the area, Waraxa had argued that because visitors to the platform mounds would pass right by his motel, they posed a potential threat to his tenants.[80] The platform mounds, Waraxa was reported as saying, would bring crime into his rooms. Gallagher and I laughed: archaeological tourists aren't really known for hooliganism. To Gallagher, Waraxa's concern for his property had become almost paranoia. One resident also noted the irrationality of Waraxa's opposition: "He thought visitors might steal things," he said with a guffaw. This informant suggested that Waraxa's unwarranted suspicion was connected, in effect, to his newcomer status. He just didn't understand where he was.

In any case, one striking thing about Waraxa's opposition to the mound project is how little the mounds actually figured in it. The desire to learn about the history of the area, the wish to make this site accessible so that others might learn—all this seems to have been lost on Waraxa in his efforts to defend his property.

The question of cost was another obstacle for the project, and in this, perhaps, the residents' fears were well founded. Trempealeau is not wealthy by any means. In 2002 the village had a total annual budget of just over $100,000. Within this context, then, questions about the cost of the project were worth asking. The grant would provide only 80 percent of the money needed for the project, with the rest coming from other entities, including the village. At an open forum on October 4, 1993, Karen Vogel,[81] the German American wife of a local Ho-Chunk man, raised questions about what the village might expect to pay for the project in the future; she also asked whether anyone had done a projection comparing expected revenues and expenses. Once the preservation and interpretive projects were completed, she wanted to know, would the archaeologists leave the village with a maintenance bill it couldn't afford? These fine points had not yet been worked out. As the village board president, Mary Kopp, said in August 1994, "I would like to see the project get going. . . . But I don't want to put the village in a financially binding position."[82] These questions became all the more pressing as the issue of authenticity was raised. As one person interviewed by a local reporter noted in June 1994, "If these mounds are fake, what's the point of spending all that money?"[83]

Ultimately, questions about the authenticity of the Trempealeau platform mounds became pivotal to discussions in the mid-1990s. How can we be sure they are real? Are these archaeologists simply eggheads who don't know a pile of dirt from an Indian mound? If the mounds aren't real, who cares about access? And, more important, why sink money into them?

As I explored the controversy, I became interested in how authenticity became an issue in the first place. On what grounds did people feel prepared to challenge the archaeologists on their own turf? At its worst, residents' treatment of the visiting scientists was churlish and obstructive. Why were people so resistant to learning about the findings of experts in this area—the archaeologists? Unlike many Native Americans, residents were not opposed to mound digging in general. So where did their recalcitrance come from?

Part of the problem, as the archaeologist Rollie Rodell acknowledges, was one of public relations. When he and Jim Gallagher first went to Trempealeau for a village meeting, they had not expected much opposition. Given the widespread distrust for book learning and outsiders, however, that was a mistake. Karen Vogel attended that meeting, and she told me years later that Gallagher came off as arrogant—as if he didn't really want to hear from the public.

Another issue was the Indian Mounds at Perrot State Park. As Karen Vogel described the scene to me, an elderly gentleman had gotten up at an early meeting and revealed that when he worked for the Civilian Conservation Corps, he and other workers had excavated three mounds and trucked in dirt for four more. That was when Harry Murray had exposed that the cherished Indian Mounds at the state park were fake, and a number of village residents became suspicious of the others. Subsequently, several elderly men insisted that the dirt that was up on Little Bluff had simply been dragged up there and shifted around in the 1930s, when the water tower was built. Some even claimed to have taken the dirt up themselves.

Furthermore, some residents felt that the information offered by the archaeologists and by the scientists' very presence was calling into question residents' knowledge of the land. Long-time residents had a sense that they knew the land well; they knew who lived where, who owned what. They had walked the land as kids, worked it as adults, hunted it, built on it. A new set of mounds was not part of their image of the place. So when outsiders came in to discuss these ancient mounds, people felt that their sense of the land was being challenged, that they were being made to play the fool. Why should some outsider have to come in and tell us what we have here, right in the middle of town? "We used to play up there, and we never knew anything about it," more than one resident told me. Put on the defensive by these outsiders—"We didn't know about any Mississippian people living here a thousand years ago"—people reclaimed their agency by asserting that they themselves had built the mounds: the mounds at the park, the mounds at Little Bluff—all those are ours.

As Roger Kennedy has argued, Euro-Americans' particular habits of thinking about history and architecture have, in many ways, left us unprepared to deal with the mounds that dot the American landscape.[84] But instead of seeking to reeducate ourselves in this area, many of us simply dig in: That's ancient history. It has nothing to do with me. Connected to this was the negative reaction to the archaeologists, which was rooted in a larger distrust of academia. Had people come to the meetings well disposed to archaeological knowledge, they might not have been so easily put off by Gallagher; they might have read his demeanor as one suggesting authority rather than arrogance. But that was not to be: when the archaeologists attempted to use signs of prowess in the field to claim authority, these were met with derision. When Gallagher mentioned that Rodell had published an article on the Trempealeau platform mounds in "the foremost journal in the field," the revelation was met with indifference. Similarly, Robert "Ernie" Boszhardt, an MVAC archaeologist, noted that at one public meeting he prefaced an opinion with the phrase "In my professional opinion." What he learned from people's reactions was that they did not give a damn about his profession, so his opinion counted for nothing.[85]

Instead of placing their confidence in intellectuals—as I do within my academic community—many townspeople turned to the local men who claimed their own authority. The most vocal of these proved to be Harold Wilber, whose version of events (discussed further in part III) proved to be key to my understanding of the project and its detractors.

15. Storytelling

My family deals with all information through stories, by telling and retelling events and encounters until they can get the plot line just right. The stories that develop are not meant to be interpretations. As they are told, they relate the way things are. People are not supposed to dicker over what they mean.

Ever since I was a teenager, I have not really been able to join in the story cycles at home, the ones played out over coffee, on the phone, at family suppers. "This happened to her . . . He said . . . And then she goes—" It seems to me that, much of the time, the very reason for coming together over drinks, cheese and crackers, or potluck is to have one's worldview affirmed. (Of course, that is also why *I* like dinners with friends.)

While I was reading a scholarly article on nineteenth-century Wisconsin, I recognized my own family. Katherine Fitzgerald writes: "A common course of conversation, especially in multigenerational gatherings, is the digression from a timely bit of gossip to the family history of the person under discussion and its connection with the speaker's family. Often everyone at the table contributes to drawing the complex web of kinship, friendship, and business connections between families, including stories of school relations, illnesses, divorces, and deaths, before the current story can be resumed. I suggest that the function of this ritualized conversation is to rehearse and preserve the family's place in and connection to the community in an ever-in-flux world of tenuous and differing memories."[86] As Fitzgerald has it, assent to a common story binds the community. Our way of the world works. Sitting around the table after a family dinner, however, I often felt that my head would explode if I heard another word. This was their story, I thought, not mine.

I started to write stories in college, largely perhaps because I felt that there were other stories to tell. But I didn't go far away; many of my stories were about my family and relatives; a gathering around the making and eating of squirrel pie; a woman with a boyfriend who makes a pass at her cousin; an old woman who does her own kind of Sunday ceremony, skipping church. For one story I adapted a plot line from my mother's family: a widowed grandmother trades her old farmhouse for her son's trailer but cannot let go of the house, cannot figure out how to live without the love of her life. My mother was bothered by the story. Despite my feeble protestations, she couldn't see that it was fiction, an adaptation; my work of the imagination looked a lot like life. That same year, my senior year, I set about writing a novella for credit; it focused on three generations of men: an elderly retired professor, his businessman son, and his college-age grandson. I was under the tutelage of a male professor—indeed, nearly all my college teachers were men—and I was heavy into the big guys of fiction: Hemingway, Faulkner, and also Malamud, Updike. I did not really pause to think about my choice of male subjects until a new faculty member in English—also male—asked me why I wasn't writing about women. In some sense I was trying to figure out how people changed social class. More to the point, however, this was the world in which I lived—both at home and at college. It was one in which the opinions and actions of men counted more. I am still trying to unlearn these stories.

One of the most troubling stories told by my family concerned the man who would become my husband. When we first started dating, I took a photo of T.S. in weak light with black-and-white film. While I was visiting my family one Christmas, I showed the photo to my mom and dad: this is my boyfriend. Then I got on the plane for Detroit, where T.S. would pick me up to visit his parents in their house near a country club not far from Ann Arbor. We then returned to our lives in Syracuse, New York, where my love for this man expanded and flowered. In May I proposed to my parents over the phone that I might bring T.S. home to meet everybody. The idea was met with silence. When I asked my sister what the deal was, she said, "Well, he's black, isn't he? He's from Detroit, isn't he?" So that was the story. Accustomed to my unorthodox ways, my parents had convinced themselves that my lover was going to be someone they would dislike. It disturbed me to have to say, "No, he's not black," knowing that that news would relieve them. What if he had been? What then? But since he was white, they could begin to tell themselves other stories, the ones about marriage and grandkids and happy, happy homes. We have managed to produce such things—to fit into their stories in that way. Although we know that those old stories have a certain hold on us, in many ways we fashion our lives against their pull.

When my son Jack and I were visiting my mother, we slept upstairs in the room that had been mine when I was a child. And before me, it had been Pam's and Debbie's and, before that, Aunt Lorna's and Aunt Darlene's. As almost-four-year-old Jack settled down to sleep, he said, "Mom, let's talk about God." *God,* you should know, is one of those words—like *infinity,* like *freedom*—that gives me a headache; I can't get my brain around it. I'm like a traditional Jew who believes you shouldn't say the Lord's name outright, so big is it. So I asked Jack, "What do you want to talk about?"

"God made everything. He is like Jesus and Buddha," he said.

"I think of God as the sacred. Like a great big spirit," I offered.

Then Jack tells me that he thinks God has something wrapped around his head. And that the only thing bad in the world is mean people. "I think," he announced, "God is like a pressure on your heart."

Another night he wanted to talk about death—people died a long time ago, he said, things die all the time. What's it all mean? he seemed to be asking. I remembered being five years old in a room below us when the fact of death hit me and I realized my mother's mortality. (My brother was playing "And When I Die" by Blood, Sweat, and Tears on the stereo.)

And the irony strikes me: while I complain about the banality of family dinner table conversations, my preschooler wants to talk about God and death. He wants some big stories.

16. Trempealeau Mountain

Trempealeau Mountain is a bluff remnant of an island in the Mississippi; standing three hundred feet high and a third of a mile across, it was considered sacred ground by the Ho-Chunk and Dakota people who lived in the region. As the legend goes, the French explorer Nicolas Perrot landed near the mountain in 1685; Linctot's trading post, established in 1731, stood within a quarter mile of its banks. Later, when Dakota people moved into the area in the 1810s and 1830s, Chief Wabasha had a village near the mountain. In 1817, Lieutenant Zebulon M. Pike camped near it and "spoke glowingly of its scenery."[87] The name of the bluff, as I mentioned, comes from *la montagne qui trempe à l'eau,* French for the Winnebago name. In *Life on the Mississippi* Mark Twain describes Trempealeau Mountain in a speech by a long-winded tour guide of panoramas. The guide pontificates about "Trempeleau [*sic*] Island, which isn't like any other island in America, I believe, for it is a gigantic mountain, with precipitous sides, and is full of Indian traditions, and used to be full of rattlesnakes; if you catch the sun just right there, you will have a picture that will stay with you."[88] When I was growing up there, local legend maintained that the Indians who used to live in the region considered "the mountain soaking in the water" to be the center of the world, the axis mundi, as Mircea Eliade would have it, around which people in the area oriented themselves.[89]

These days Trempealeau Mountain is part of the Wisconsin state park system, though it used to be private land, as my family will attest. My dad's boyhood friend Dale Critzman used to own an arm of land off the mountain. My brother talks about being able to walk across the bay in the 1960s; my mother recalls being out on the mountain and nauseated with pregnancy; after a sip of cold coffee from a smelly thermos, she threw up. She was pregnant with me, she thinks. My family's boaters and water-skiers used to picnic and launch from the banks of the mountain, until the state condemned the land in order to seize it for the park.

Although the banks of the mountain were well trampled by my family, there is something foreboding about climbing its peak. Even now my uncle Clyde expresses surprise that I, a forty-year-old mother of two, would scale the mountain by myself in the dead of winter. Hiking just for pleasure is not really in his book. Other things conspire to keep people off the island and mountain too. For one, you have to walk on the railroad tracks to get there. When I was a kid, I believed it was illegal to go there; perhaps because the railroad had put up forbidding signs; perhaps this was a story told by parents and other knowing adults. It added to the fun, in any case. To be sure, the number of trains on these tracks make going there a bit risky. In the old days part of the way was on a trestle over the river, and if a train came while you were crossing, the only place to go was in the water. Recently, however, the railroad has added a footpath to this bridge; hikers and fishers use it, even if a sign proclaims it as the land of the Burlington Northern: keep off. Even now, though, if a train comes while you are on the tracks, you have to scramble down the bank while a hundred cargo boxes from China go barreling up the river. When I was a kid, other things kept you off as well: the rumor about rattlesnakes, which Twain cited. This rumor was repeated by my grandma Hovell, who, after one of my visits there, cried out in dismay: "You can't go there! There are rattlesnakes out there!" I doubt my grandmother knew she was echoing Twain; I assured her I'd never seen a snake, that I was careful. Certainly, she could not yet imagine that I would soon go to India, where cobras and vipers (and their owners) sometimes come knocking at the door, and snakes have their own special holiday. Anyway, she couldn't keep me away from the mountain—it was as exotic and romantic as I could get in those days, the center of someone else's world.

As a high-schooler, I probably went to Trempealeau Mountain three times a year, mostly alone. Romantic notions about Indians drew me, as did something about its forbiddenness. One time I was able to convince my cop brother and his fiancée to join me, and we scrambled up the rough trail to take a good look at the bluffs all around, the places where the land was reclaiming the bay in which we used to swim and water-ski, the trains, barges, and boats passing, the river running below us. At other times, when I climbed nearby Brady's Bluff with a camera, I always took some shots of the mountain, which from that height rose out of the water like an isosceles triangle, or, in other terms, echoed in gigantic fashion the shape of the burial mounds constructed on it and that lined the opposite bank. The mount meant something to my dad too. His grandfather and dad helped build the road that limned the river (and thus the mountain) and extended into the state park. He had his memories of playing and boating in its shadow. Our shared attraction to the place gave my dad and me some connection. From his basement studio my dad turned out paintings of the mountain in many lights, at many times of year.

The centrality of the place to local self-conceptions is suggested by the decision to use the name of the mountain for the county when it was incorporated in 1854. Shortly after, in 1856, the name of the village also changed to Trempealeau. And Trempealeau Mountain continues to orient people there. The local cafe sports an enormous painting of the mountain. Pictures of it adorn park brochures.

A county tourist pamphlet notes, erroneously, that "The French called the mountain, rising out of the Mississippi River, La Montogne qui [*sic*]. That is how the county got its name."[90] In the 1960s a local band director wrote a "tone poem" about the site—"La Montagne qui trempe à l'eau"—that, in his words, explored something of what the place might have meant to the native peoples here. Most recent is Harold Wilber's Trempealeau Mountain Golf Course. I am not immune to the mountain's pull, either. While staying in the area recently, I set out for a walk in the direction of the mountain and felt that old sense of excitement and reverence for the place.

That there are effigy mounds on Trempealeau Mountain is little known. Below a drawing of the mountain itself, brochures for Perrot State Park include images of the effigy mounds found on parkland: mounds in the shape of birds, deer, dogs, ovals, and wide straight lines, as well as conical burial mounds, but the park people don't tell you where to find them all. Archaeologists maintain that the effigy mounds were built sometime between 600 and 1200 CE, by the Late Woodland people, who have since become other peoples, changing their lifeways and taking on different names as time passed. Even though archaeologists cannot be certain who succeeded the mound builders in this region, members of the Ho-Chunk Nation, now the dominant native group in the region, believe that they were the mound builders. As the Ho-Chunk anthropologist Anna Funmaker told me, the mounds are clan totems.

Most local people know nothing of the effigy mounds on Trempealeau Mountain, and those who know where they are like it that way. And while most people these days have forgotten about them, there are also twenty-two burial mounds on the mountain, all of which were desecrated by amateur archaeologists and Sunday treasure seekers, by George Squier himself. "Can you imagine digging in a cemetery? It's the same thing," John Ebersold said.

John learned of the effigy mounds on Trempealeau Mountain from copies of Theodore Lewis's extensive survey of mounds in the region from the 1880s. No one told John where to look; he had to scramble the steep banks until he found the right humps of dirt. John says that late spring is the best time to go looking, when the snow is gone but the brush has not yet grown tall enough to obscure them.

Although it was high summer, John took T.S. and me out to see them in July 2001, surprising us by suggesting that we should go in the afternoon because the snakes would be sleeping then. (I had assumed that snakes were simply part of an old grandma's tale.) Because it was July, the brush was thick and had the potential to obscure the eroded figures. But John knew where to look. And, sure enough, after tramping through the brambles, he found the linear mound, a hump of dirt that sloped down the hill, and, below that, the shape of a bird mounded in dirt, facing the river. John held his arms out like wings to show us the shape of the bird, and then we could see it. Perhaps forty feet long and forty wide, the bird is poised at the edge of the slope, its wings spread wide. John reported that sometimes Ho-Chunk people come out here to pay their respects, leaving little packets of tobacco tied up in red-and-white thread strung up in the trees.

Effigy mounds, burial mounds, center of the world: The convergence of so many sacred structures in such a small area—Trempealeau Mountain—leads Rollie Rodell to posit that this part of the river area created a place of notoriety—others might say sacred power—among native peoples that continued into the seventeenth century. Rodell suggested to me in conversation that it may have been this fame that led Perrot to the area in the first place, directed by Ho-Chunk guides who left him at the Wisconsin River to find his own way. Certainly, the mountain and its effigies represent something of the sacred for a number of native groups. The Ho-Chunk claim them; the Dakota have their own stories about them.

And John told us one: Dakota people came into the area from Minnesota in the early nineteenth century. They too honored the mountain and maintained that, like themselves perhaps, it had floated down the Mississippi from upriver, from what is now Red Wing, Minnesota. When the mountain turned up missing, they sent scouts down to search for it; they made the seventy-mile journey by canoe. There, nestled among the other bluffs, they found the mountain and on it the thunderbird and linear effigies, still safe and sound, protected as they were by spirits—spirits in the form of rattlesnakes.

John put it together: there may well be snakes on the mountain, yet the story of rattlesnakes and the forbiddenness of the mountain was the tale—altered and rewritten—that Twain had passed along,

2.14. Trempealeau Mountain (1982), painted by Robert Ray Hovell Sr. and presented to his mother.

the one my grandmother had told me, the one my dad had heard tell of—"There are rattlesnakes out there!"—a story transformed and translated but, as it was passed on, still intimating something of the holy out there.

17. Rendezvous

After my first brief encounter with a latter-day gathering of voyageurs, settlers, and natives at Perrot State Park in 2000, I was eager to see a full-blown rendezvous. In the summer of 2001 I traveled to a rendezvous at French Island, downriver from Trempealeau, near La Crosse. Before I went there, I stopped to look at the controversial Indian statue that stands in Riverside Park, near downtown La Crosse. The statue caricatures a Plains Indian; it had recently come under fire for its depiction of a Native American. The Indian stood there obstinately, arms crossed in front of him.

Across the water the rendezvous was getting under way. The vendors were setting up shop, a blacksmith was at work, a man was making a barrel in the old-fashioned way. The first participant I saw was a large white woman in a buckskin dress with her thin daughter, who was similarly attired. The baby the woman was holding wore disposable diapers. I soon ran into Phil Palzkill, a ranger at Perrot Park, who was dressed as a voyageur in a calico, buttonless shirt, and breeches, with trade beads around his neck. While most folks there dressed as European settlers and voyageurs from various historical periods, some took on native garb. A woman in a ribbon dress sold beadwork she had done. Another woman in a fringed leather dress had a headband with a feather tucked in it. Some men were shirtless in buckskin trousers—it was hard to tell what they were supposed to be. And one fortysomething man wore only a short loincloth, his tan line showing on his exposed upper thighs. He called himself Blackheart. I overheard one man in polo shirt and shorts say, "If I dressed up, I'd have to be an Indian. They are the coolest."

I talked for a while with a woman and her grandson who were selling fry bread. She and a patron were discussing the difference between various fried breads. "The elephant ears you get around here are not like the real ones," she said. "Real elephant ears are from India and they are salty, not sweet. They are served with split pea soup." That sounded like a South Indian *dosa* to me, but I kept my mouth shut. "And did you know," she said, "that there were three kinds of Indians? The turban-wearers, the ones who wear nose-rings, and the ones who wear dots on their forehead." She said she'd been to Asia many times and loved it. "Asia is a shopper's paradise," she claimed.

While she was talking to me, she bargained with a man who wanted to buy a cowhide she had for sale. She goes around to a lot of such fairs, she said, so I asked her if she went to powwows. "When I go to powwows, I go to dance," she said. "But we never eat there. We eat at the casinos." She is Mexican and part Apache, originally from San Antonio but now lives in Hayward, Wisconsin. Her grandson, Steve, was burning sage, and the scent reminded me of Tibetan juniper. He showed me how to pull the smoke toward me, to purify myself. He pointed out where I could buy some. When I went to the nearby tent, the burly white shopkeeper handed me the sage, saying, "It's a great mosquito repellent."

In my shorts and tank top I interacted with folks by taking photos, and every person I asked obliged. It takes a lot of effort to put together the costumes—or a persona, as some serious rendezvousers have it—and people seemed happy to have someone record their efforts. An adolescent girl tagged behind me, "Oh, lady with a camera! Lady with a camera!" She asked to have her picture taken and posed jauntily in her long cotton skirt.

Tom Hunter has been a janitor at Trempealeau Elementary since I was a kid. The last time I had seen him was at the Perrot State Park gathering, where he had dressed like some kind of native. This time, though, he was a voyageur in leather and calico. When I asked him why he came to these things, he said he does it out of an interest in history. "I'm really interested in 1750." He said he has learned a lot just by trying to put together a costume—each part means something. He pointed to the trade silver on his bandana as an example but added that he knows the French probably cheated the Indians on trades. For him, adopting a persona and going to rendezvous is a way of remembering the past, a way of participating in community: "You learn a little from everybody"—what's authentic, what things mean. He spoke of his wire-rimmed glasses—how he tried to get them to look like they came from the period. And because rendezvous folk try to do everything from the period, "The camping is much harder than modern camping," he said. There are no sleeping bags, no handy cookstoves, no flashlights. Later he and the park ranger Phil Palzkill fashioned fishing poles from branches and string for a kids' fishing contest. When I asked Tom how he got started in all this, he said he went to the Perrot Park rendezvous the year before on a lark and spent the weekend in a tepee. He found he didn't want to go back to work on Monday.

Tom admitted that a few rednecks among the rendezvous folk make comments about Indians' being savages and backward, but most folks are decent, he felt. We talked for a time about the Redmen mascot issue at the local school—he is against the mascot—and about the platform mound project—he was for it—and I noted how much his politics coincided with mine. But that, of course, also put him on the margins of Trempealeau's power structures, which were occupied by businessmen and Lions Club members. It strikes me that if I had stayed in the area and not gone away to college or been able to travel abroad, I might well have become one of the rendezvousers, dropping my usual persona for a weekend, finding another way to be in that place. And going native was, in some ways, as far

2.15. Rendezvousers, French Island, July 2001. Photo by author.

away from yourself as you could go. But it was also very familiar, another, more elaborate, way of playing Indian.

The rendezvous folk frequently imagine their participation in these events as a way of wresting something authentic from the snares of modern life. In this way, they imagine the rendezvous as an escape from the workaday world. But, of course, that world works its way into the proceedings—into their perceptions of rendezvous history, into their images about settlers, natives, and voyageurs, into their buying and selling. Theirs is a peaceful, quiet gathering—a kind of elaborate dress-up party—a recasting of history. On the edge of the encampment I bought a hotdog and a diet Pepsi from the La Crosse Lions Club.

I wandered among the tent shops, buying rock candy for my sons. I spotted a Native American man in shorts and T-shirt with long black hair and a younger man, who appeared to be his son, as they made their way through the exhibits—tepees, traders' hut, vendors' tents. As they were heading out, I approached the elder and blurted out, stopping his progress: "Excuse me for being so forward, but what do you think of all this?

He stopped and looked at me. "Not much," he said. "There's nothing really here. It's a way to make over past history. We go to powwows at Prairie du Chien, and this is really nothing much."

"Yes, I don't notice any Native American participants," I observed.

"No, our people don't come here. The rendezvous people have an attitude. They use a lot of stereotypes."

"I've seen white guys dressed up as Native Americans," I ventured.

"The people here will even go so far as to use modern-day stereotypes. They walk around with a beer, stagger around, and say, 'Look at me. I'm a real Indian.'"

"That's really offensive," I agreed.

"That's what we think," he said and moved on.

The rendezvous offers a seemingly benign history—a history of trading, intermarriage, exchange. In that sense it is a way of remembering without acknowledging what else happened, what else followed: death by disease, war, removal, seizure of land, murder. The scene at the rendezvous is complacent and cheerful. There is a tomahawk throw at 1 p.m. A Celtic band plays at 2. A children's fishing contest and a dance. Native American games and contests. And for this remembering, no Native Americans are really required, the white folks having taken their part. We can be our own mascot.

18. Arrowheads

The school at Galesville has a long history of using Indian images as part of its identity. The yearbook has been called *The Arrowhead* since 1914, and Plains-style Indians in headdresses have adorned class rings for decades. Although residents sometimes claim that the origins of Gale-Ettrick-Trempealeau High School's "Redmen" mascot similarly stretch back into the mists of time, the first reference to the Redmen that I can locate appears in a front-page story about the basketball team in the *Galesville Republican* of November 1, 1956. The adoption of *Redmen* as the team name gave official sanction to habits of remembering others and imagining oneself that had gone on since the early part of the century. While supporters of Indian mascots sometimes argue that they intend to honor Indians, exploring this local school's use of Indian images over time illuminates something about how white residents have imagined themselves. Indian mascots have allowed local people both a way to play Indian, as Philip Deloria has described it,[91] and a way to distance themselves from Indianness. Indeed, in the efforts of white students and residents to revise and re-imagine their relation to Indians and Indianness, there is something of the compulsive—a sense that this matter cannot be dispensed with once and for all. This ambiguity, not surprisingly, has also shaped recent debates about the fate of the Redmen mascot and logo.

A brick school for all grades was built in 1908 in Galesville on the bank above Lake Marinuka, a body of water named for the Ho-Chunk "princess" who was buried on its edge long ago. Said to be the former site of an Indian camp, the school's location allowed residents—and students in particular—to imagine themselves as taking the place of those who had gone before them. That there was some anxiety as well as pleasure in the claiming of this land is suggested by the repetitive nature of the plays performed by students in 1914 and 1915, both of which dealt with the winning of the West. (In 1914 and 1915 the Indian wars were still part of the recent past.) The 1914 photograph of the cast of *Burley's Ranch* shows students dressed as soldiers, settlers, and Indians; the characters include Roaming Bear, chief of the Ute tribe; Black Eagle; and Wakita, daughter of the chief. In the end the settlers win out; as the synopsis notes, "Roaming Bear demands surrender. Troops arrive." And Steve "save[s] the day." This victory, however, seems not to hold, for the next year the students enact *On the Little Bighorn,* a "comedy drama" in four acts. The massacre of Lieutenant-Colonel George Armstrong Custer and the Seventh U.S. Cavalry takes place off stage; this play ends with the happy reconciliation of "Rose of the Mist, a Sioux maiden," and the white hero.[92]

The pleasure of playing Indian—John Cance,[93] for example, played a chief in both plays—is available elsewhere as well. With the inception of the *Arrowhead* in 1914, student editors of the yearbook imagine their "annual" as a native artifact and, by implication, take up for themselves the place of Native American artisans. Consider this foreword to the 1932 *Arrowhead:*

> This volume of the Arrowhead, emanating from the very sod on which our high school stands—an Indian camping ground—is filled with the heart of the student and the lore of the Indian who left his tradition behind.
>
> Many a tribe before us has passed out from council on this historic spot.

It is our sincere hope that this book may be a living memory of friends and associations for years to come.

In this passage white presence in the region is indigenized; the yearbook becomes something of human design that simply rises out of the earth. The version of local history here suggests a kind of benign succession—first there were Indians, then we came along—with no account of the violence and political forces that attended white settlement of the area. In this construction native tribes simply "pass out" from council, leaving their tradition behind to be cared for by those who come after them.

Over the years students took up Indian motifs with varying zeal. The makers of the 1926 yearbook, for example, made extensive use of Indian motifs. Images of an Indian brave in pigtails, single feather, breeches, and loincloth organize the sections, directing readers. With his hand stretched out to the sky this Indian can be seen dedicating the yearbook to a Mr. Abraham; the brave looks into the vague horizon in the foreword; he dons only a loincloth so that he can run on the page announcing "Athletics." In these images the Indian caricature gestures lightheartedly toward who "we" are.

In the 1932 yearbook, students made a more sober connection between themselves and their Indian predecessors. Excerpts from Henry Wadsworth Longfellow's immensely popular poem "The Song of Hiawatha" are included with each section heading, lending the volume its honorific solemnity. As the section head to "Scenes" beckons:

> Ye who love the haunts of Nature,
> Love the sunshine of the meadow,
> Love the shadow of the forest,
> Love the wind among the branches,
> And the rain shower of the snow storm,
> And the rushing of the great rivers
> Through their palisades of pine trees,
> And the thunder in the mountains,
> Whose innumerable echoes
> Flap like eagles in their eyries:—
> Listen to these wild traditions.

The excerpt from Longfellow posits an identity between the romanticized Indian and the local lover of nature. Because both Indians and whites love the land in common, white settlers can imagine taking the place—even continuing the work—of the Indians who have gone before them.

Such white presence, of course, depends on Indian absence or displacement. The 1928 yearbook represents this idea graphically and overlays photographs of the town's current features on a drawing of the Indian past: photos of the steel bridge over Beaver Creek and Lake Marinuka, the downtown storefronts, the "East Side Camping Place," the "grave of Indian Princess Marinuka," and "Indian Mounds" are pasted over a simple drawing of a brave in a canoe, another beating out smoke signals, an Indian village in the far distance. Indian life has given way both to the Indian dead—in the form of graves and mounds—as well as to the modern—bridges, stores. With native culture safely consigned to the past, students—like their elders—could forward their own versions of the place and of themselves.

Students in the 1920s made ample use of Indian images and motifs, replaying the legend of Princess Marinuka and her burial on the edge of the lake that bears her name, finding different ways to present Indian people and artifacts. Longfellow's Hiawatha is at work in both the 1932 and 1938 yearbooks. In 1952, except for the *Arrowhead* name, nothing about the yearbook is Indian at all. But with the use of the Redmen name beginning in 1956, a new crop of Indian imagining is possible. Images of the Redmen in the 1958 yearbook lack the old solemnity of some earlier yearbooks; it is 1958, after all, and—like everybody else—Redmen just wanna have fun. So this yearbook offers the cartoon Indian, the happy smiling Indian, an Indian who reads yearbooks, chews bubble gum, drinks soda pop, milks a cow, drives a tractor, and plays basketball—hey! They are just like us! This Indian, though largely male, can also go bowling and fills out a cheerleading sweater quite well, thank you. The artist who drew these cartoon Indians, Gloria Grover, is herself part Native American; her great grandmother, Mary Ann Farnham, was the daughter of the "half-breed" Agatha Wood, who later married James Reed, one of Trempealeau's earliest settlers. In this year, at least, students can deal with the Indianness of both the artist and the mascot if it is not too alien, not too scary. If the identity was ambivalent in previous years, by now "we" are the Redmen.

Later the Redmen image would be awarded a new dignity. My letter jacket, for example, bore the profile of a Roman-nosed brave in a headdress. As a high schooler I never thought to ask where the "red man" came from; I didn't even know which tribes had a local presence. As noted in Paul Radin's *The Winnebago Tribe* (1923), in their traditional dress Ho-Chunk men wore "a comb-like ornament woven from deer's hair and generally dyed red" to which was attached an eagle feather; the ornament was decorated with horsehair and rattlesnake rattles. [94] The Ho-Chunk did not opt for feather headdresses. While Dakota Indians are known to have worn war bonnet headdresses made of feathers, it is more likely that our image of Indians came from the movies than from the desire to emulate the ceremonial dress of a local native group. And, to be sure, the appearance of contemporary Indians was nothing we wanted to emulate: Tom Thunder and his prominent nose, the impoverished Indians by Hunter's Bridge, and Susie Kramer in her pastel frock were not who we wished to honor. Our heads were full of Hollywood Indians, and our hearts were full of local pride.

19. Local Informant

I was finishing work on the book about Tibetan-Western encounters and was beginning to think about seriously beginning the platform mound project. I was in Trempealeau one winter weekend and stopped by John and Lu's house that Saturday. I woke John up from an afternoon nap; he had shaved his head completely since the last time I had seen him. He showed me his arrowhead collection— more than one hundred pieces—all things he has found in the area just by looking on the surface. He figures that most are about seven hundred years old. He reported that some relatives of George Squier's had come to town recently; John helped them locate Squier's then-unmarked grave in the public cemetery. John passed along a recent rumor that "some rich lady" wanted to buy the land on which the platform mounds stand; he swore me to secrecy. It wouldn't do to let the opposition get their dander up ahead of time. We spoke about the Redmen mascot controversy; the school board had just voted—again—to keep it, despite some vocal opposition. Back in Ohio I was involved in discussions about the Wahoo mascot with Larry Dolan, owner of the Cleveland Indians and a trustee of Oberlin College, where I teach; I asked John his opinion on the mascot issue. He said the Redmen mascot doesn't really bother him. Like many in Trempealeau, he said he'd rather that the team just was called the old Trempealeau Bears.

After interviewing an elderly Trempealeau resident one Friday morning the following summer, I took a drive around the village. I pressed my palms together in a gesture of respect before the platform mounds, checked on the garden planted in the platform mound at Third and Jay, looked at the houses where my dad used to live, and circled my old elementary school. Down by the Duck Pond I saw a pickup with a Village of Trempealeau sign on the door and a man using a weed whacker to tidy up the edges of the pond. It was John at work. He shut off the machine and we chatted for a while. At forty-seven he had just become a grandpa, so I congratulated him. We made plans to meet up that night to hear the band Indigenous;

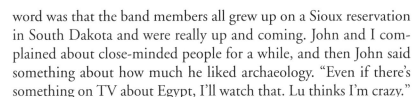

word was that the band members all grew up on a Sioux reservation in South Dakota and were really up and coming. John and I complained about close-minded people for a while, and then John said something about how much he liked archaeology. "Even if there's something on TV about Egypt, I'll watch that. Lu thinks I'm crazy."

"Did you ever think of going to college and studying it?" I asked.

"Naw, I couldn't do that. I'm too old now."

John knows just about everybody in town and has raised two kids in Trempealeau. He knows its woods and rivers, where to hunt, fish, and trap. He knows where to look for artifacts—though he won't tell. Born in Trempealeau, the youngest of eight kids, John has never lived anywhere else. But rather than shutting him down, the place opens him to the world.

That night John introduced me to Gus Vogel, Karen's husband. We were all at the performance of two Native American bands—Bill Miller's and Indigenous—on the lawn of the Trempealeau Hotel on a cool August evening. It proved a fortuitous meeting for me; not only did Vogel, a Ho-Chunk man who works for the nation in Black River Falls, become a key informant, he also put me in touch with Anna Funmaker, who does research on the Ho-Chunk and who had played a role in the platform mound controversy. But just after I spoke with Gus, John started to get worried. "You'll be nice to these people, right?"

I didn't really understand his question. "Of course. What do you think?"

"Well, I've never seen you speak with a First Nations person. I don't know how you'll treat them." He was probably remembering things I'd told him about other informants, the ones I had described in exasperation: those who had blocked the platform preservation project out of ignorance or self-interest. "John, I've worked in India and Tibet and interviewed people there. My approach is always to let people know—respectfully—what I think and to try to listen to what they have to say." In Trempealeau my status as a Hovell—a family of long-standing association with the town—opened a lot of doors for me, a person who had become something of an outsider in the twenty years since I'd left the place. At the same time, my status as a woman meant that many of the town leaders I spoke to—all men—didn't feel threatened by me. Sexism, ironically, gave me some advantage as an interviewer. But John was worried about how I treated native people and what I would do with their words. For the truth was, as respectful as I was during my interviews, I could be very critical when reporting what I'd heard. So John worried: Would I show respect? Would I be properly reverent? In his own way John could romanticize Indians as much as the next person. It was an attitude I struggled with too. And there was something else: Because he was my link to Gus Vogel and Anna Funmaker, he worried about what might happen. And after I left, he'd still be there.

20. A Thing of the Present

Past hopes, past excuses, past regrets lay thickly upon his soul, like fat on a side of bacon. Memory was always a thing of the present to the Indian. All he had to do was walk past a piece of dirt and he would be reminded of the sorrows of Little Wolf. The cries of the past could never die in a man who dwelt on the soil where his ancestors were buried. They became the cries of his children today.

David Seals, *The Powwow Highway*

Gus Vogel describes himself as half Ho-Chunk, half German. These days he works for the Ho-Chunk Nation in Black River Falls. He and Karen moved to Trempealeau in the early 1990s. When I spoke to him, Gus was not particularly interested in the platform mounds.[95] More meaningful to him is Trempealeau Mountain, with the Ho-Chunk stories that circulate around it, the ones he sees recorded in books and hears from elders, in tribal ceremonies, and that his grandfather passed on to him. For Gus, Trempealeau is marked by the graves of his ancestors—and also by the sites of their former graves. "There are a lot of remains we would like to have back," he said to me when we talked of such matters. As he sees it, native burials are all over the landscape around Trempealeau and Black River Falls, despite many white people's unwillingness to see them. When the white people came, he said, "we lost everything. Our religion, our culture, our names." Despite archaeologists' interests in these remains, Gus is suspicious of the field. In particular, he is troubled by the way that archaeology deals with burials. If, as Gus described it, everything was taken from his people when the whites came, then archaeology has served only to wrest another aspect of his people's history away from them, putting the bones and artifacts of ancestors in display cases and the cabinets of museums.

Vogel's conceptions of archaeology connect to larger criticisms of the field leveled by native activists and others. In his 1969 book *Custer Died for Your Sins,* Vine Deloria Jr. indicts the field of anthropology on several counts. The anthropologist—or "anthro," as Deloria shortens the term—is a person who comes into the field with a sense of discovering something new but with a firm sense that "he ALREADY KNOWS what he is going to find."[96] In the case of archaeology in particular, Deloria describes a certain dig in Minnesota in which archaeologists failed to "understand they were not helping living Indians preserve their culture by digging up the remains of a village that had existed in the 1500s." Instead of recognizing that native peoples might have their own views about digging for burials and artifacts, "the general attitude of the whites . . . was that they were the true spiritual descendents of the original Indians and that the contemporary Indians were foreigners who had no right to complain about their activities."[97]

This critical perspective on archaeology also informs the views of Anna R. Funmaker, who obtained a master's degree in anthropology at California State University. Funmaker researches the history of her tribe and lives in Black River Falls, about fifty miles from

Trempealeau, in Jackson County. Like Vogel, Funmaker was not particularly interested in the platform mounds; she doesn't think they are the work of her people. She has a sense of the land and its history that departs in many ways from standard archaeological knowledge. Educated in the era of the American Indian Movement (AIM), Funmaker suspects archaeologists of not having native interests at heart.[98]

In one example of her ability to go against received knowledge, Funmaker rejects many archaeological terms and categories. For example, like Lance Foster she finds the designation *Oneota* unsatisfactory because it distances the archaeological evidence produced by that culture from any living nation or tribe. These days we know the names that nations use for themselves—Ho-Chunk, Dakota, Ojibwa, Potawatomi, Ioway—but for her, Oneota is an artificial name invented by archaeologists that distinguishes these people from any historical tribe. "They [archaeologists] say it was a different group [from us]," Funmaker said. But she claimed, "No, it's the *same* group."

Criticisms like Funmaker's have indeed been integrated into a strand of self-questioning within the field of archaeology. As the archaeologist David Hurst Thomas argues, and many more have come to recognize, archaeology has tended to ignore or discredit native knowledge about the past since archaeology's very creation as a professional discipline. Larry J. Zimmerman describes the situation: "Pasts created by archaeologists have been imposed on Indian pasts without a chance for debate."[99] Furthermore, within the profession archaeologists have, until recently, tended to discredit oral tradition. Funmaker is especially critical of this tendency. Because the many mounds in the area were built by native people—whether her tribe or some other—she feels that there might well be stories connected with them, stories that might shed some light on their meaning. In the case of the platform mounds in particular, as she sees it, the archaeologists never sought out these stories. Speaking of the lead archaeologist, Jim Gallagher, she said: "He should have gone out to hear the stories."

Funmaker, then, does not accept the tendency to see archaeology as scientific fact and oral tradition as fancy; for her, the stories of the elders connect to the land; even if they are scientifically unverifiable, for her they represent a higher truth.

In another critical departure from archaeological knowledge, Funmaker is assertive about her tribe's connection to the effigy and conical mounds found in the region, whether they are called Hopewell or Late Woodland. She maintains that they were made by her people: "We were here first," she said. "These are the things left behind. Maybe these were generations before us. They left them [the archaeological artifacts] here. I have to assume they're mine." It's not clear if Funmaker is identifying with Ho-Chunks here or with native people more generally. Although the claim that the Ho-Chunk are connected to all these mounds would put her at odds with many contemporary archaeologists, it nonetheless echoes and perhaps even depends on the views of scholars in the early twentieth century, including George Hull Squier. In Radin's 1923 book, *The Winnebago Tribe,* the anthropologist writes: "One of the most interesting and important features of the area occupied by the Winnebago is the large number of earth mounds found. That these mounds were made by the Winnebago or the Sioux there seems to be little doubt. The participation of the Sioux in the construction of these mounds seems, however, to have been confined entirely to the so-called linear and conical types. The effigy mounds seem to have been the work of the Winnebago exclusively."[100] In this way, what Funmaker presents as memory may well be part of quite recent knowledge, even a product of colonizing culture itself. W. C. McKern suspected Radin's influence on Winnebago self-perception, noting that the Winnebago did not claim effigy mound authorship until 1910 or 1911, after Radin had spent two years working among them.[101] The likelihood of such influence does not preclude the possibility that the Ho-Chunk were indeed effigy mound builders, however. Given the devastation that the Ho-Chunk Nation has experienced over the past centuries, a great deal of traditional knowledge has been lost; indeed, Rodell pointed out to me in conversation that by the nineteenth century the Ho-Chunk had lost all memory of being toolmakers, though that would have necessarily been part of their heritage.

Funmaker is well aware of the possibility that aspects of Ho-Chunk tradition have been reinvented; she acknowledges the ways in which the colonizer and colonized had, in effect, created shared cultures. Concomitant with her criticisms of archaeology and anthropology, then, Funmaker recognizes that Ho-Chunk culture is already entwined with, and in some ways has depended on, the knowledge produced in those fields. She laughingly recalled a conversation with her ninety-seven-year-old father in which the elder held off a question of hers by saying, "I can't give it up," intimating that what she wanted to know was in the realm of secret tribal knowledge. "But Dad, it's in the book already!" she replied; the "secrets" had been published in 1923 in Radin's book. At times, then, Radin's book is not just a representation of tribal knowledge—it's a source of it.

While archaeologists are becoming increasingly sensitive to the importance of involving local informants,[102] considering oral evidence, and exploring the possibilities of collaborative work, Funmaker suggests that there is still a long way to go—largely around the issue of human remains. As David Hurst Thomas notes, the 1906 Antiquities Act, by permitting only "professionally sanctioned archaeologists to remove antiquities from federal lands," shut out Indians, who, in effect, were designated as amateurs. The professionalization of archaeology, Thomas argues, "encouraged generations of professional archaeologists to view the archeological record of America as their exclusive intellectual property because, by law, it essentially was."[103] Cognizant of this heritage, both Vogel and Funmaker say that, in their view, archaeologists and Native Americans split over this fundamental difference: some of what archaeologists see as data, many Native Americans see as the remains of their ancestors. From this perspective, when scientists disturb these remains in the pursuit of academic knowledge—even if they believe they do so respectfully—they are inherently disrespectful to native culture. For this reason the Ho-Chunk policy across the board is "Don't dig." If the nation wants to know more about the graves and remains of its ancestors, it makes use of a high-tech ground-penetrating radar (GPR), a costly bit of equipment that works like an x-ray to detect artifacts and bones under the earth's surface—without disturbing them. Funmaker attested that someone in the nation uses it every day.

In my interview with her it became evident that Funmaker's critiques of archaeology spring in part from the field's own debates and shibboleths. Nonetheless, she also expressed a view of the past that was very different from archaeologists' and in which she was completely integrated. Rather than imagining history as something distant and disconnected from her, she posits an almost organic connection to her ancestors. In discussing the history of the Ho-Chunk tribe, she tends to speak as if she was there—at all times and places. Of the Ho-Chunk removal to South Dakota in 1863, she said: "That was a bad one. That's *plains*. We like the woods." Similarly, in her critique of archaeological cultural categories such as Woodland and Oneota, she expressed a sense of connection to the mounds and the long native presence that they represent. She spoke of white residents who were proud to trace their heritage back 150 years. "They don't know their background. They don't know where they came from," she said. By contrast, as Vogel and Funmaker both suggested, they need only to consider the ground around Trempealeau to know where they came from. As Vogel believes, there are Indian burials all over the place, and the GPR can help find them. Some burials were in the mounds, of course, but some are more recent and tell different kinds of stories When, for example, smallpox hit the tribe in the eighteenth and nineteenth centuries, "people died, and they'd bury them, and then move on," Gus said. "The elders remember these things." Furthermore, despite most residents' ignorance and, at times, active denial of this presence, Vogel maintains that there are native burials in valleys, on hills, on Trempealeau Mountain, in parks, on farms, under parking lots, and below manicured lawns. Indeed, as Funmaker expressed it, "I have a theory about the state of Wisconsin: it's a huge burial grounds."

21. View

When in the mid-1990s there was hope that the platform mounds might become part of an educational center, a local troop of Boy Scouts cleared all the brush from the surface of the mounds. Seeing the site back then, I could easily make out three distinct platforms and the nearby borrow pits from which dirt had been shifted, basketload by basketload. That was some years ago now. That was why, on that Friday afternoon in July 2001, John, T.S., and I decided to visit the mounds again. We'd already been to Trempealeau Mountain and Nicholls Mound that day; just after John parked his truck below the mounds, a black-and-white cop car cruised past us, and I saw my brother, Bob, in the driver's seat. I wished he could go with us, but he was on duty, serving papers. Although the mounds were right there, he'd never been up on the bluff and tended to doubt their existence.

We scrambled up the bank, grabbing on to the thin trunks of bushes that struggle for a perch on the hillside. At the top John was appalled at how overgrown the site had become; it was hard to see anything unless you already had the image in your head. The mounds seemed such unobtrusive things, really, given all the fuss about them. And it seemed weird—improper—to be walking right on top of the 950-year-old structures. But village workers had already driven trucks up there and busted up the largest mound with the water tower; you could see the holes they'd made. John, who works for the village plowing snow, moving garbage, and maintaining public spaces, said he used to drive a truck up there to check on the air raid siren that had been posted on the edge of the bluff. T.S. had not seen the old maps and photos of the mounds, so he had a harder time imagining them. But soon enough he could put together the picture from our descriptions, the terraces at three levels leading out to the bluff's edge with their borrow pits gouged out behind them. From the lowest platform we could look out over the village of Trempealeau, the river, the railroad line, the lock and dam. "No wonder they picked this place," we said of the mound builders. "You can see the village hall perfectly from here."

That same summer, while staying in Trempealeau, I stopped at the gas station to fill up the car and ran into my uncle Kenny. Kenny is my dad's younger brother and has grown into the same big belly my dad had. This Hovell tendency to put on weight suggests a settling-in that is both physical and psychic; Hovells can have a tendency to dig in, to not want to move. This propensity is often tempered by a wicked sense of humor, a willingness to joke; but at other times it turns on itself and becomes self-pity. As much as I can, I try to exorcise this self-pity and recalcitrance from my own life, but it's a hard thing to do when you're in the middle of believing the whole world has wronged you. If the settling in has less-than-savory aspects, its positive force involves an abiding attachment to people and situations. In my father this sometimes involved a desire to see things never change and, by the time I went to college, had manifested as an outpouring of tears every time I left home; in my sister Pam it has meant her unflagging willingness to put herself out for her family and friends. Running into Uncle Kenny at the gas station, then, was more than just a chance encounter to me; it was, in a sense, a meeting up with family history. But this time when I met Kenny, he was jovial, and I had put my own baggage aside. We met in the present, in a sense. As we pumped our gas together, I felt like a native, felt like I lived there, could imagine that I had never left. He asked me if I had been to see the "tree walk" over by his house. "They planted a tree for your dad," he said. I promised I would visit.

The tree walk stands on land where we used to ice-skate as kids, but my dad's and uncles' memories go further back: this was pasture when they were young; this was a plot of land right next to their old barn, right between the house occupied by my dad's parents and his Beardsley grandparents. The barn and the houses are still standing. I looked across the street to where Kenny Drugan used to live, where my cousin Tammi and I used to stay over sometimes, talking late into the night about boys and friends and what we'd be; she died of cancer when she was twenty-five. Next to the Drugan house was the ball field where I remember seeing John run hurdles, where they held the centennial celebration. Not far away was the house my uncle Kenny Hovell still lived in, a place that used to be the home of my great grandparents on the Hovell side. The place was thick with memory. Then I went on my tree walk.

The tree walk followed a path past trees that couldn't be more than a couple years old. Each tree had been planted in memory of someone, and next to each one stood a small post with a sign stating in whose memory it had been planted. A birch for a boy who died suddenly in the middle of a high school basketball game. A pine for Kenny and Elvira Drugan. A silver maple for my dad. And I am moved again by these young trees, these recent memorials, these names and faces that place demands on me: don't forget, for you are tangled up with us.

Part III

What's at the Bottom

1. Scientific Method

My brother, Bob, is eleven years my senior. He has long been known for his encyclopedic knowledge. When I was growing up, any time anyone had a history or science question, the answer was simply, "Ask Bobby." (To be sure, I frequently sought his help with details for this book.) As a child I looked up to him, and although his greatest act of teenage rebellion involved sleeping on the floor surrounded by candles, I identified him with the defiant aspect of the 1960s in which he came of age. (It helped that in 1972 he made a solo trip to Montana on a Honda 160 that he'd refurbished.) In some ways my romanticization of Native Americans, my attraction to India, even my early experiments with drugs stem from my idolization of him and his era. These days he works in law enforcement for the county and has 190 acres of hilly land that he tramps and hunts. Deer come down from the hills and raid his blueberry trees; he goes up the bluffs to pick apples, gather hickory nuts, and collect sap from box elder trees.

In the summer of 2001 T.S., the kids, and I rented a small house in Trempealeau near the Mississippi for two weeks so I could study the mound controversy, and Bob, his wife, Ellie, and daughter, Amanda, came over for dinner. It was hot—one of those humid July nights when the air conditioner cannot cut the heat, and the conversation was going poorly, interrupted by the needs of small kids, left to languish by an overworked brother, upended by my overenthusiasm, and cut short by the recognition that we see things very differently from each other. I was telling Bob about what some local people had said about the platform mounds, how they fought against preserving them, how they resisted caring about them. When I asked our uncle Kenny, for example, what he knew about the mounds, he had said, "Oh, yeah, I remember them. Some archaeologists wanted to put an escalator up Little Bluff." I guffawed when I repeated the story for Bob, laughing at our uncle's muddling of things. And I told Bob about the great efforts to which people went to discredit the archaeologists and their project, saying that the mounds were built by horse and wagon, with another uncle asserting that someone had built them with a Cat bulldozer, insisting that there was nothing up there. Bob didn't say much.

As he was heading toward his car, though, and as we were saying good-bye, Bob said, "What about the scientific method?"

"What do you mean?"

"It sounds like you have your mind made up. Aren't you supposed to remain objective?"

I tried to explain to him that, although I have some problems with the field of archaeology, from what I could tell, the archaeological evidence for the mounds was good and that, yes, when I spoke to people, I tried to listen carefully to what they said to me. But I still had a point of view. And, anyway, I thought that with my brother I could be open about what I really thought. I said that in this project I was trying to seek out a diversity of opinions—that I wanted to write a book that presented a complex view of peoples' attitudes toward Native American history and artifacts—that I thought that would be much more interesting than writing a book that simply said these folks are all jerks. Besides, I said, I don't even see it that way; when I write, I try to understand how people come to hold the views they have. But even as Bob and Ellie got in their car and backed down the driveway, I knew he wasn't satisfied. As the air conditioner whirred away that night in the bedroom of the tiny rental house and trains rushed past on the tracks below the house, I dreamed and woke repeatedly, all the time stewing about what he had said to me, convincing myself that he understood little about the interpretive nature of what I was doing, and planning what I'd say to him when I saw him again. Scientific method! There is no way to *truth,* brother, I imagined saying. There are only educated guesses, categories and habits of thinking that pass for knowledge. I saw myself spouting defiantly that even the knowledge produced by archaeologists does not represent the ultimate truth about anything—theirs are only interpretations based on the data at hand, interpretations made in a particular time and place and thus subject to change, interpretations that in turn bear weight on what subsequent interpreters are able to think and imagine. It seemed to me that Bob was asking for an objectivity that didn't exist, while I held fast to the belief in a multiplicity of views, a multiplicity I hoped to represent but that would inevitably be filtered through my own partial view. I took Bob's resistance to my approach personally, of course, and developed arguments against what I imagined to be his view. To me, "scientific method" suggests a presumption of objective truth that is part of the problem, helping to create people who impose their view of the world onto the world in the name of truth—people who believe they somehow stand apart from land, from things, from history; this kind of universalizing objectivity presumes to take people out of particular places and times and—despite claims to the reverse—allows people *not* to see where they are, encourages them not to recognize the complex and vexed forces that work on us all and keep us from finally knowing anything for sure. It seemed to me then that Bob wanted me to be able to stand apart from my own consciousness; in a way, he seemed to want some cold hard facts with which to prove the case: a smoking gun, some fingerprints, a tell-tale scrap of writing. In this respect he had much in common with the archaeologists themselves, who considered their work science. In this he seemed to me to be like many other townspeople who asked for proof even after the archaeologists offered it—those who persisted in believing, in some sense, that the platform mounds should produce a body.

2. Gale and Squier

Mounds were in George Squier's consciousness. He studied mounds in farmers' fields, mounds on Little Bluff, mounds at the park, and his work tried to make sense of those mounds, at least in archaeological terms. But even before Squier another (neo-)local man considered mounds a worthy topic and pondered a population that left behind "the graves of their fathers and the temples of their god."[1] George Gale was the founder of the nearby town of Galesville and a leader in the incorporation of Trempealeau County in 1854. Born in Vermont in 1816 and largely self-educated, Gale came to western Wisconsin in 1851; as Merle Curti notes, "It is likely that the assurance that he could be county judge of the new La Crosse County was an important factor in Gale's decision to move to the Mississippi River country in 1851."[2] There Gale bought and sold land and became, as Curti notes, a "one-man mortgage company."[3] In the 1860s Gale founded a town, established Gale College, and became "the father of Trempealeau County."

Gale was also something of a scholar. In his 1867 book, *Upper Mississippi,* this town and county father offers a history of the region that ranged from the era of the mound builders to his day. As denoted by the subtitle of his book—*Historical Sketches of the Mound-Builders, the Indian Tribes, and the Progress of Civilization in the North-West; from A. D. 1600 to the Present Time*—Gale sees European and white American settlement of the region as advancing civilization. At the same time Gale posits the decline of the first inhabitants of the area; although he recognizes some affinities between contemporary Indians and the mound builders, Gale tends to differentiate the groups, seeing the latter as superior to "the dusky savage [who] pursues the chase and the war-path, heedless of the sanctity of the ground on which he treads."[4]

In the late eighteenth and nineteenth centuries a number of educated Euro-Americans were fascinated by the many mounds that marked the American landscape, which in Wisconsin alone numbered fifteen to twenty thousand. As to who built the mounds, Alan S. Downer notes that "two competing explanations of [the mounds'] origins were offered. One explanation held that the mounds had been built by the ancestors of contemporary Indians. . . . The other explanation attributed the mounds to 'the Moundbuilders.' In one version or another of this view, the mound complexes were attributed to almost any ethnic group other than Native North Americans: for example, the Lost Tribes, Danes, Tartars, Romans, Aztecs, and even Hindoos."[5] Like others of his era, Gale is impressed by the knowledge of geometry and the enterprise evidenced by those who built the mounds in the region, and he works to distinguish them from "modern Indians" at every turn. Referring to the work of Albert Gallatin, one of the preeminent scholars of Indian culture in the new republic, Gale asserts that "there is not, and there was not in the sixteenth century, a single tribe of Indians (north of the semi-civilized nations) between the Atlantic and the Pacific, which had means of subsistence sufficient to enable them to apply, for such purposes, the unproductive labor necessary for the work; nor was there any in such a social state as to compel the labor of the people to be thus applied."[6] Gale uses Gallatin to dismiss the possibility that native peoples could organize and work hard enough to build mounds; then he turns to another expert, Samuel George Morton, whose science of "craniometry" seemed to give concrete support to the notion of race at the same time that it correlated race and intelligence. Morton believed that the cranial capacity of the human skull accurately measures brain size and thus intellectual powers. Filling skulls with lead shot, Morton tabulated the brain power of different "racial" groups by the volume displaced. (Given the racial prejudices of his day, it is not surprising that Morton determined that Caucasians had the largest brain capacity—87 cubic inches—and thus the greatest intelligence.)[7] Gale is interested in other of Morton's findings as well; as Gale writes, Morton came to "the conclusion that there is a great similarity in the *cranial* development of the Mound-Builders, the Mexicans, Peruvians, and all the modern tribes of Indians." But for Gale the difference in the cranial capacities of "Mound-Builders" (85 cubic inches) and "American Indians" (82 cubic inches) marks an important distinction.[8] And while Gale cites similarities between the mound builders and modern Indians—evidenced in their use of tobacco, corn, tools, and their common lack of a written language—and while he notes that they share a "uniformity in . . . physical appearance," for Gale the hypothesis that these peoples are related "is nearly destroyed by the radical difference in many of the tribal tongues and the total absence of the custom of building mounds" among contemporary Indians.[9] Altogether, then, Gale finds modern Indians "less civilized than the Mound-Builders."[10] For him, the reasons for the existence of the latter remain a mystery that, nonetheless, is part of a larger, orderly Deist plan: "We can only conclude that Deity filled, with that populous nation, some important *niche* in the great temple of humanity."[11] Gale's insistence that modern native peoples had no connection to the mounds in the region serves to clear the space for white settlers like himself to claim them.

Squier (who was thirty-three years Gale's junior) accepted the idea that the mounds had been built by the ancestors of contemporary native peoples, a position that had been decisively argued by Cyrus Thomas and Squier's own mentor, Frederick Ward Putnam, in 1894. Writing on the mound-builder question forty years after Gale, Squier argues that "the studies of the past thirty or forty years have . . . wrought a pretty thorough revolution in our knowledge of the subject. It is now definitely established, though once the contrary was held, that many of our Indian tribes were in the habit of building mounds."[12] Not only does he maintain that these mounds were the work of Native Americans, Squier connects them to local native groups. While many archaeologists are hard pressed to make a direct connection between the modern Ho-Chunk and the builders of various mounds, Squier accepts the working assumption of the time and—like many Ho-Chunks today—credits the construction of effigy mounds to the Winnebago.[13] Squier writes: "When the whites first entered the region the area was claimed by, and in part occupied by, the Winnebago tribes, the members of which appear to understand the significance of the effigies. They are simply visible representations of the clan or gens totem."[14] Observing that there are several types of mounds in the region—in one article he uses the categories of conical, elongate, true linear, taper linear, and platform to identify them[15]—Squier takes an interest in all of them for what they reveal about the people who inhabited the land before him.

Unlike those of Gale's day, the parameters of archaeological knowledge of Squier's time allow him to connect human remains and artifacts with living native peoples. Nonetheless, like Gale, Squier is more interested in the distant past—represented by artifacts—than in the contemporary cultures represented by living peoples. This was not unusual for an archaeologist, of course; in the early twentieth century even the branch of anthropology that concerned living native peoples was, in a sense, focused on the past; living informants were considered valuable insofar as they could help anthropologists reconstruct and "salvage" the cultures that had once existed. Anthropologists tended to discredit the customs and ideas that sustained the current culture (which was often imagined as decrepit and disappearing). More specifically, the field of archaeology was a science of the material past. (Only recently have archaeologists begun to acknowledge the value of consulting native peoples about archaeological remains—but even now they debate the value of using native informants more broadly.) As amateur archaeologists during the field's infancy, Gale and Squier largely overlook contemporary Indians, focusing instead on the material past of ancient peoples and cultures, represented by mounds, artifacts, and bones.

In standard archaeological fashion Gale suggests that history can be read in the very earth one lives upon, if only one knows how to discover it; as Gale sees it, the unknown people who built the mounds "have left the graves of their fathers and the temples of their gods so unceremoniously, that their very name has disappeared with them; and we only know of their existence by their decayed walls and tumuli, and by their bones, exhibiting human form, although in a far-gone state of decay."[16] The archaeological and anthropological models of his day allow Gale to imagine a gap between his superior civilization and that of the mound builders; thus Gale has no ethical problem in digging up graves or excavating mounds. He describes the remains discovered in one man-shaped mound near Galesville in which he found "pieces of the crushed skull, upper jaw and teeth, the left side of the lower jaw and teeth, both thigh bones entire, one shin bone, and many others of less importance. . . . His skull varied from three-sixteenths to one-fourth inch in thickness; his jaws were round and full, but not distorted; and his teeth were of the usual

number and variety of the white race. These bones are now preserved in the 'Upper Mississippi Historical Society' at Galesville."[17]
Gale's distance in time from the mound builders seems an important
component of his archaeological method; without it he may not
have assumed the privilege to disinter these remains.

For Squier too, digging up native graves does not seem to have
presented any ethical problems. It was only a few years after the last
Ho-Chunk removal when Squier returned from Cambridge and
began his research; archaeological theory and method gave him the
rationale and the means to analyze and survey the platform mounds.
Squier also dug into one mound on what is now Perrot State Park
land; in a published article he describes what he found there. A foot
below the surface he uncovered a thick layer of ash and charcoal;
within this were three extended, charred skeletons laid side by side
with their heads toward the east. No artifacts accompanied them.
Three feet lower he found a single skeleton in a seated position.
Excavating further Squier reports finding a basin-shaped subfloor
burial pit that extended four feet into the rocky substrate and eight
feet below the top of the mound. In this pit he uncovered seven or
eight disarticulated skeletons within a small space. These skulls were
arranged together with some pottery on top of them; the leg and
arm bones radiated outward from the skulls. After excavating conical mounds in Perrot Park, Squier sent his findings along to Putnam
and the Peabody Museum.[18]

Such excavations are, of course, the stuff that archaeological
knowledge is built on. But they also suggest the proprietary role that
archaeologists have often taken toward such burials and artifacts.
Graves are disturbed in the name of science; skulls and bones become not the remains of somebody's ancestors that should not be
disturbed but data. Because native tribes had been largely removed
from the land by 1873 and placed on reservations by the turn of the
century, the land—and the graves and artifacts buried in it—became
sufficiently "clear" for Squier, in a sense, to claim it for himself. Removal makes the earth a suitable site of investigation; few Indians
are around to question such actions.

Although Squier probably would not have approved of the looters of the time who dug into mounds, he accepted that educated

men had a right to the artifacts, that the artifacts—these old bones—needed men like himself to tell their stories. Thomas Biolsi and Larry Zimmerman, archaeologists themselves, describe an attitude that, until quite recently, shaped how most archaeologists conceived their work; Biolsi and Zimmerman maintain that a discourse of the vanished and vanishing race of Indians "made it easy for archeologists to believe that they—and not contemporary Indian peoples—are the inheritors, and the appropriate protectors and interpreters, of the Indian past."[19] Or as Vine Deloria Jr. notes in another context, "Most whites . . . did not know how to relate to living Indians. Their education had taught them that almost all the Indians were dead [or, in the nineteenth century, dying], so they promptly began to search for dead Indians."[20]

If we think of Gale's and Squier's attitudes and work as forming layers of memory, these layers differ from each other. Although Gale admires the mound builders, he plotted them in a line of progress that was somewhere between that of the inferior "dusky savage" and that of representatives of white civilization. Squier, on the other hand, in his discussion of the settling of the Trempealeau County region, recognizes a connection between white settlers and ancient Indians in their shared attraction to the land.[21] At the same time, he argues for a connection between mound builders and contemporary Indians but notes that the latter were in decline when they came into contact with whites.[22] Different as they are, both men assume a prominent place for themselves as archaeologists—mound diggers—to investigate and speak for the region's earlier inhabitants. This layer of memory still informs how people in the town think about and imagine the past, giving them a sense of ownership of the land, encouraging a sense of superiority to native cultures. It takes a lot of effort to think differently; a lot has to be moved around.

The attitudes and beliefs that Gale and Squier held toward native people surface in complex ways in contemporary understandings of mounds and archaeology, yet the specific ways in which these scholars themselves are remembered vary greatly. Despite Squier's contributions to knowledge about local archaeology and his own scholarly productions, he is seldom memorialized in the village, though, of course, his name was often repeated in the debate about the platform mound project. When I asked people about Squier, the answers tended to peg him as a college boy, not really from around here, an academic type. Squier moved to Missouri in the 1920s with his son. When he died, his body was brought back to Trempealeau. He was buried next to his wife in a large plot.[23] For years Squier lay in an unmarked tomb, near the pauper's section of the public cemetery and near the Indian graves. In 2001 William Green, some of his colleagues, and Squier's descendants—who now live elsewhere—had a simple stone memorial erected for Squier and his wife, May Button. George Hull Squier, it reads, and in smaller letters: Scholar.[24]

George Gale, on the other hand, is well remembered, at least in name. There is the eponymous town of Galesville, and the old Gale College (whose Old Main Hall was recently renovated by the Garden of Eden Preservation Society) up by the kindergarten. Gale's given name was passed on first to his son and then to his grandson. (The local phone book today lists no Gales.) And the first George Gale—along with his namesakes—was given a memorial worthy of a town father. After his death in Galesville in 1868, Gale was buried under a stone pillar on a fenced-off site near Gale College, near the place where, as Squier noted, a bear effigy mound used to stand. Even by Squier's day the effigy had been plowed under.[25]

When I was a senior in high school, I gave the Founder's Day speech in honor of Gale one summer morning; I was evidently the highest-ranking senior with a Galesville zip code. I didn't even have to research Gale's life myself; instead, I was simply given the information I needed to work into my text. I knew nothing about Gale and cared even less. (Nor had I ever heard of Squier or the platform mounds, for which I might have had more sympathy.) My head was full of plans to go to college, where I planned to study anthropology, archaeology, "Eastern religions," and go to India as soon as possible. I stood next to Gale's monument and repeated the old praises.

3. Platform Controversy Again

With my brother's doubts about my methods still nagging at me, I continued to try to learn what I could about the platform mound project from the early 1990s. The trail was pretty cold by 2001, but most players were still in the area, and the minutes from village meetings and newspaper reports could help fill in the gaps.

Harold Wilber, a distant relative of mine and, as I mentioned earlier, the owner of a lucrative quarry business, initially supported the platform mound project. But as one informant recalled, Wilber made an abrupt turnaround by the second meeting and took up the question of authenticity as his cause. The minutes from an October 1993 meeting suggest that Wilber was ready to conduct his own archaeological investigations on the site. The minutes state that Wilber "requested being allowed to do borings at the Platform Mound site. He would hire Twin City Testing[26] and have 20 core samples taken. He would not object to having the archeologists present or sending samples to them for their review. Mary [Kopp, village president] did not feel comfortable giving permission to tamper with something that has been put on the Historical Registry.[27] Norma [Van Vleet, village clerk] should find out the reason why the archaeologists are saying 'don't bore.'"[28] Wilber's offer was an attempt to determine for doubting residents once and for all whether the mounds were real or not—an attempt to take the verifying of authenticity out of the archaeologists' hands. Professional archaeologists, however, held that twenty borings would only further destroy the already compromised mounds. And as far as the archaeologists were concerned, they had done their homework. In 1991, as part of the investigation into the platform mounds by the Mississippi Valley Archaeology Center (MVAC), the geomorphologist Michael Kolb made a single auger coring in the north platform. As Green and Rodell note: "At 1.82 m small fragments of mussel shell were encountered, and associated with the shell or immediately beneath it was a silt layer that exhibited blocky structure. Both appeared out of place in relation to the deposits immediately above and below them. The shell could only have been introduced during construction of the platform. The level may represent a prepared surface in the construction sequence of the mound."[29] For the archaeologists, this single auger sample was sufficient to confirm the historical and material evidence they already had collected; these included Lewis's 1884 survey; Squier's maps, photos, and descriptions of the mounds, as well as his descriptions of pottery finds; and pottery shards collected from Squier's garden in 1991. Of this evidence, as Jim Gallagher told me in 2001, the strongest pieces are Squier's and Lewis's historical documents; the material evidence is circumstantial, he said—it wouldn't stand up without the historical evidence. But in terms of archaeological knowledge the material evidence confirms and corroborates the historical evidence.[30] Given archaeology's methods and interpretive structures, and given the current state of knowledge about Middle Mississippian earthworks elsewhere, the archaeologists felt they had enough evidence to affirm the authenticity of the mounds.

But archaeological method and its forms of interpretation seemed too imprecise, too small and tentative to Wilber. Wilber and others tried to discredit Squier as an outsider, a weirdo, someone who sought fame; while Squier's work was key to the archaeologists' arguments, it counted for nothing to the Wilber faction. And the coincidence of Squier's finding the mounds on his father's land was too much for some people. As Jim Stull told me in 2001, "Squiers [*sic*] made [the platforms] himself. The dirt he would have brought up himself."[31] When I asked Stull about Lewis's corroborating survey, he claimed to know nothing about it: "Never heard of it." Wilber, on the other hand, had heard of Lewis but argued that Lewis's own papers cast doubt on the authenticity of the mounds. Academic knowledge in general was suspect, and Wilber discredited the work of both Squier and Lewis specifically; slivers of pottery and tiny bits of mussel shell revealed by a single auger hole were not enough. The only evidence that was going to convince him was something more tangible—something big and real. That the mounds were those very things—big and real earthworks—Wilber seemed unwilling or unable to recognize.

The fear of the fake is underlined by Wilber's persistent effort to take matters into his own hands in authenticating the site. By June 1994 he had decreased the number of auger holes desired but persisted in his wish to find material proof of the mounds' authenticity. Minutes from a meeting that both Gallagher and Rodell attended give this account: "Harold Wilber [wanted to] hire an independent firm to bore half a dozen samples from the sight [*sic*] (after first obtaining permission from the State of WI). Both Mary & Bill expressed an unwillingness to grant permission to drill on Village property without complete State approval, because of the potential liability to the Village."[32] In his 2001 recollections of events Wilber told me that the archaeologists were opposed to pursuing ways to prove the authenticity of the mounds; from the minutes of the village's Platform Mound Committee, however, it appears that the resistance comes from within the village government itself, as board members were concerned that such augerings would violate state laws about historic sites. The likelihood that this intrusion would further damage the mounds, of course, was also very real.

As is suggested by Wilber's repeated offers to auger the mounds, he seemed to focus on digging the mounds, on doing something *to* them. The archaeologists were done with their digging and had proposed to begin reconstructing the mounds. As Wilber recollected the controversy in 2001, however, he emphasized the notion that the archaeologists wanted to *dig*.[33] Perhaps this preoccupation came out of Wilber's own work as a large-scale earth mover; perhaps it came out of the common image of archaeologists as excavators with shovels and toothbrushes. Wilber spoke bitterly of the delays caused when his work in the limestone business unearthed objects of potential archaeological or paleontological value: flakes, tools, bones. Scientists had to be called in—work had to stop—while the archaeologists went about their painstaking project of digging, digging very slowly, usually never to turn up much of value. He could not seem to accept that that is how archaeological excavation works: you dig not because you *know* you will find something but because there is the chance—the educated guess—that you might.

And Wilber was not interested in interpretations. He wanted the truth and found other ways to challenge the mounds' authenticity. At one public meeting, as Wilber attested to me in 2001, he offered the archaeologists $5,000 of his own money if they could come up with decisive proof of the mounds' authenticity—one way or the other. Because the archaeologists did not follow up on this, Wilber maintained that they didn't think that they could prove it.[34] But several factors were at work. As far as the archaeologists were concerned, they had already made their case; there was proof enough for them. Furthermore, if an archaeologist accepted money from a private citizen in this manner, it would seem to bias the proceedings. More practically, Rodell noted that he didn't really have a problem with such a monetary arrangement, but from his point of view Wilber's offer was not genuine; it was made only once and in the context of a public meeting. The offer seemed more a chance for Wilber to display his wealth—and thus his power—than an expression of a sincere proposal. Furthermore, Wilber did not formalize the offer, and Rodell told me that he was not about to pursue Wilber and give him the pleasure of seeing the archaeologists beg him for his money.[35] In his conversations with me Wilber spoke of his $5,000 offer as a major event in the controversy, but when I asked Jim Gallagher about it, he didn't even remember it.

Wilber had other tactics as well. As he told me in July 2001, he made contact with the prominent Ho-Chunk leader Anna Funmaker to see what she thought of the project. As he presented it, her response helped to finish off the project.

I interviewed Funmaker in September 2001. At that time she remembered getting a phone call in 1993 from an anonymous man, telling her about a meeting in Trempealeau scheduled for the same night, and suggesting that it might be of interest to her. Funmaker made the trip down to Trempealeau, but she said that at that point she didn't know anything about the platform mounds. The Ho-Chunk assert their relationship to the effigy and conical mound builders of Wisconsin. But as Funmaker told me in 2001, "Someone else must have made the platform mounds." She also told me, "I haven't heard a story [about the platform mounds]. I wouldn't say." I understood Funmaker to mean that without a story she couldn't connect the Ho-Chunk specifically to these mounds. I also sensed that her reticence was political; in some sense this knowledge was none of my business.

What is perhaps more important, Funmaker described archaeology as something that frequently desecrates Native American sites.

Like the American Indian Movement (AIM) activists who "did not believe their ancestors had buried their dead for the express purpose of providing summer adventures" for whites, as Vine Deloria Jr. said, Funmaker maintained that archaeological sites are not simply grounds for scientific exploration. They might be the tombs of ancestors; they are sacred sites. Because of this, she said, "Ho-Chunks don't dig."

At the meeting in Trempealeau, as she described it, Funmaker iterated these things: We don't know if they are ours. Don't dig.

Taken separately, these two statements do not deny the authenticity of the mounds. The first reflects the uncertainty about who made the mounds; the second takes a political and ethical stance on the issue of archaeological excavation. But as Wilber remembered events, Funmaker's presence worked to deny the authenticity of the mounds.[36]

The meeting in question was actually a talk given by Rollie Rodell to a library club on regional prehistory. Rodell recalls that when he asked for questions, Funmaker stood up and said, "We're opposed to what you are doing." He also recalls that she said something to the effect that the archaeologists secretly planned to excavate the mounds.[37]

In any case, because Funmaker is a Native American and a Ho-Chunk leader, her opposition added credibility to Wilber's efforts. In this way, Funmaker's insistence on the sanctity of the native past became allied with Wilber's efforts to block it from his consciousness; together these two views were used to oppose those who wished to remember and imagine the native past through archaeology, as well as some people who wanted to be able to remember more than the white past. When the village held a referendum on the issue, 65 percent of voting residents weighed in against the project. It was dead in the water.

4. Opening Day

It was Opening Day in Cleveland, 2001. Thousands of Cleveland Indians baseball fans sailed past us while we stood in a line with our handmade signs. Our signs said things like "People Not Mascots," "This is not a chief; you are not a Tribe: Stop the Racism," "What if they called them the Cleveland Kikes, the Cleveland Wops or Niggers?" We were a ragtag bunch: white folks, a Legal Aid lawyer, college students with pierced lips, a half-Ojibwa Catholic brother, urban Indians connected with the American Indian Education Center. We were clearly outnumbered and stayed close together as the fans passed by us. Some slowed to read the signs. Mine said: "Cleveland Baseball Fans: You are Better than This"; since I am also a baseball fan, I wore a blue baseball cap with a red "C" on it, a reproduction of a Wahoo-less "Indians" cap from the 1940s.

It was a sunny April day, and Wahoo regalia were out in full force, shiny and bright. Large Wahoos on the back of jackets; collectors' versions of the 1948 caricature (the last time we won the World Series); little Wahoos on caps, on children, Wahoos on butt rests, Wahoos on signs, on T-shirts, sweatshirts, Wahoos stitched over fans' hearts. New Wahoos emerged from the team shop; several fans stopped in front of us and slowly and theatrically placed their new Wahoo caps on their heads. Many fans waved a forearm at us as if to push us away. An older woman shook her head at us, as if we were the ones who should be ashamed. Two middle-aged women passed by and tsk-tsked. A lone man passed and shouted indignantly: "You wanna call it the Cleveland Kikes?!" He was angry; we'd hit a nerve. Two men, on separate occasions, said they'd love to see the team called the Cleveland Wops.

Several people shouted out at us: "Get a job!" It was 12:30 on a Monday afternoon and they were going to a baseball game. They called us losers. Someone said: "None of you guys look Indian." A man passed by in a felt costume that was supposed to look like buckskin and a dime store feather headdress. The fans are the Indians on Opening Day, and they don't want anyone to tell them otherwise. "This is honoring Indians!" one guy yelled. "You just don't get it.

Honoring!" A number of men, apparently drunk, passed by and did the "Woo-woo-woo" thing we learned to do as kids, like the Hollywood Indians. A young woman made the sound too, laughing as she passed by. Sometimes the eyes of a passerby met mine; sometimes I smiled. Though the stereotype of a drunk Indian is common, the protesters were the sober ones. As Robert Roche, head of the American Indian Education Center, said laughingly about one fan who took objection to our presence: "That guy was so drunk I could hear him slosh."

I was on the end of the gauntlet of protesters for a while and felt exposed, protected only by my flimsy sign. I tried to think about the Dalai Lama and to pour out compassion on everyone to keep from feeling scared, to keep from hating them. Two women, on their lunch break from an office downtown, approached with little photocopied signs and asked to join us. Most people, however, tended to keep a distance between us and them and even at times seemed to try to push us away with their arms and gestures.

The fans wear Wahoo on their body; he is next to their skin. It's as if their gestures say, don't make me think about this. Don't get close to this. A young protester of Umatilla descent remarked, "It feels like we're in the middle of a strange cult," a cult that rests on the wearing of a red-faced, buck-toothed decapitated head with a red feather, a cult that lets people say, "I belong to something. Today I am an Indian." While we stood there, outside Gate C, the ceremonial first pitch went out. A cry rose up from the crowd in the stadium, lifted toward the sky, and fell out to us there with our paper signs and protests. The Indians had taken the field.

5. Mascots Again

In the 1970s the use of Indian mascots for sports teams became a hot topic around the country. Stanford University, the University of Oklahoma, and Dartmouth all traded in their Indians for other mascots; Syracuse University abandoned the Saltmen Warriors for the Orangemen. While debates about the use of Indian mascots raged on elsewhere, at G-E-T High School we blithely pitted our Redmen against Arcadia's savage-looking (Indian) Raiders and Holmen's Vikings.

More recently, professional sports teams such as the Cleveland Indians, the Atlanta Braves, and the Washington Redskins have been challenged both by Native Americans and non-natives on the teams' use of Indian imagery. Not far from the Trempealeau area, the issue of Indian mascots received national attention in 1992 when a large crowd came to the Metrodome in Minneapolis to protest the appearance of the Washington Redskins at Super Bowl XXVI there. Many protesters maintain that the casual use of *redskin* covers up a violent history; Suzan Shown Harjo asserts that the term "has despicable origins in the days of Indian bounty hunting in the 1600s and 1700s. Bounties under a dollar were paid for Indian children, women, and men, dead or alive. . . . It quickly became too cumbersome for bounty hunters to transport wagon loads of bodies and gunny sacks of heads, and too bothersome for bounty payers to dispose of them. Thus began the practice of paying bounties for the bloody red skins and scalps as evidence of Indian kill."[38] Reacting in part to the histories of such naming practices, since the mid-1990s both the University of Wisconsin and the University of Minnesota "have instituted policies prohibiting their athletic departments [which field teams called, respectively, the Badgers and the Gophers] from scheduling games against institutions with racist icons."[39] In part as a result of these policies and discussions, the Redmen name and Indian logo have come under discussion at my alma mater. What some see as a way to remember an aspect of our nation's and our region's past, others see as the blatantly racist use of stereotypical Indian images—an insulting way of playing Indian.

The debate about the Redmen mascot reached the G-E-T school board twice in the 1990s. In 2000, 75 percent of the district's teachers signed a petition asking the board to change the school's mascot. One high-ranking administrator is strongly opposed to the mascot—"It makes us look like hicks," he told me—and said that he is embarrassed to use school stationery with the profile of a brave in headdress stamped on every piece.[40] It's especially problematic, this administrator said, when G-E-T plays a school such as Black River Falls, whose students include a large Ho-Chunk population. Indeed, other districts in the area have already changed their mascot: the logos of neither Arcadia's Raiders nor Independence's Indies use Indian references any more. Many Trempealeau residents are indifferent to the Redmen mascot and suggest they would like to return to the old Bear mascot, which dates to when Trempealeau was an independent district. But the depth of feeling about the Redmen mascot—particularly in Galesville—has prevented the school board from making a change.

In 2000 the debate about the mascot was carried out in school board meetings as well as in a string of letters to the editor in the local paper, the *Galesville Republican.* Much of the debate centered on the nature of mascots. Those who support the use of Indian mascots often argue that they are designed to honor Indians and that they were instituted to pay homage to local tribes. This attitude is evident in Phil Lamke's letter of July 20, 2000; he asks "the hand-wringing politically correct persons of our school district to take a moment and examine the G-E-T mascot issue from a non-emotional aspect. First: what is a mascot?" Lamke goes on to argue that mascots are a way of asserting pride and support for "American Indians for their teamwork, love of sport, community support, and high moral standards with regards to respect for God, the earth, and each other."[41]

As Lamke's letter suggests, when questions are raised about such mascots, they are frequently attributed to the politically correct or to outsiders. Former Galesville resident Roy Suttie, writing from Colorado, blames "egg-head [*sic*] radicals" for trying to destroy the Redmen. He suggests that the mascot's "detractors have been taken in by what is called 'political correctness.' This movement involves more than just doing away with certain names and logos. It's also the re-writing of history, doing away with old text books, pitting various social, racial, economic, etc. groups against each other, curtailing free speech, the promotion of divisiveness instead of unity, and various other efforts to make the U.S. look bad."[42] In his own revision of history Suttie lists himself as a member of the "Redmen Class of '45." In 1945, however, while there were Indian images aplenty, the Redmen was not an official team name. Teams generally were identified by their town of origin; uniforms simply said "Galesville."

Like Suttie, Galesville native George Christiansen suggests that "a lot of objections to the logo come from those who are relatively newcomers to the school, city and area; and, therefore have no knowledge of what transpired in the days the Winnebagoes [*sic*] lived here."[43] Outsiders have a difficult time making the connection between the all-white residents and this Indian logo, but, as Christiansen suggests, to live in the area is to connect to the Indian past.

For mascot supporters like Christiansen, part of the history memorialized in the Redmen name and logo centers around the figure of Tom Thunder. Thunder lived in the area and was reputed to have fought for tribal treaty rights in Washington, D.C.; most people remember him as a poor man who farmed a bit in the Little Tamarack area. (He died in the 1950s.) Stories about Tom Thunder constitute a kind of Redmen charter myth. One writer notes: "The Redmen name is the gift that the community gave to Tom Thunder personally out of gratitude and appreciation for all that has been given to the community by him and his ancestors."[44] Such appeals to history fail to explain that when the use of Indian imagery first began, there was no mention of honoring Tom Thunder. Furthermore, the Redmen image is of a Plains Indian in full headdress, while Thunder was Ho-Chunk. Many people recall seeing Tom Thunder around town; Christiansen remembers seeing "Tom Thunder and his brother, Harry, walking in the shopping area of town to make purchases."[45] Presumably, they were not wearing feather headdresses.

Tom Thunder is only part of the complex of memories for supporters; as many see it, the mascot is part of local tradition and history—it's a way of remembering. Suzy Fonfara's letter of August 10, 2000, details what she sees as the Redmen mascot's connection to local history. She notes that Judge George Gale received help from Chief Decorah[46] and other Winnebago when he first attempted to settle the area:

> It is not written, that I could find, how long Chief Decora and his tribe had been here before Judge Gale arrived, but it was long enough for them to understand this land. Chief Decora and his tribe helped to establish trading to begin industry in this town, which was Judge Gale's main focus for settling here.
>
> Chief Decora also showed Gale how to use the waterways to get to the Mississippi River. With the help of the Winnebago's [*sic*], a town had begun to form and people wanted to live here despite the inhibition of the Winnebago Tribe.[47]

Fonfara then goes on to detail the creation of a high school in 1898, the inception of the *Arrowhead* in 1902, and, erroneously, the creation of the Redmen logo in 1926. As Fonfara sees it, the logo is a way of honoring the past. "You see, for many years the community has shown gratitude and been thankful to the Winnebago Nation for the sharing of its heritage that is still with us today." She points out the places in the area that have been given Winnebago names as other examples of honoring and goes on to list prominent Winnebago: Tom Thunder with "his huge red nose" again, as well as Chief Decorah, Chief Winneshiek, and Princess Marinuka, whom she identifies as "a teacher of the Winnebago heritage to all children no matter their race. She was loved for her gentle manner and the way she treated everyone equally. Her grave is marked with a permanent headstone on the place of burial next to the Arctic Spring, her favorite place."[48] As Fonfara sees it—and rightly so—these people are an important part of the town's history. According to her, "Thanks to these Tribal people is continually shown in the way the original names of streets, roads, peaks, flats and the school logo are used."[49]

And although she asserts that the mascot commemorates the native past, Fonfara offers a novel approach to the Redmen name, one that, in an interesting twist, claims it for white settlers: "The history proves that this community did not choose to be the Redmen because of stereotyping from the media. The word Redman actually means 'man of the earth,' which is quite appropriate for this farming community and the use of water and land for food is about as down to earth as we can get."[50] In this etymology local Indians are practically done away with—to be replaced by farmers. This is no stereotype, she suggests: The Redmen are us.

For Fonfara, the mascot connects us to history. Such a view of the mascot is also offered by John Lofgren, a leader in the campaign to change the logo and a guidance counselor in the local schools. But for him, the history that the mascot recalls is less happy. The *Galesville Republican* of August 17, 2000, summarizes Lofgren's argument before the school board. Lofgren argued that when people claim that the mascot honors Indians, they "ignore history which was not always kind to Indians." The *Republican* noted that in order to illustrate something of this forgotten history, Lofgren "read [aloud] a 1898 front page article from the *Galesville Independent* which ridiculed Native Americans who came to town to trade. He implored the board to honor local Native American heroes like Chief Decorah and Tom Thunder another way. He said that although the logo may have been adopted with the intention of honoring Native Americans, today it is viewed as a putdown."[51]

In an August 3, 2000, letter to the editor, Lofgren further develops his argument against the logo. Lofgren attributes his involvement in the logo issue to the documentary *In Whose Honor?* a film by Jay Rosenstein that details the debate about Chief Illiniwek at the University of Illinois–Urbana-Champaign and focuses largely on the activism of Charlene Teters (of the Spokane tribe).[52] According to Lofgren, the program taught him two things. First, many Native American groups have spoken out against the logos: "The leadership of the twelve federally recognized Indian tribes that make up the Great Lakes Inter-Tribal Council, Inc., are jointly concerned about how the perpetuation of Native American stereotypes can be damaging to a Native American child's sense of self and native cultures as a whole . . . because they keep the public image of 'Indian' grounded in the ancient past."[53] Second, Lofgren claims that, since viewing the documentary, he has begun to understand the unintentional forms of racism perpetuated by the use of logos. For example, while the logos may have been adopted with the intention of honoring Indians, their use in athletic competitions invites opposing teams to view their "Indian opponent" in a negative way, leading to homecoming floats like the one in La Crosse last fall depicting dead Indians with ropes tied around their necks being dragged through the streets.

It's true that the same thing could happen with a team called the Vikings [another local mascot], but what makes these images uniquely appalling is the fact that they are reminiscent of the only federally sanctioned genocide that actually took place in America.[54]

There. He has said it: genocide. And not only that: federally sanctioned genocide. (On hearing these words, many will point a finger back at him: politically correct!) As Lofgren sees it, the dominant culture's use of Indian mascots both covers up and, in effect, reenacts a specific history of genocide. In this view of events, although mascots may not be used with the intention of causing harm, they have a way of perpetuating stereotypes about Native peoples; these images have a way of putting a proud, strong face on aspects of history that many of us have learned to forget.

As these letters suggest, one subtext in the mascot debate is the very nature of racism. For many people, racism is something enacted consciously and deliberately; one's intentions matter very much. But for others, racism is something more insidious, something that is carried out on an unconscious level and is thus both affected and expressed by images, language, mascots. In her letter Suzie Fonfara represents racism as made up of intentional acts: "Changing our high school logo will not erase bigotry or racism practices toward Native Americans or anyone else for that matter. It is an individual choice to practice racism and an individual choice to be offended by it."[55] For Fonfara, racism is intentional discrimination—something one both chooses to perpetrate and chooses to perceive. For Lofgren, in contrast, racism can take other forms. As Lofgren writes: "Isn't it amazing how the pervasive use of stereotypes can lead adults, as well as kids, to be blind to the horror of these images, and the negative effect these images have on the Native American community in particular, and the larger community as a whole?"[56] In this understanding of things racism can take unconscious forms. Although it is only suggested in Lofgren's letter, racism can be constructed and perpetuated through signs and images that work on people—despite their own best intentions.

In a letter published on September 14, Bruce Lehman notes that part of what is at stake in the mascot debate is different notions of what racism is and how it works: "I think it's important here to say that no one is accusing the people who want to keep the Redmen name of intentionally being racially insensitive. But until someone has walked in the shoes of a downtrodden minority, he or she is not qualified to make the judgement [*sic*] of whether it's insensitive or not."[57] Lehman, a 1973 graduate of the then newly minted G-E-T High School, gestures toward a number of "indignities that were inflicted upon" Native Americans—indignities so numerous that "it would be pointless to list them all here. But you only have to look back a few years in time to see the racial epithets and hatred that were directed toward them for simply exercizing [*sic*] a fishing right that was guaranteed them in one of the many treaties their forefathers signed in good faith with our forefathers."[58] Lehman refers here to the Chippewa/Ojibwa battle about spearfishing rights that took place in northern Wisconsin in the 1980s.[59] At that time, for example, bumper stickers appeared on pickups declaring "Spear an Indian" and "Spear a Squaw."[60] At the same time, local police officers, such as my brother, were hired to try to keep a rein on violent encounters between the Ojibwa and the fishing rights protesters.

Lehman is an insider—Galesville born, bred, and resident—who, despite townspeople's tendency to identify "us" white folks as Redmen, points to a gap between the townspeople and the Redmen logo. Instead of seeing the Redmen as a representation of white residents, he argues that "we are not qualified to decide what is offensive and what isn't to an ethnic group that we are not a part of."[61] He calls on people to remember that "tradition goes far deeper than what a school's sports teams are named."[62] In this way, for Lehman the mascot becomes something that is expendable.

Those who support the mascot, however, tend to take a proprietary attitude toward it, seeing the mascot as a representation of themselves and their history. From this perspective only those local people who are apprised of local history and local ways of doing things are qualified to make a decision about the mascot; others are branded as outsiders or seen as tainted by foreign ideologies. Through a contradictory logic, however, some mascot supporters also make a different argument. When it comes to mascots, they argue, the people in this small Wisconsin town should not have to be the first ones to take up the burden of history. As George Christiansen writes, "If logos are to be made an issue, why start with the school system in a small place like Galesville? Instead of making this local, why not begin with 'bigger fish' and work on down? Take the professionals like the Cleveland Indians, Atlanta Braves and the Kansas City Chiefs, for example."[63] Apparently unaware that protests have been lodged against such teams since the 1970s[64]—and with great success in the specific case of the Chiefs, which have dropped the Indian logo[65]—Howard Hare, a distant relation of mine and a contemporary of my father's, makes the same point: "Start at the top. Indians, Braves and Redskins."[66]

Within the local setting mascot supporters frequently imagine themselves as benevolent victors, the ones who settled the land through cooperation with and respect for Indians. When the debate is placed in national perspective, these residents imagine themselves as downtrodden little guys—why pick on us? The reluctance of many local people to consider the racism of their own use of such mascots is profound. The extremes to which people go to defend their position is suggested elsewhere in Hare's letter.

Hare works to establish that he bears Indians no ill will; he points out that his parents often traded with Indians in the Trempealeau area—the Little Bears, the Funmakers—and that "if it were not for the help of an old Indian," he himself never would have learned to trap properly in the 1940s.[67] So, he suggests, he's got nothing against Indians. He goes on, however, to describe a school board meeting at which people in attendance speculate on "what a deceased Indian 'might say' [about the mascot] if he were at the meeting." Speaking for this dead Indian, Hare imagines that he "would be proud to be recognized as a school symbol." The notion that one might actually ask living native peoples in the region what they think of the mascot escapes Hare at the moment and, at the same time, demonstrates Lofgren's assertion that the trouble with such logos is that they make us think Indians are simply part of the past. But Hare is not done. Hare, probably referring to the history of broken treaties, writes that at the school board meeting "there was also mentioned of [sic] a dirty trick that was played on some Indians long ago. There have always been, and still are, those who will play dirty tricks on those who are weaker or are not quite as bright, as most of their fellow men, regardless of race, creed, or color." Hare uses the phrase "regardless of race, creed, or color" to underline his nondiscriminatory attitude; in effect, he argues that mean and ignorant people can be found everywhere. But in casting the situation in this way, Hare's depends on an old racist credo that Indians are ignorant and inferior: White people tricked Indians not because they were Indians but because these Indians were stupid. Hare comes to a racist conclusion in the guise of equal opportunity.

And, like others, Hare is worried that if he gives up the mascot, other things with Indian names will have to go too. While William Crogan asks facetiously about the fate of Winnebago campers and his Tecumseh lawnmower,[68] Hare notes: "There are a lot of cities and towns, also, that have Indian names. Should we then rename them to satisfy what could be a minority? Or have we lost what our forefathers fought and died for. The concept that this is a democracy and 'Majority Rules.'"[69] That others may have lived and died in the region—sometimes at the very hands of his forefathers—is lost on Hare. Democracy, as he construes it, is a form of might makes right. Hare seems unwilling to consider just what his responsibilities might be as a member of the white majority in the area—unwilling to imagine that democracy might also involve protecting the rights of others.

Given the dominance of the white majority in the area both numerically and ideologically, it is hardly surprising that few people thought to consult local native people about what they thought of the mascot. Hare, for one, is ready to speak out on behalf of dead Indians. Suttie is similarly ready to speak on the behalf of Indians, declaring, "Indians have lived in Wisconsin for many years, and few, if any have ever complained about being demeaned by the many Indian names or references to their race. If they have, I've never heard it."[70] Suttie's assertion is doubly ironic: for one, he has not apparently sought out native responses to mascots before making this claim, and, second, he lives in Colorado and thus severely restricts his chances to hear what Wisconsin Indians might think. But while some people simply assume that they already know native perspectives, others seek out more information. Fonfara claims that she had "interviewed a Winnebago woman who thanked her for researching the issue."[71] Just what this woman thought of the issue, Fonfara does not report. Lofgren is one of the few participants in the debate to include data from Native American groups.[72] Not only the "politically correct" have come out against the use of Indian mascots. Across the country numerous groups and tribal councils have announced their opposition to Indian mascots. These include the NAACP, National Education Association, Great Lakes Inter-Tribal Council, Menominee Tribe of Indians (Wisconsin), Oneida Tribe of Indians of Wisconsin, Wisconsin State Human Relations Association, "Indian" Mascot and Logo Taskforce of the Wisconsin Indian Education Association, Minnesota State Board of Education, KOLA (an international human rights organization established by Native Americans), United Indian Nations, American Indian Movement, National Congress of American Indians, National Indian Education Association, Institute of American Indian Arts, Affiliated Tribes of Northwest Indians, and American Indian Cultural Support. Additionally, a number of Christian and Jewish groups have come out against such mascots. Furthermore, in April 2001 the U.S. Commission on Civil Rights made a statement that reads, in part: "The Commission believes that the use of Native American images and nicknames in schools is insensitive and should be avoided. In addition, some Native American and civil rights advocates maintain that these mascots may violate anti-discrimination laws. These references, whether mascots and their performances, logos, or names, are disrespectful and offensive to American Indians and others who are offended by such stereotyping. They are particularly inappropriate and insensitive in light of the long history of forced assimilation that American Indian people have endured in this country."[73] To be sure, the commission's statement was made after the most recent round of discussions in the G-E-T school district; nonetheless, it is clear that a number of prominent groups oppose the use of such mascots. Faced with such opposition, however, the supporters of the mascot in the G-E-T district can always fall back on their standard line: outsiders need not apply to interfere in this very local business.

At a school board meeting about the mascot in 2000, one local white man, confident of his position, stood up and declared that because no native Americans lived in the district, the mascot was really a nonissue. Yes, he suggested, the mascot may be offensive to Indians, but in our case there are no Indians around to offend. Unwilling to recognize that as a white man he perhaps ought to think about why some people find the mascot offensive, he made a bold challenge: "All I need to hear is one Native American say, 'Get rid of the mascot,' and I'm ready to change it." He stood up in a sea of white faces, certain of his position. But in the room was one Native American, Gus Vogel. As one of the few native people in the district, he was reluctant to put himself and his family at the center of the controversy. When he first heard the challenge, he sat still in the silent room.

"Just one Indian person. Just one!" The man smiled tightly, satisfied he had proved his point.

Still Vogel sat. The room was quiet. Then slowly, slowly, Gus leaned forward, then got up, stretching out to his full six feet. "Get rid of the mascot," he said firmly. The people in the room were stunned. They hadn't known he was there.[74]

In October 2000 the school board, representing the majority opinion of its constituents, voted to keep the Redmen name and mascot.

6. Genealogy

Bob's research on the Hovels shows that Thomas was sixteen when he came to Wisconsin in 1858 from Cambridgeshire, England, from the town of either Upwell or Outwell. Although one genealogy links the Hovel name to the royal family of Tancred de Hauteville, which ruled Sicily in the twelfth century, Thomas's father, Robert, is listed on a marriage certificate as a farm laborer. Despite the exalted genealogy, the English word *hovel* itself suggests more modest origins. The 1870 census lists Thomas as illiterate; ten years later he could read and write. Family history has it that he curbed and dug wells for a living, in addition to farming.

For a dozen years my brother's research was confined to this continent, but in 1997, when T.S. was leading a college study abroad program in London, Bob came to visit. Bob had never been out of the United States before; indeed, he said it was pretty much "against his religion" to go any farther east than Wisconsin. But he made the trip so he could find out more about Thomas. At the time I wasn't much interested in the whole genealogy business, but when we arrived at the records office in Cambridge and it became a research problem, I was hooked. It was like piecing together a puzzle made of names that repeated themselves over the years—William, Robert, Thomas—a riddle made up of baptismal and death records, and marriage certificates signed only with an X. We searched the cemeteries and churches of Upwell for more records; a gravestone yielded some information. And although I had been concerned about the ability of my rural-dwelling brother to manage being abroad and to navigate a foreign country, I was impressed by what his desire to know about our father's side of the family led him to do. But I was troubled by the way that naming practices and patterns of marriage led us to pursue the father's line. Public records and family trees tend to confirm that same old story: what men do matters most. But when I looked at my father's side of the family, I saw men who had been worked hard by life—men who had hunkered down. Their tendency to dig in was expressed in their bodies: some of these men got stodgy and moved with difficulty. Partly because of my ambivalence about my origins, I had taken my husband's last name when we married, shoving the Hovell to the middle, where it might be remembered and forgotten as the occasion warranted.

Bob has also researched women's roles in the family tree, but the lines are harder to follow. He has learned that Thomas's wife, Mary Amanda Wilber, came to Wisconsin in 1856 as an adolescent from New York or Connecticut; the family traveled in covered wagons and flat boats. But to know more about her, you have to keep track of her changing names. Before wedding Thomas, Mary first married a man named Truman, who went to the Civil War and didn't come back. After Thomas died, Mary Hovell, *née* Wilber, married twice again. We can keep track of her only if we know whom she married, if we remember her father's name, her brothers' names. (The men seem to have been a fairly industrious lot. Bob says that plat books for the village of Trempealeau from 1877 are full of Wilbers—they owned a lot of the land there.) Ultimately, delving into women's lives will take the researcher back to men.

My mother's ancestors are German. On her mother's side they come from the far northern region near Kiel, practically in Denmark. They are so far north, their German is almost English. The Standard German word for "door"—*Tur*—becomes something like "Dur." Mom's maternal grandmother, Emma Schwanabeck (b. 1883), came over from Germany when she was seven. My mother's maternal grandfather, Jakob Storm (b. 1879), came over when he was fifteen; the story goes that his older brother was in line to inherit the family farm, but because the brother wanted to be a carpenter, he killed himself rather than become a farmer. Exercising his own options, Jakob came to America. He met Emma in Minnesota, they married, and they worked land near Winona that my mother describes as "all rock" before finally settling into the Centerville area, not far from Trempealeau. Mom's father's people are from what used to be East Germany; no one knows exactly where. When her ancestors came to the United States, their name—whatever it was—was changed to Bockenhauer. They made their way west to Dunkirk, New York, then moved farther west, to Wisconsin.

My mother's parents met as teens, when they were both working on a farm near Fort Atkinson, Wisconsin. My grandpa Earl was lanky and handsome, loose limbed, and ready to laugh. My grandmother Viola was short and in later years prone to stockiness. She loved to have fun and knew a good thing when she saw one. They eloped when she was fifteen and Earl was twenty-two. My mother was born the next year, in 1930, the oldest of eight. As for my grandparents, despite all those children, they seemed to always remain in love—my grandmother so devoted to her husband that she nearly forgot her children sometimes. The kids grew up learning that laughter and gaiety were good, reading was a pleasure, and more difficult feelings—like sorrow, loneliness, self-pity, fear—were best ignored. If you don't see them, they can't exist, seemed to be their motto.

A bright tomato red became the family color of choice; we call it Bockenhauer red. There developed a distinct kind of laughter among the Bockenhauers: a pound-your-fist-on-the-table, throw-back-your-head-and-holler kind of laugh that is best practiced in large groups.

During the world wars those of German ancestry were frequently suspect; my mother, who grew up in a largely Polish area, recalls being taunted for being German while she was in school during World War II. When the immigrant grandparents died, the German language was all but forgotten in our family. (It seems strange to me now that when we played war games as children, the Germans were always the bad guys.) Later, in the 1970s, my grandmother Vi embraced her Germanness, and we learned that she had been corresponding sporadically with Storms in Hohn, Germany, where Jürgen Storm still lived on and worked the family farm, where distant cousins ran the Bäkerei Storm. My grandmother, a farmer of few means and fewer resources, had the audacity to travel there in the early 1980s, where she rekindled a friendship with the German Storms. Soon after, while on side trips from India, I traveled to Hohn with my mother and sister Pam, and later with them and my father. What was most striking to me about these visits was how unexotic they were. The farm life, the gaiety, the refusal to acknowledge difficulties, the alcohol-filled town celebrations, the gatherings around coffee and pastry (though the German varieties of both were supe-rior): these were coupled with living one's life out in a small town, the contentedness that members of both families had about the world they had constructed around animals, food, and relatives. Most people in both families were satisfied with this. Of course, such contentedness always spawns rebels—the relatives who left Germany in the first place, my cousin Jonny, me, and now a distant German cousin near to me in age, Rainer Storm. When, on our first visit to his hometown, Rainer expressed a desire to study in the United States, I helped arrange for him to study at my college in ex-change for work as a German teaching assistant. (Later he would live in Japan for years, teaching English, while at the same time I me-andered around India, Nepal, Tibet.) On our second visit to Hohn, after Rainer had returned from his U.S. travels, he and I stood on a dike and looked out toward Denmark and raged against the easy satisfaction of our elders, about the limited ways with which they approached the world, their seeming inability to ask questions of their lives and their world and where it had come from. Things just *were* to them—no need to ask why. Delving into the past, entering into one's pain or the pain of others, could bring only misery. Better not to look there.

Ours was, in some sense, the anger and conviction of youth. But it was an anger that shaped the choices we would make in our lives, an anger that fueled the promises we made to rend the curtain of propriety and detachment we saw in our elders—to escape what W. G. Sebald calls "the extraordinary faculty [Germans possess] for self-anesthesia."[75] Ours was, in its way, a very German rebellion.

While in Hohn, we took time to visit the church graveyard and tried to decipher Aunt Helga's German explanations of kinship. Jakob, Jürgen, Heinrich, Anna: the names repeated down the family line. And, indeed, in Hohn as in Trempealeau, the dead keep one rooted into a place. In a small town, where people don't move much and know each other face to face, the dead are remembered—you can't get away from them—old relatives, neighbors, classmates, friends. They live on in conversation, in name, rooted in the very earth that you live on.

7. Names

The land has its rivers, its bluffs, its rich soil near the river, its sand on the prairie, its trees, heavy winters, humid summers. There also are traces of what people have done to the land: hearth rings, the blackened soil left behind by old fires; the geometry of cornfields; solitary oaks encircled by fields; the river shaped and directed by the dam and the Army Corps of Engineers. The land bears traces of the people who have lived on it: rock art, artifacts, mounds, of course, but also the crops in fields and the chemicals put on them, the overpopulation of deer. While Middle Mississippians—at least in the Cahokia region—were known to test the limits of their environment—and there's plenty of evidence that native peoples set fire to forests—the work done to the land since white settlement almost obliterates the signs of those who had lived here before. One has to look hard for them. One has to be reminded, for often we have chosen to remember other things.

Names form one part of this remembering. My father was named in memory of his grandfather, Robert Damon Hovell. My brother is named for my father, Robert Ray Hovell. My cousin Clyde Jon was named for his dad, and his younger brother was named Stanley Earl for both grandfathers. I am named for my mother. Studying the Hovell family tree in England, my brother and I kept running into the same names: William, Thomas, Robert, William, Thomas, Robert, as if the repetition of names confirmed their presence in the place. Later their American descendants would repeat the names of ancestors to root them to a new place: Thomas, Robert. Amanda, Sarah. Laurena, Laurie.

But the family is only one place for such remembering, for such rooting. Place-names too are often kinds of memorials, forms of honoring. When white settlers laid out the village of Trempealeau, they built up from the river, numbering the streets along the way, from First to Tenth. Cross streets, however, were named after people: among these are Jay (for the Federalist John Jay), Sumner (for Charles Sumner, the abolitionist), and Fremont (for the explorer and general John Charles Fremont). There's even a tiny dead-end street named for George Gale. The old high school—Healy Memorial—was named for Benjamin Healy, the moneyed nineteenth-century land speculator. Brady's Bluff, now part of Perrot State Park, was named for the farmer who once owned the land on which it stood. Nicholls Mound and the Schwert and Shrake groups of mounds were named for the farmers who owned the land on which these Hopewell mounds were built, just as the name Hopewell itself came from a landowner in Ohio whose farm was dotted with mounds.

Place-names in the area suggest layers of history. Reed's Landing, Caledonia, Galesville all refer to white settlement by Scots and Yankees. La Crosse,[76] La Crescent, Perrot Park all recall the presence of the French and the fur trade. The Frenchified name Trempealeau is a transitional term to another layer, that of the Indian past. This past has been memorialized by white settlers in such place-names as Mississippi, Winona, Minnesota, Wisconsin. Place-names suggest layers of history, but they can't tell us what happened.

George Gale, of course, named Galesville in his own honor and was instrumental in choosing the name Trempealeau for what had first been Reed's Landing, after the first white settler, and then Montoville, after a nearby bluff. The town of Trempealeau was named for the bluff remnant in the Mississippi; the French *la montagne qui trempe à l'eau* was derived from the Ho-Chunk name Hay-nee-ah-chah, "the soaking mountain." (The Dakota name, Pah-hah-dah, "moved mountain," seems to have been left out of this lineage.)[77] The name Trempealeau lent the place some antiquity, linking it to the past. It skewered layers of history, connecting white American settlement to French presence to the Native American past but also helping to disconnect the place from Europe. The tendency to refer to Native American words in naming places was part of a larger trend among Euro-Americans, and it was a practice with roots in colonial America. As the Yuchi and Seminole anthropologist and historian of religion Richard Grounds argues, "After independence and a rising self-confidence coupled with the growing Romantic Movement came an increasing fascination with Indian names as the proper choice for new Euro-American political entities. . . . These Native-derived names served two important and interrelated purposes. They helped to sever what was felt to be an overreliance on

European origins. They also provided a new, intentionally distinct identity that more directly linked Euro-Americans to the so-called American continent."[78]

The adoption of the name Trempealeau seems to connect past and present seamlessly and without pain, violence, disease, or removal. The name is a kind of palliative; Trempealeau Mountain is still there, after all, tranquil, covered in trees, the home of deer and birds, the Mississippi still lapping gently at its feet.

Lydia Howard Sigourney's poem "Indian Names" asserts that Native Americans survive in place-names, even if they seem to have disappeared (this version was published in 1856):

> Ye say they all have passed away
>   That noble race and brave
> That their light canoes have vanished
>   From the crested wave;
> That 'mid the forests where they roamed,
>   there rings no hunter's shout;
> But their name is on your waters
>   Ye may not wash it out.
>
> 'Tis where Ontario's billow
>   Like ocean's surge is curled
> Where strong Niagara's thunders wake
>   The echo of the world;
> Where red Missouri bringeth
>   Rich tribute from the West,
> And Rappahannock weetle sleeps
>   On Virginia's green breast. [79]

She goes on to list Massachusetts, Ohio, Connecticut, Kentucky, and other native-derived place-names. In Sigourney's vision Indian names seem to arise organically from the earth to contradict settlers' misperception that Indians have all disappeared. But as Katherine Fitzgerald has argued, naming places was something in which white settlers were actively engaged; appropriating Indian names was a way to lay claim to the land. "Even when the white name is the same as the Indian name (in French or English accents and orthography), it is the codification and preservation of the name in white people's maps, records, and narratives that preserve it as a 'real' name."[80] Furthermore, as Grounds suggests: "Native-derived place-names, like

public monuments, function to promote the forgetting of the in-
humane details of the past and the misremembering of the meaning
of those events that were ties to the expropriation of Native names.
They serve to sanction the national enterprise by guarding the national pride, creating the illusion of bridging the chasm between
American self-conceptions and the historic and ongoing heartless
treatment of the Native inhabitants of the land."[81] Red Wing. Marinuka. Decorah Prairie. Wabasha. Trempealeau. Mississippi. Wisconsin. The names survive, are altered, and acquire new meanings.

This habit of using indigenous place-names is not unique to the
Upper Mississippi. Half the states in the Union have Indian-derived
names; perhaps as many towns and cities have indigenous names—
Mackinac, Tallahassee, Miami—as have been named for the men
Americans count as heroes: Washington, Lincoln, Jackson, Co-
lumbus.[82] But as Grounds argues, "There [is] a doubleness about
these Indian names, remarking the existence of Native Americans
while simultaneously relegating them to the past, appearing to
bestow honor on them while cloaking the destructive deeds of Euro-
American society."[83] Some will say that the use of such names is designed to honor, to remember, just as they say that Indian mascots—
Redmen, Indians, Redskins—honor Native Americans. But if we
don't know even the broad strokes of the history of contact—if that
remembering depends on certain kinds of forgetting—where is the
honor? If we can live in these places named after Indians, if we can
pass through Jackson County and not think about policies of removals and trails of tears, our remembering is a symptom of amnesia.

8. Dead Indians

Chief Decorah and Princess Marinuka have been central figures in white remembering of the native past. Decorah Peak perches over Decorah Prairie, looking down on a major county highway; Lake Marinuka spreads out below the town of Galesville. The stories told about these two figures—grandfather and granddaughter—emphasize their heroic stature. The Ho-Chunk chief is remembered as a brave fighter and leader who evaded an attack by Sioux or Chippewa warriors (accounts differ) by hiding inside the limestone tower that would bear his name. Princess Marinuka is recalled as a gentle Indian woman who died young and whose body was buried at the edge of the mill-dam that would later bear her name. (In my imagination I see the princess as the woman on Land O'Lakes butter, in buckskin, beads, and feather.)

Their stories have passed into legend. Searching out accounts of their lives, I found that the same stories were retold and recycled. Newspapers and pamphlets simply reprinted the same stories, whether the year was 1913, 1926, or 2001. These were our local Indian heroes.

The name Decorah probably came from the French De Carey or De Corrie or something similar; Gale lists Decorah's Ho-Chunk name as Wadge-hut-da-kaw, or the Big Canoe; he is also known as One-Eyed Decorah.[84] Decorah, who fought in Indian wars, was the great grandson of a Frenchman who married a Ho-Chunk woman. In 1825 Decorah signed a treaty with the United States government at Prairie du Chien. In 1834 he turned in the warrior Black Hawk to the government forces at the same place. In 1837 Decorah went to Washington to sign a treaty that relinquished all Winnebago lands in Wisconsin to the federal government. He moved to Iowa but died in Monroe County, Wisconsin. The chronology of his life echoes the myth of the disappearing Indian, the Indian who stands proudly, then retreats silently into the forest, as it were.

Parallel to stories about brave but disappearing warriors are stories of Indian princesses, of which the Marinuka legends are part.

Honorable, gentle, though ultimately powerless, the princess myth allows a tranquil remembering, a romantic story of a lovely girl, now passed on to the happy hunting grounds. She becomes an ancestor of a sort, the kind that white people can live with. As Vine Deloria Jr. writes in another context, "A[n Indian] male ancestor has too much the aura of the savage warrior, the unknown primitive, the instinctive animal, to make him a respectable member of the family tree";[85] as a youngish woman Marinuka poses no such threat. Further, the honored woman is not just any woman: she is royalty—a princess, like Hiawatha's bride—who bestows on the town a certain prestige. But our memory of her is often slight. Growing up, I knew almost no details about her, and when I asked my mother what she knew about Marinuka, she could say only, "She was an Indian princess— daughter of a chief. Her grave is at Arctic Springs."

In making Marinuka into a legend, people had to make some effort. For one, the woman's name, Marie Nunka, was given a pseudo-Indianized form: Marinuka. More burdensome still was her corpse, which needed to be buried and buried again before its proper resting place could be settled upon. In this handling and rehandling of her bones and the stories told and retold about these burials and reburials, something of the anxiety about—something of the desire and fascination for—dead Indians emerges.

I see this anxiety in the simple repetition of her story, the basic details of which I will repeat here: Born in the 1850s, Marie Nunka was the daughter of Chief Winneshiek, granddaughter of Ho-Chunk Chief Decorah. She died in an Indian encampment just outside Galesville in 1884 on land owned by G. Y. Freeman and was buried that same night in the presence of both Ho-Chunk and white observers. In 1911 she was reburied because her grave lay in Freeman's new barnyard. In 1926 she was reburied again at Arctic Springs.

Students writing for Galesville's high school yearbook offered two versions of her story. One reproduced a poem written by a "schoolgirl," Dorothy S. Emmons, from 1910; this version depends heavily on Longfellow's "Song of Hiawatha."

> By the shores of Marinuka,
> By the shining smooth pond water,
> Lies the princess of the Redskins,

Lies the daughter of Decorah.
And the day was dark and dreary
And the sky weeping softly,
When the maid was brought for burial,
Brought to sleep and rest for ever.[86]

As the poem continues, her "suitor, / Bravest of Docorah's [*sic*] warriors," comes to mourn beside the body of the dead maiden. His tears fall next to the "earthmound" that is her grave; he "christens" the water with her name: Marinuka.

In this schoolgirl's story the Indian warrior names the lake after the princess. In practice, however, it was white Americans who appropriated native names. As Grounds insists, "Indian place-names became symbols of the national ideology of conquest and the right to Indian lands as well as an expression of American mythology about the disappearance of Native peoples."[87] Accommodating whites' need for an empty landscape, in this girl's poem the Indian brave in the story obligingly disappears. He hears the water murmur back its new name,

Then he strode into the forest;
And he ne'er again was heard from
'Mongst the warriors on Docorah [*sic*].[88]

With the "princess of the Redskins" entombed and the warrior safely disappeared, legends rise up around them.

Yearbook-making students in 1928 repeat the standard story: "Princess Marinuka, daughter of Chief Winneshiek and granddaughter of Chief Decorah lived with a party of Winnebago Indians near the present site of Arctic Springs. At her early death in 1884, several interested towns people [*sic*] visited the camp, and Charles Freeman speaking for the whites requested that the Princess be buried at the head of the lake which has since been named Lake Marinuka in honor of the Princess. The Indians were at first skeptical but later complied with the suggestion. A number of white people took part in the burial ritual which was performed in true tribal fashion at midnight."[89] But neither the story nor Marinuka's body can be finally laid to rest; students in 1928 would have been present to hear firsthand of yet another reburial. They note:

The grave of Princess Marinuka has twice been moved, the first time because the grave was practically under one of the dwellings erected.

In 1926, when the Galesville Fire Department purchased the Arctic Springs and converted it into recreation grounds, Princess Marinuka's remains were restored to their original burial place. The grave is marked by the original stone slab and is enclosed with iron rods. Beside it stands a concrete wigwam as a memorial to the dead Princess.[90]

Not only does the appropriation of Marinuka's name for the lake suggest residents' "effort to work out [their] own troubled relationship to the land,"[91] her many burials are suggestive of townspeople's need to come to terms with the past. Like her bones, Marinuka's story is handled and retold—in the yearbook and in local newspapers. In September 2001 a local newspaper, the *(Melrose) Chronicle,* saw the need to tell the story again and reprinted Charles E. Freeman's 1884 account of the burial together with Bert Gipple's 1941 version of the reburials in an article titled "The Midnight Burial of Princess Marinuka." (Gipple's version, incidentally, reprinted part of a 1926 account that I found in a file on Marinuka at the Galesville Public Library.)[92]

The 1926 article from the *Galesville Republican* adds a whiff of mystery to the story by noting the following:

> In an old desk sold at the auction of personal effects of the late Charles Freeman was found a copy of an old school newspaper, which contained an article by Mr. Freeman touching upon the burial of the Princess Marinuka.
>
> This is a valuable bit of history right now when Arctic Springs and the grave of the Princess are receiving so much attention.[93]

Freeman's story and its reprintings form the basis of the Marinuka myth.

Charles Freeman had been a pioneer lawyer; in 1884 his father, George Y. Freeman, owned land at Arctic Springs just outside Galesville on the banks of the mill-dam; some Winnebago people were camped there. In his account the younger Freeman notes that he learned at supper one Saturday night in 1884 that "an Indian woman had died" and that "the men at the wigwam wanted to bury her on the Artic [*sic*] Springs property." The elder Freeman was willing to allow the burial on his land as long as it was done that night. As the younger Freeman was then superintendent of the Presbyterian Sunday school, he "could not get away to be present at a real Indian burial the next morning"; Charles proposed to a couple of friends that "we row up the lake that night after [Odd Fellows] lodge and get the Indians to consent to an interment at once."[94]

Charles Freeman's narration of the burial and his encounter with the Ho-Chunk is charged with spookiness.

> When we neared the head of the lake we heard the Indians pounding a drum and chanting. It was between 10 and 11 o'clock, with a glorious moon making it very light.
> We found two wigwams in a thicket by the lake. . . . There were two families sitting by the light of a lantern in a circle in one tent, and one of the men was beating a monotonous tum, tum, tum, tum, tum, on a drum and they were singing a melancholy song that sounded weird enough, among the black shadows and the moonlight. A squaw [*sic*] came up from out of the shadows and challenged us, as we came up to the tent. She evidently was watching the body, which laid inclosed [*sic*] in a rough pine box in the other tent.
> We told them that "Preeman" as they called Mr. Freeman had consented to permit the body to be buried on the Artic [*sic*] Springs grounds, provided they buried it that night and that they fix the grave in regular Indian fashion.[95]

As Freeman's account suggests, the Ho-Chunks gathered there had doubts about the white men's participation in the burial; as he recounts, "They hesitated, and talked among themselves in the Winnebago language and then, turning to us, said, 'You no come, when we gone away, and dig up the "meat" and sell it to Chicago?' We assured them the body should be undisturbed." Despite Freeman's assurance, this was not to be.

The proceedings around the burial are shared by both white and Indian participants. When the Winnebago consent to the burial, it is the white men who collect the body, which, as Freeman notes, showed the deceased to be "a woman of about 30; slender and clad in a calico dress with a small shawl about her shoulders." (No buckskin here.) They carried the body out to and along the road, over to the point where the grave now is. We dug a grave, due east and west, about two feet deep, as they directed, and lowered the body with the head to the west. Then the speaker of the two Indians stopped us and standing at the south side of the open grave said some kind of farewell speech in Winnebago and sprinkled tobacco in the grave and began a chant. They stepped across the grave and moved in a circle once or twice and stopped; and then, he said in broken English: "Great Spirit, he is God. He Pader (Father). He pader white man. He pader Injun. All same Pader; White man, Injun, he brudder."

After that, we quickly filled the grave and they promised to cut poles and put a fence about the grave, which they did later. We then came away much moved by the strangeness of it all.

Aware, perhaps, of the attraction of Indian bones and artifacts for white settlers, the elder Freeman made it clear at the time that "any desecration of the grave will be resented by him to the full extent of the law."[96]

For the time, then, all was well and good. But in Charles Freeman's absence from the area, his father constructed a farm near the burial, and this placed Marinuka's shallow grave, as the son puts it, "in the barnyard." After consulting with town leaders and "also some Indians" for their permission, the younger Freeman exhumed the body in 1911. The following is from Bert Gipple's account: "Unaided, he opened the shallow grave and with minute care removed the skeleton. The pine box in which the Princess was buried, had wholly rotted away, leaving the skeleton imbedded in earth. When all was removed, he assembled the skeleton. Versed in anatomy, he made careful examination and found that only a few small bones had been turned to dust. A considerable number of beads and some trinkets buried with the body were found. He sifted the soil of the grave to preserve all these."[97] The account of Freeman's handling of Marie Nunka's skeleton has a clinical detachment; Freeman proceeds like a scientist—an archaeologist, even, sifting the soil—and works to preserve what he can. Freeman treats her remains in a respectful manner; after all, people of his day were accustomed to seeing and touching the dead, and it was not unusual to disinter and reinter remains.[98] But Freeman is scientific in another respect; like archaeologists, who until recently have routinely disturbed graves, Freeman disturbs the burial of the Ho-Chunk woman, despite his earlier promise. Yes, there is the problem of the barnyard; yes, she had had a shallow and decrepit grave. It is not that he treats her bones like those of a dog; she is, instead, a kind of specimen that must be preserved. Marinuka's is a special case; she is a relic of sorts, sanctified both by her connection to a notable Indian chief and her status as one of a dying breed. And she must get out of the way of progressing farmers and townspeople to a safe place. When the skeleton was placed in a new pine box and reinterred, "a committee of citizens" assisted in and witnessed the reburial.[99]

But this was not yet her final resting place. Fifteen years later, in 1926, when the barn at Arctic Springs was torn down, "a number of citizens suggested that the remains of the Princess should find a permanent resting place near the spot of the original burial."[100] As one article notes, the Boy Scouts "were to participate [in this reburial], but not a lad showed up."[101] Before the final interment Marinuka's remains were handled again and more intimately examined by Dr. M. J. Senty, head of the Galesville Boy Scouts. As Gipple notes in 1941:

> The larger bones of the skeleton were still in a good state of preservation. Some of the smaller ones had "returned to dust." The skull was perfect. In this, Dr. Senty was deeply interested. He took it to the springs, held it under the outlet pipe, washed it thoroughly and then for a quarter of an hour or more, studied the teeth. With the exception of one, which had a small cavity, they were perfect.
>
> This time the skull and bones were placed in a metal container and taken to the present location, on a point probably 30 feet from the original place of the burial.[102]

The skeleton and skull are handled with scientific detachment and inspected according to medical and perhaps phrenological interests. Indeed, Senty's examination recalls the cranial studies of Samuel Morton as well as the work of some archaeologists today. There is a proprietary air here, an assumption of privilege, a reassertion of an Indian as a different order of being. Despite the concerns of the Ho-Chunk when Marinuka was first buried, it was not the "meat" that the white citizens were interested in but the bones, her skull. These, however, were not sent to Chicago, as Marinuka's companions originally feared; they stayed in Galesville. As the good citizens of Galesville desecrate Marinuka's burial, they crown Marinuka their princess, exhume and reinter her body; they take her name, change it, and give it to the lake in town.[103] In 1926 a concrete tepee was erected over the grave by the Wisconsin Order of Redmen,[104] a group of white men who dedicated the site while attending a convention at Galesville.[105] With the perception that Indians have disappeared into the forest, into the ground, these men assume the epithet Redmen and play the part of caretaker of the dead.

All this handling of Marinuka's skeleton might make residents today squeamish, but during this period white settlers were handling Indian remains all over the region.[106] Farmers sometimes ran across artifacts and bones. Looters and amateur archaeologists had been digging into Indian burial mounds since they first settled the area. Picnickers on Trempealeau Mountain had lunch and dug in burial mounds for fun. In Trempealeau around the same time, townsmen encountered bones and burials as they dug the road around Perrot Park. Squier had already excavated a number of mounds. Euro-American occupation of the region depended on the dispatching of these bones—through entombment, plowing, collecting, remembering, and forgetting. One of Thoreau's descriptions of settlers' behavior in Massachusetts is apt here as well; he writes of the white man, "pale as the dawn, . . . who buys the Indian's moccasins and baskets, then buys his hunting grounds, and at length forgets where he is buried, and plows up his bones."[107] He will then go on to memorialize what he has dug up.

Memorializing and naming practices like those described in the Marinuka case are hardly unique to Galesville. As Richard Grounds writes: "The U.S. landscape, littered with place-names derived from Indigenous peoples, can be viewed as a great onomastic reliquary, a bone yard where Indian names are brandished from the highest spires of America's cities. . . . As accentuated in this hermeneutics of American place-naming, Native people and cultures were literally decapitated and symbolically stored in place-names, as if the veneration of the names could mask over the hostile relationship to those ancestors and their lands."[108] Gus Vogel contends that remains of his ancestors are buried all over the region; Anna Funmaker suggests that the state of Wisconsin is a burial ground. For Grounds, not only is the landscape littered with bones, indigenous names themselves become reliquaries, sites in which certain memories and ideas are locked away, cemented over. The name Marinuka becomes such a repository.

When the town fathers give Marinuka's name to their man-made lake at the center of the town founded by George Gale, they wed the feminized Indian past and the masculine white present. Galesville and Marinuka, land and water, man and woman, are joined. White men become Redmen. Decorah's name is taken for a peak and a prairie. (As Freeman writes, "Decorah's Peak and Decorah's Mound, together with Decorah Prairie, still keep in mind the fact that this American Switzerland was once the home of the red man. The smoke of the wigwam has passed, but the rocks keep sure vigil over this great chief's name.")[109] Around the same time that the high school gave up its site above the shores of Lake Marinuka in 1956—moving, like the reburied princess, to a new site—the students took her name for themselves and became the Marinuka tribe; when the school kids finally left the old camping grounds, they became free to become the "Redmen."[110]

9. Natural History

A poet friend of mine, Lynn, grew up in Tennessee, far downriver from Trempealeau. She recalls that when she was twelve she went with her father and brother on a YMCA Indian Guide trip for fathers and sons. (Her dad's Indian name was Big Wind to his son's Little Wind.) Some archaeologists had excavated a burial site along the river in anticipation of a Tennessee Valley Authority damming project. After the scientists had removed all the human remains they could find, they opened the site to the public and allowed people to look for arrowheads. Lynn's father, an independent type, walked away from the crowd at the now empty grave and went into a nearby cornfield. There he stuck his shovel in, announcing that this was where he would dig. After he dug about eighteen inches down, he hit bone—toe bones. A crowd gathered to watch as Lynn's father dug with his hands. Soon he uncovered an entire skeleton laid out parallel to the river. It was that of a man, apparently, with one bony hand at his side and the other pillowing his head. Her father picked up the skull; under it were treasures of a sort: a tooled bone awl, a tomahawk head, mussel shells. People started to claim the bones. One retrieved finger bones, another ribs. Her father selected the skull, Lynn the femur. Lynn rode home that day in 1967 in the passenger seat of the family Chevy, holding a skull in her lap. She remembers being surprised that the skull was full of dirt, and, as the dirt crumbled into her lap, it came to her that this was what was left of someone's brain, someone's mind. Nonetheless, as she described it, this realization of mortality and the sense that they had violated something when they dug up the bones was "overridden by the exotic, this sense of the other." Later Lynn kept the skull and bones in her closet.

Only after she was out of college did the incident come to bother her. Reflecting on the scene years later, Lynn said, "If we had thought we were digging up a white person's grave, I don't think we would have felt entitled. I can't imagine feeling [entitled] if it had been the first homesteader." She tried to understand her attitude back then. In part, she said, we had the sense that Indians were "part of prehistory—we didn't have their stories." Instead, "there was this feeling that they had vanished." The bones seemed to belong to another order of being.[111]

10. Trempealeau Mountain Again

I knew some stories about Trempealeau Mountain—center of the world, home of rattlesnakes—but I wanted to hear more, wanted to find out something of what it meant and means to native peoples, wanted to find out how the layer of stories that I knew are connected to other layers of stories. The mythologizing that townspeople had done about the mountain—putting it on paintings, naming golf courses after it—was only part of the most visible layer of meaning ascribed to the place.

I asked a Phil Palzkill, the Perrot State Park ranger, if he knew any stories about the place. "You want to hear legends?" he asked wearily. He repeated the old Maiden Rock story, a version of which is also told in Twain's *Life on the Mississippi.* (Indeed, when I was a kid, our family used to vacation in the Twin Cities, where my dad was working for the Army Corps of Engineers; on the way up, we'd stop and read yet another version of this story at a historical marker in Maiden Rock, Wisconsin.) Palzkill told the story this way: There are these star-crossed lovers from different tribes. She is a "maiden"; he is a "brave." The tribes live on opposite banks of the Mississippi; he must swim the wide river to see her. Conniving people tell the maiden that her lover has drowned trying to reach her. Despondent, she jumps from a cliff that towers over the river; this we now know as Maiden Rock. This was the story as I had known it, as it had been retold in the roadside historical marker. But the ranger added a new aspect to it: When the brave learns of his lover's death, he kills himself as well. And at this point the Great Spirit itself takes on a role and avenges the crime. A tremendous storm rises up, breaking off a piece of a bluff, which floats down the river. This is Trempealeau Mountain, "the moved mountain," Pah-hah-dah in Dakota.

Karen Vogel told me a Ho-Chunk story about Trempealeau Mountain, in abbreviated form. She had first heard the story orally but noted that I could also get a copy of the story at the La Crosse Public Library. In this tale a grandfather takes care of twin boys until one dies. The remaining child seems all alone, but the truth is that when the grandfather goes away for the day, the spirit of the dead

3.1. The northeast side of Trempealeau Mountain. Photo by author.

child comes over from Trempealeau Mountain to play with his brother. They cause a lot of mischief together, she said, and get into trouble downriver.

Gus Vogel told me another story. It was about the removals. As the website for the Ho-Chunk Nation reports, "The memories of living Ho-Chunk contain stories of their elders being rounded up at gunpoint, loaded into boxcars and shipped to 'their reservation' in Nebraska."[112] Gus's grandfather had a story from this time: During the Ho-Chunk removals of the midnineteenth century, the Ho-Chunk who managed to escape the soldiers and trains that were going to ship them west made their way to Trempealeau Mountain, walking across the shallow bay to its refuge.

11. The Removals

White possession of the land around Trempealeau was predicated on surveying, settling, and naming it. According to Frederick Jackson Turner's notion of the "empty frontier," only through such actions was the land perceived as wilderness transformed, made into a known and manageable place of borders and private property, made into a civilized place. For this reason, French traders, white settlers, and their descendants have often been blind to other ways of dwelling with and on the land.

Although there appears not to have been a native village at Trempealeau when Nicolas Perrot landed there in 1685—some say this is the precisely *why* he was able to land there—it does not mean the place was not meaningful to native peoples. As Rodell suggested to me (and as I mentioned earlier), it is likely that at the time of Perrot's arrival the Trempealeau area was well known to native peoples as a powerful site, as it was the place of large Hopewell burial mounds, numerous effigy and conical mounds, platform mounds, and Trempealeau Mountain itself; indeed, Perrot may have first learned of the place from Ho-Chunk guides because of these landmarks. In any case, native peoples clearly had a long connection to the place.

The fur trade, along with intertribal disputes and alliances, brought about great movements of people in Wisconsin.[113] Perrot's account of the area around Trempealeau lists a number of tribes—people we know as the Ioway, Dakota, Ho-Chunk, Kickapoo, Mascoutin, and Miami; from his account I get the sense of a place traversed, rather than a site of permanent settlement.[114] We can't forget that by the late seventeenth century native populations were already being ravaged by foreign-borne diseases. Smallpox took a huge toll; influenza, typhus, whooping cough, measles, and many other diseases took more lives than any battle; later, some of these were deliberately introduced into native populations. The subsequent arrival of the British in America and then the construction of the United States further transformed cultures, lands, and patterns of habitation.

Although in the discussion that follows I will be emphasizing the history of the Ho-Chunk, who continue to have a presence in the

Trempealeau area, I want to look further into the fate of other tribes who lived in the Trempealeau region and whose cultures were transformed and shifted by government policies and European settlement. For while the standard narrative is that Indians once lived in our area but then went away, there are reasons for their absence. Disease was but one; more to the point were the policies of removal and the people who carried them out.

As Americans of European descent determined to move westward in the nineteenth century, the presence of many native peoples in those regions became a problem, a problem dealt with in different ways at different moments. In the 1820s and 1830s the government adopted a policy of "separation" and moved eastern tribes out of areas of expected white settlement to lands largely west of the Mississippi. When these measures proved insufficient to accommodate whites' desires to expand, the government undertook a policy of "concentration" in the 1840s; this plan further reduced Indian landholdings and initiated the reservation system. Native resistance to this policy led to the Plains Wars of the 1860s and 1870s. The third policy undertaken by the government was that of "Americanization"; initiated in the 1870s, this policy paired land reform with education and attempted to assimilate Indians into Euro-American culture.[115] One aspect of this policy involved taking Indian children from their parents' care and sending them to boarding schools, where they were forced to learn English and forbidden to speak their mother tongues; they also were encouraged to learn a trade. As Richard Henry Pratt, the founder of the Industrial Indian School in Carlisle, Pennsylvania, argued, the goal was to "kill the Indian and save the man."[116]

When the policy of separation was implemented, the Ioway, like many tribes in this period, were forced to cede all their lands in Missouri (and east of the Mississippi) in 1824; they were then removed to Kansas. One faction of the tribe moved to Oklahoma in an effort to retain the traditional way of life. It is impossible to know the population of Ioway in, say, 1600, but J. O. Dorsey and Cyrus Thomas noted in 1912 that the number of Ioway was estimated as 1,100 in 1760, as 800 in 1804, 1,000 in 1829, and 470 people in 1843.[117] The *Statistical Record of Native North Americans* lists the total population of Ioway in three states in 1930 as 173.[118] After the ravages of removal

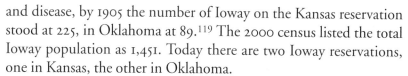

and disease, by 1905 the number of Ioway on the Kansas reservation stood at 225, in Oklahoma at 89.[119] The 2000 census listed the total Ioway population as 1,451. Today there are two Ioway reservations, one in Kansas, the other in Oklahoma.

During the nineteenth century the Dakotas' story is also one of lost land and diminishing numbers. The government seized all Dakota lands in Wisconsin in 1837, pushing the Dakota across the river to Minnesota. With the Santee Sioux uprising in New Ulm, Minnesota, in 1862, the U.S. government under Lincoln removed the Dakota again—this time to Nebraska. The Dakota population was largely resettled in South Dakota. Today there are four federally recognized Dakota communities in Minnesota, three reservations in South Dakota, and one in Montana that is shared with the Assiniboin; today the Dakota in the United States number in the tens of thousands.

Like the Dakota, Ioway, and other eastern tribes, the Ho-Chunk lost their landholdings in the late 1820s. Earlier in that decade the U.S. government had recognized the Ho-Chunk as a sovereign nation. But after the Red Bird War of 1827 the Winnebago were forced to leave the lead-mining region of southwest Wisconsin. In treaties in 1829 and 1832 the government confiscated all Winnebago land south of the Wisconsin and Fox rivers. At the time the U.S. government promised the tribe a $10,000 annuity for twenty-seven years; it also agreed to give the Ho-Chunk land west of the Mississippi, as well as funds for a school, a blacksmith, oxen, plows, and "demonstration" farmers (such as the early Trempealeau settler James Reed had been for the Dakota). In turn, the tribe had to promise that no Ho-Chunk would live, hunt, plant, or fish on any part of the tribe's former lands.[120]

While it seems clear enough that possession of the land and access to its resources was the issue here, white settlers offered moral arguments for removal. In the 1830s Henry Dodge, who had been a commander in the Black Hawk War and would later become Wisconsin territorial governor (1836–41), reasoned that the Winnebago had to be transported elsewhere because their contact with whites had debased and depleted the Indians: "I have no hesitation in expressing my opinion that the wretched remains of this people can only be saved by the humane and protecting policy of the government, by removing them."[121] In Dodge's logic removal is a form of protection: the Indians will be saved by being shifted. Others used a converse argument for removal: white settlers had to be protected from Indians. As the historian Mark Wyman notes, "The concept of removal gained strength in part because it drew Indian-haters and Indian-lovers into brief alliance: both decided that the Indians east of the Mississippi had to be moved to open lands in the West. Some whites wanted Indian lands; others saw it as the only way to save the tribes from annihilation."[122]

Given these two strands of argument, there were more treaties. After talks in Washington, D.C., in 1837 the Ho-Chunk lost all their land east of the Mississippi. Wyman notes that the Winnebago treaty of 1837 "dropped the government's treaty-making ethics to a low point: the tribe's negotiators were kept in Washington all winter and were finally assured they could remain another eight years on the ceded Wisconsin lands. With that promise, the Winnebago gave up all their remaining lands east of the Mississippi. When they returned home, however, they were informed they could stay only eight months."[123] Henry Merrill, a Wisconsin pioneer who witnessed the negotiations, notes in his memoirs that the interpreter had lied to the Indians, and "at length (the Ho-Chunk) yielded not to their judgements [sic] but to the pressure brought on them."[124] The government forced the Ho-Chunk to move to Turkey River, Iowa.

In his 1876 memoirs John T. DeLaRonde, a soldier employed by the infantry division of the U.S. Army, described his part in the Ho-Chunk removals of 1840 at Portage, Wisconsin. The soldiers invited the Indians to Portage, ostensibly "to get provisions; but instead of that, as soon as [the Indians] arrived, they were put into the guard-house, with ball and chain, which hurt the feelings of the Indians very much, as they had done no harm to the government."[125] Later, while carrying out his duties, DeLaRonde encountered "two old [Winnebago] women [who] came up, throwing themselves on their knees, crying and beseeching Captain Sumner to kill them; that they were old and would rather die, and be buried with their fathers, mothers and children, than be taken away; and that they were ready to receive their death blows. Captain Sumner had pity on them, and permitted them to stay where they were, and left three young Indians to hunt for them."[126] Further on, DeLaRonde describes how other Ho-Chunks asked for a chance to say good-bye to their ancestors before being removed. "They said they were going to bid good-bye to their fathers, mothers and children," DeLaRonde writes. "The captain directed me to go with them, and watch them; and we found them on their knees—kissing the ground and crying very loud—where their relations were buried."[127]

Although it may be tempting to imagine DeLaRonde and others engaged in removal as unfeeling thugs, DeLaRonde's descriptions of the removals is tinged with remorse and suggests the ways in which white soldiers were moved by Indians' displays of emotion and their connection to their homeland. Watching those who grieved to leave the land of their ancestors, DeLaRonde writes: "This touched the captain's feelings, and he exclaimed, 'Good God! What harm could those poor Indians do among the rocks!'"[128] Nonetheless, both captain and infantryman carried out the government's instructions.

The Trempealeau historian and physician Eben Pierce offered this account of Ho-Chunk removal in his 1917 history: "By the treaty of October 13, 1846, [the Ho-Chunk] agreed to cede the tract assigned to them in 1832 [in northeastern Iowa], and to accept in return a large tract north of the Minnesota and west of the Mississippi. The larger part of the tribe was removed to Long Prairie, in the central part of Minnesota, in 1848, and small bands were moved from time to time in the years immediately following."[129] Writing some years after DeLaRonde, Pierce uses language that underplays the racism as well as the force involved in carrying out the removals: the Ho-Chunk "agreed" and "accepted" the treaty. The unvigilant reader of 1917 (or the present, for that matter) might be forgiven if she imagined the Ho-Chunk "disappearance" from Trempealeau County as the unfortunate and simple result of bad treaty making. Pierce's language also plays down the active role played by settlers and soldiers of both white and mixed descent: he uses the passive voice to describe how the tribe "was removed" to Long Prairie and how "small bands were moved" by an unnamed hand.

Antoine Grignon was a man of French, Sioux, and Ho-Chunk descent who also played a role in the removals; he spent his final years in Trempealeau and is buried in a neglected cemetery outside town.[130] Born in 1828 at Prairie du Chien, Grignon was a former fur trader who worked as a soldier as well as an Indian trader among removed Indians. In his "Recollections," collected and edited by Pierce, Grignon describes his service to H. M. Rice during the Long Prairie removals in the 1850s.[131] Grignon presents a pathetic scene. The men ride a steamboat downriver from St. Paul to seek out "Indians camps near the river." Having spotted smoke, Grignon goes to locate the camps near Sugar Loaf, a high bluff just up and across the river from Trempealeau, near Winona, Minnesota. Grignon writes that, arriving at the Ho-Chunk settlement,

> I told the Indians my mission and they at once began breaking camp and loading their canoes. When they were ready, I accompanied them to Trempealeau where they remained all night. Mr. Rice, S. B. Lowry and David Olmstead who were working in the interests of the government in removing the Winnebago to the reservation, stayed all night with Mr. Reed [presumably this was James Reed], and next morning we all went to La Crosse, taking our band of Indians with us. A few miles above La Crosse we located another Indian camp on French Island and took them also with us to La Crosse. There the Indians were loaded on barges and into boats and taken by steamboat to St. Paul, whence they were carried overland by wagons to Long Prairie, Minnesota.[132]

Grignon's account portrays the Indians as docile victims who willingly submit to removal, and in this way the account undercuts the violence inherent in forcing people to give up one place—their home—for a place they have never seen and for which they have no association. Grignon's language, through Pierce, keeps both violence and remorse at bay, and in this way his words contribute to the current situation in which many residents remain entirely ignorant of the history of removal. That Indians were collected from French Island, for example, was lost on many of us who attended a rendezvous there in the summer of 2001. That Trempealeau was a way station in these removals is not part of the historical tours. That Indians were forcibly removed from Trempealeau—I didn't know that until I began this research. These chapters in local history have been all but forgotten among white residents. Indeed, in a truncated version of Grignon's recollections that Pierce published in *History of*

Trempealeau County, he deleted Grignon's account of the removals; they were not part of what was to be remembered.

But the memory of these removals remains among the Ho-Chunk. The journalist Susan Lampert Smith interviewed a number of Ho-Chunk men and women during Wisconsin's sesquicentennial in 1998. As she writes:

> Ho-Chunk Ken Funmaker Sr., 65, heard his grandfather talk of the day soldiers arrived in his village, which was on the Mississippi River, near present-day Trempealeau.
>
> "The soldiers rounded up the people and they burned everything," Funmaker said. "[My grandfather] was just a little guy. All they let him keep was a pair of (ice) skates."
>
> The tribe lost many of its sacred religious items in the round-ups; the name for one former village near La Crosse is "the place where the war bundles burned."[133]

The Ho-Chunk would be subject to three more removals. After Long Prairie they were moved again, this time to Blue Earth, Minnesota, in 1855. In 1863 the Ho-Chunk Nation hit another low point when Lincoln, in reaction to the Dakota uprising at New Ulm, ordered the tribe out of Minnesota. This new reservation was on the plains of South Dakota, an environment alien to people who had lived in woods. Some Ho-Chunks shifted to the Omaha reservation in Nebraska, where they were granted land or, in some cases, purchased it from the Omaha. Meanwhile, as Emma Blair notes in her 1911 account, "many of the tribe (more than 1000) had remained in Wisconsin, and in 1873 the government attempted to remove these people to Nebraska. Several hundred of them were sent thither, against their will; the removal was even more cruel than the previous ones, many dying on the way or after reaching their destination."[134] According to the Ho-Chunk Nation's website, today the memory of "elders being rounded up at gunpoint, loaded into boxcars and shipped to 'their reservation' in Nebraska" is part of Ho-Chunk oral tradition.[135]

Throughout the removals many Ho-Chunk nonetheless refused to leave their homeland for the poor lands offered by the government. Others who had been removed took desperate measures to get back home. As Smith notes, "Histories tell of Ho-Chunk carving canoes from cottonwood trees, and paddling down the Missouri, then back up the Mississippi, to get home to Wisconsin."[136] There those who returned—and others who had remained—faced the 1873 removal mentioned by Blair. As Smith notes: "In December 1873, U.S. soldiers surrounded Ho-Chunks gathered for a religious festival and herded them, at bayonet point, into railroad cars. They were left on the plains of Nebraska with little shelter or food. Another 240 died of starvation that winter, and, when the survivors returned to Wisconsin in the spring, they found their belongings stolen or destroyed."[137] Smith does not pinpoint the place of such roundups, but it is clear from Pierce's history that white settlers in Trempealeau County opposed the Ho-Chunks' return. Pierce writes: "A new movement was on foot to compel them to return to Nebraska, and by a display of military force, hundreds were again removed to that region in the winter of 1873–74. During the troubles attending the forced removal, no less than 56 Indians were arrested in Trempealeau County."[138] Pierce mutes the role of American settlers in opposing the Winnebagos' return: through "a display of military force, hundreds were . . . removed." Again, Pierce does not assign this force full bodily presence and agency in his account; instead, a movement simply "was on foot." Only forty years had passed by then, and the memory of both the violence and the regret may still have been palpable. In any case, white settlers who opposed the Ho-Chunks' presence were thwarted when the Indians persisted in their determination to return home—to a place only recently settled by Americans and Europeans. Pierce's romantic description of the Ho-Chunks' insistence on returning to Wisconsin emphasizes their relation to the land; it also echoes Andrew Jackson's notion that Indians have a particular attachment to the "graves of their fathers":[139]

> Taken to far away Nebraska, the people of the unfortunate race still longed for their native woods and streams, and their thoughts wandered over the old hunting grounds and berry fields of Wisconsin. In the pine woods were the graves of their dead, which made the soil more sacred in their minds, and there were the camping grounds where all of their festivities were held, and they hungered for the scenes and associations of the olden days.
>
> The homeward trail was soon thronged with the returning stragglers and within a year, half of the tribe were back. This time Fate was kinder to them, for in 1875 the government gave them the

homestead right, which enabled them to gain a home of their own by building houses and doing a certain amount of improving on their land.[140]

In this context the violence of removal and the Ho-Chunks' receipt of permission to return are presented as tricks of "Fate" rather than the result of governmental policies; in this way, Pierce draws parallels between the Ho-Chunks' efforts in the area and those of the white settlers and farmers of his day who also want to build houses and "improve" the land. White tolerance for the Ho-Chunk was commensurate, then, with Ho-Chunk willingness to assimilate to Euro-American cultural and agricultural practices.[141]

Ho-Chunks have lived and moved through Wisconsin for a long time. There has never been a Ho-Chunk reservation in Wisconsin, but there have long been Ho-Chunk people, despite the forces mustered to expel them. As Ken Funmaker told Smith, "That's how we are [—] that's why we act so stubborn. We didn't want to go away."[142] Despite widespread myths that Indian people are part of a colorful bygone era, indigenous peoples did not just disappear or vanish into the forest. As Anna Funmaker protests to the people, laws, and ideologies that would relegate the Ho-Chunk to the past: "We're not extinct. We're not disappeared. We're here!"[143] When so many have died, their names and land taken, that is not a small thing to say. And the memory of that violence, the sadness and meanness and regret that accompanies it, is something that shapes who we think we are, where we think we live.

12. What We Tell Ourselves

The following appeared in the *Winona Post* in August 2002:

> For the earliest inhabitants of present-day Fountain City [twenty miles upriver from Trempealeau], local Indian nations posed a true threat, but not because they had harbored any animosity for the white settlers. The Indian nations of the area were at war with each other, and as the small town grew, residents were often caught in the middle of the bloody battles between the Chippewas, Winnebagos and Sioux. Stories handed down for generations describe battles in which the very city itself was caught in the crossfire, leaving muzzle loader blasts in buildings and residents cowering under furniture as warring tribes attacked each other.
>
> By 1860, most Indian tribes [had] left the area, but they were quickly replaced by German and Swiss Settlers off steamboats from Galena, Illinois. In the rugged peaks and rolling valleys, these early immigrants saw their homeland, and they came in droves to make a new home.[144]

In this account the only conflicts are between Indian and Indian, while white settlers cower in fear. In this version of things the situation is resolved when Indians simply and conveniently depart, making way for European settlers.

13. Epiphany

After my dad died, I told my uncle Clyde that he'd have to be a kind of grandpa to my kids, seeing as he was Dad's closest brother. That made him tear up some. Clyde is now the oldest living Hovell, and we turn to him for points of family and local history. It was he who told me—or perhaps I finally paid attention to his telling me—the story that my dad had told me earlier: that their father and grandfather had worked on the road to Perrot State Park with teams of horses. So one July day in the summer of 2001 I walked across the road from Mom's to hear more.

"Tell me something about Grandpa Hovell's work on the park road," I said.

Clyde had been told I was researching Native American history. "What's that got to do with Indians?" he asked. When I told him I wanted to know about archaeological sites and local history, he told me that his dad—S.J., they always called him—was the first to drive his car around the park—a 1926 Buick touring car. (S.J. signed his name S. Hovell and was thus sometimes called "Shovel.") Clyde said that S.J. used to take equipment out to the park—and that people used to be able to drive their cows out there and let them graze. As far as he knew, there wasn't much more to tell.

Then I asked him what he knew about the platform mounds. I could see him smile a little. And then he said, "Harold Wilber told us about that. His dad and brother moved all that dirt up there with a Cat" when they built the water tower. This was not what Wilber told me later, but this version of things shows how a couple stories had become one: Harold Wilber opposed the project + somebody claimed to have dragged dirt up there in the 1930s = the Wilbers built the mounds themselves. I tried to tell Clyde about the 1884 surveys, the 1905 photos that clearly show the platform mounds: "But they don't look like that any more, do they?" We let the subject drop.

It's true: there are big holes in the northern mound where they mounted the water tower—and from where they pulled it out in 1991. But the town fathers had known about the mounds even back in 1938—the Milwaukee archaeologists had urged them to hold off their digging, to slow down. The village went ahead anyway: nothing could stand in the way of progress. After this disappointing exchange with my uncle, I headed to the Galesville Public Library in the flashy red car that my mom had bought after Dad died. As I was driving past the bean fields formerly tended by my dad and that now suffered from lack of rain, it dawned on me: even if the platform mounds had been completely busted up and dumped on by these men who were in charge of things in the 1930s, until then *they had been there*—until then they had survived. And for some reason I started bawling, mourning for the mounds, mourning for what we had let these guys do to them, for what we had let happen to ourselves. They had taken what power they had and tried to make the land into something they understood. What this meant for the land, what this meant for Indians, for mounds, for our own sense of connectedness to each other was violence, repression, forgetting.

◆

14. Excavation

Let me try to make sense of what happened by using an imaginative reconstruction. Some details come from my father's writing and some from the recollections of my father, my uncle Clyde, and Barney Stephan. Other details come from my own memories of my grandfather, and some come from half-remembered and overheard conversations.

Stanley pulled his pants on one leg at a time, like anybody else, tucked in his chambray shirt, and cinched the belt. Ruth had been up for an hour already. Kenny had a cold and woke up early crying, so Ruth had him in the high chair and was busy making coffee, which she had just bought from Stanley's last pay in these lean times. They always had a farmer's breakfast even though they lived in town: eggs, bacon or sausage, potatoes. Stanley sat down at the table to wait for it. Ruth called for the older boys and they came straggling in, dressed for school, and sat down. Ruth made Clyde go and wash his face at the basin; Bob had already done so, slicking his hair back with the comb he kept in his back pocket. After breakfast S.J. lit a cigarette on his way out the door and climbed into his car. (Clyde remembers it as a 1926 Buick touring car, my dad as a Model T Ford.)

S.J. took the road through town and along the river on his way to Perrot Park. For the past few years he had been working out there whenever they needed him, ever since he had helped to make the dirt road passable for cars. The Civilian Conservation Corps guys had come into town then to help work on it. S.J. himself had been the first one to drive his car around the park. Some of those CCC guys had stayed on. Like Floyd Johnson. That man could not drive truck for nothing. He crashed one truck up on the quarry road so Barney Stephan had to take over his job, and Barney rode around like they made him king. The CCC guys had stayed in tents out near where Perrot Post is; their horses slept in tents too. Both S.J. and his dad had worked out there, grading the road. Although S.J. was proud of his car, he was also proud of the way he handled horses. He'd learned everything from his father. It wasn't something everybody could do: you needed a good team, horses you knew. He remembered one time when they had been leveling the road around the rocks on the south side of the park. The horses were digging with wheeled scrapers,[145] and he couldn't use reins, only voice commands, because one horse had to be three feet higher than the other on the bank. They took a picture of how they did it.

Now all the talk was about Lock and Dam No. 6, and that brought men flocking into the area looking for work. You could only work thirty-two hours a week, and they paid you in cash, in an envelope. When he wasn't working there, S.J. worked at the park, where there was still plenty to do. Picnic sites to build, a road down to the bay. And S.J. was known as someone who could run machinery well, someone who could be trusted, so his name had come up as a guy who could fill in. Heck, everybody was hurting for money.

He had been working on leveling the land out by Trempealeau Bay. The place was full of mounds. They had already plowed some of it for picnic sites. Now the idea was just to level it off a little, make it so a car or a team of horses could get around the park without too much trouble. He climbed into the tractor and started her up. Up there on top of that machine he felt powerful and liked the way that—working by himself—he could move a lot of dirt around, the way the machine showed its muscle, at least when it was working right. Once, while they were working on the road, he found an arrowhead; he had given it to Bob, who kept it with his other treasures in a cigar box. When they first dug up the dirt around by Perrot Post, S.J. had seen a few things he imagined might be Indian bones. Floyd claimed to have dug up a mound and found a skull, but Stanley never saw nothing like that. Just little things. Anyway, if you run that machinery over it enough times, it's just going to get crushed and covered up. Ashes to ashes, dust to dust, he joked to himself, but of course none of these Indians had had a Christian burial.

S.J. surveyed his work, walking along the busted-up sod. You could hardly see where the mounds had been any more. He squatted in the dirt, rolled a cigarette, and, while he smoked it, looked across the bay to Trempealeau Mountain. From here it looked like a big green pyramid.

15. No Fools

First there was a canoe, then a bone, then some mounds.

The canoe was banked up on the ice in the middle of the river in the middle of winter. A lot of people have canoes, aluminum, fiberglass—but this was carved out of a single tree—a dugout. The park ranger who found it said it was really old—maybe it was Indian, from before white people ever came around here. Maybe they used it to run along the shore of the big old river, paddling back into the bays around Trempealeau Mountain or around where the refuge now stands. Harold Wilber told me that some archaeologists took some tests on it and said it was five hundred years old. Harold and others in town thought it would be a good idea to preserve it, make a glass case for it, have some signs put up saying what it was. "I would give my own money for such a thing," Harold declared.[146]

People in town got excited—they'd do it. As Harold saw it, school kids could use it to learn about the area; it was something everyone could be proud of.

But pretty soon a letter came from a woman across the river in Pickwick, Minnesota. It wasn't a five-hundred-year-old canoe, she said. It was a *five*-year-old canoe—something her husband had made just for fun and that had got away from him in the river.

Everyone was mad, Wilber recalled: "It made us look stupid." Harold said they went back to the archaeologists to ask how in the world they could make that kind of mistake. They told him, "Well, the tree was five hundred years old, but we can't say for sure when the canoe was made." That made Harold sick. "Now, Laurie," he asked, "How can archaeologists make a mistake like that?"

And then there was a bone. Harold's crew found it on a job site. It was sticking out of a bank. So they had to stop work, call in the archaeologists, let them have a look at it. "You always have to do that now," Harold said. "Sometimes it takes days. So they came down and had a look, and they said it's a dinosaur bone. A dinosaur bone—right around here! Everybody was pretty excited about that. Then the farmer who owned the land came over to have a look.

211

'That's no dinosaur bone,' he said. 'That's a horse. My dad probably buried it right there fifty years ago.'"

That was when everyone started hearing about the platform mounds. "Who's ever heard of platform mounds?" People knew about the Indian mounds out at the park; they were supposed to be burial mounds—turns out they are fake too, Harold said. "But I'd never heard of platform mounds." Some archaeologists came to a Lion's Club meeting and told the members about them. That they were supposed to be a thousand years old, built by some people down near St. Louis, and the archaeologists wanted to build steps up to Little Bluff so people could see them, put up some signs, put in a parking lot.

Well, this time the people in Trempealeau weren't going to be fooled.

16. My Meeting with Harold

As my mom says, Harold Wilber is a "shirttail relation" of mine; we share common great, great, grandparents, Mary Amanda Wilber and Thomas Hovel, the one who spelled his name with one "l," who came to the area from England in the 1860s. When I met Harold, he was one of the most successful men in the area—he ran several businesses, flew his own plane, and embodied the image of a successful man with deep roots in the town. He had gone to high school in

Trempealeau—before it became part of G-E-T—then joined his dad's limestone business and made a success of it, without even a college degree. The grand house he built on a bluff outside town overlooked the Mississippi and had a lawn like a golf course. (Seeing it, I could not help but think of the site the Middle Mississippians had chosen a mile away for their own view of the river.) People in town—some of them, anyway—had been ready to listen to him—or to respond to his authority, whether they understood the grounds of his recalcitrance about the mound project or not.

A number of those who supported the platform mound project mentioned Harold's name in disgust. The soft consonants had a way of rolling around in their mouths and getting stuck in there, like a too-thick peanut butter sandwich. An archaeologist and park worker had taken to calling Harold "Doctor Wilber" for the knowing attitude he adopted in discussions of the mounds. One person said with some relish, "Harold is not long for this world." That was the summer Harold was facing his second bout with cancer.

While on a research visit in the summer of 2001, I knew I had to talk with him but, as in other situations where I had to talk to the town muck-a-mucks, I found myself a bit nervous, as if I were still a little girl knocking on the big man's door, knowing that as a woman and an outsider I would be suspect. For even though we were distant relatives, I had never met him before—I was not sure I'd ever even seen him before. My sister Pam spoke of Harold's cancer and called his mother to ascertain his health. When Pam heard he was doing okay, she called Harold at his golf course to set up a meeting. He told her that I should come to the course any afternoon that week; somehow I didn't make it. On Sunday my mom happened to see Harold at a fiftieth anniversary party for mutual relatives, and he told her I should come the next day for lunch at the club. "Lunch is on me," he said.

Monday was my last day in town. I dutifully showed up the next noon, Mom in tow. After we'd taken a table, the cook, Irene—John Ebersold's sister, as it happens—told us that Harold had gone to Arcadia to play golf. "I'll put your lunch on his tab, though." We ate our sandwiches looking out at the manicured course on what used to be farmland—"*poor* farmland," my mother said. Harold had named the place Trempealeau Mountain Golf Course. (Indeed, sometimes folks referred to his course simply as "Trempealeau Mountain," disregarding the original entirely.) Lining the fairways were smooth grassy hemispheres that looked for all the world like well-tended burial mounds. The décor inside the clubhouse was plaid and neat. A drawing of Harold and his wife hung above the bar with these lines:

It's Just Beautiful! Doesn't it Make You Proud.
    Harold D. Wilber

We ate our sandwiches in the air-conditioned clubhouse; I was angry that he had wasted my time. Did he just forget? Was he afraid to see me? I decided that he thought he was just too important to have to remember his invitation to me. We paid for our own lunch.

I went on to other things that afternoon—another trip to the Galesville library, a stop-in to say good-bye to John and Lu, a visit to the offices of the *Galesville Republican*. At the office of the small weekly newspaper, I wanted to look up information on the mascot from the 1950s in the paper's archives. The editor made a special trip to remind me to "be very careful with the pages. They are very brittle." I didn't tell him that when I looked at eighteenth-century manuscripts at the British Library, the people there had not felt the need to make such admonitions.[147] Then, while walking in downtown Galesville—nearly abandoned in the heat of the July afternoon—I had a déjà vu feeling, as if I were seventeen again, and I remembered why I wanted to leave home in the first place. It was the smallness of it all. The limited ways of telling stories, the narrow way of imagining the world.

While I was out, Harold called my mom's house and said I should come to the clubhouse at 5:30. I got home at 5:15, got the message, and went right back out the door. At the course Harold was sitting at a table in the clubhouse waiting for me, while his wife ran the vacuum. He wore a Trempealeau Mountain Golf Course ball cap over his bald head. Chemotherapy had claimed all the hair on his body, and his face was shiny and soft looking, almost infantlike. He seemed to want me to sit beside him, but I sat across from him, facing him. We started, of course, with discussion of our mutual relatives, old Tom Hovel, what the nature of our relation was. Harold said that in the 1970s he had started studying his genealogy. "When I started researching the Wilber family tree, I ran into my mother before my father; I guess we're a little retarded."

I offered, by way of analogy, "My brother says we're related to the Hares two different ways."

"I guess you're a little retarded too," Harold said.

I gave him my spiel: that I was interested in people's attitudes toward Native American history, especially archaeology. "And whenever I talk to people about the platform mounds, your name comes up," I told him.

Harold described how his distrust of the mound project got started: the dugout canoe and the embarrassment it caused him and other village leaders. (Later, Phil Palzkill, the Perrot Park ranger, would tell me a different story about the canoe: that it was found and promoted not by archaeologists but by an interning park naturalist. For Harold, archaeologists, naturalists, park rangers, and the Department of Natural Resources (DNR) seemed all to be one and the same.) Then came the incident with the horse bone and the needless delays it caused his business. And then came the platform mounds. As Harold saw it, the idea of the platform mounds depended entirely on the word of one man, George Squier. Harold said that everybody considered this Squier "a weird duck." Even George Gale, who founded nearby Galesville, said Squier was a strange man, Harold claimed, adding, "Now I don't know if it's true or not." But, Harold said, it troubled him that all the evidence for the mounds comes from this one man. (It doesn't.) And it bothered him that the mounds, coincidentally enough, were all found on Squier's property. And that the platforms did not meet Harold's expectations of what mounds should be. "Why are there no artifacts in those mounds?"

I explained that platform mounds were not burial mounds, that they were like stages, and would not necessarily have anything inside. In any case, I noted, Squier had found some artifacts in the vicinity: shards of red paint pottery that suggest the relationship of the Mississippians at Cahokia to the platform mound builders in Trempealeau.

"You're going to take a piece of pottery this big—" he held up his fingers and figured a seedsize morsel "and tell me that's enough to prove it? I don't buy it, Laurie, I don't buy it. You see those mounds

out there?" he said, pointing to the pseudomounds constructed between fairways on his golf course. "What if I write something right
now that says these are Indian mounds? In a hundred years someone's going to find that and say, 'Yes, those are Indian mounds.' It's
the same thing."

I mentioned that Squier was not the first to describe the mounds,
that Theodore Lewis had surveyed the region in the 1880s and documented their existence then. Harold said he had looked into Lewis's
papers and that they actually cast doubt on the mounds. He said
that when he showed these papers to Jim Gallagher, head of the Mississippi Valley Archeology Center, he thought Jim was going to rip
them up. (What Harold may be referring to here is that Lewis's and
Squier's surveys differ somewhat from each other. Lewis was a trained
surveyor and Squier an amateur; indeed, Squier noted the difficulty
of taking exact measurements because of the changes "wrought by
the elements and the trampling of animals [cattle].")[148]

As Harold and I talked further, it seemed to me that he did not
understand the differences between and connections among platform, burial, and effigy mounds. (Indeed, I was just beginning to
learn about their characteristics and the archaeological discussions
about them.) Harold tended to speak in generic terms of "Indian
mounds." He said that the archaeologists had told him that there
were mounds similar to the Trempealeau platforms elsewhere in
Wisconsin, so he flew his plane to see them, "near Stoughton." Although he couldn't remember the name of the place, he probably
went to Aztalan to see the mounds there. "But those aren't anything
like our mounds," he said.

Aztalan State Park has both conical and platform mounds.
Earlier, when I had looked up photos of Aztalan on the park's website, the mounds it showcased were all effigy mounds, but documented Mississippian constructions are located there as well, including platform mounds and palisades. Showing my own ignorance at
the time, I told Harold, "Those *aren't* platforms. That's a different
kind of mound." In any case, it is possible that Harold had simply
seen what I had seen: effigy mounds. I went on: "To see something
like the platform mounds you have to go to Cahokia, and there you
will find the most significant archaeological site in the United States.

But even those don't look exactly like what's on Little Bluff. Many of Cahokia's mounds are quite built up; ours are low."

"Maybe it helps to think of it in this way," I continued. "Cahokia was like Rome; Trempealeau was a kind of outpost. The platform mounds in Trempealeau were built by some offshoot from the capital—a group connected to Cahokia who made their way up north but who didn't have the population or the resources of Cahokia. This was a different kind of place."

I wrote *Cahokia* on a slip of paper and asked him to look it up on the Internet. He put the paper in his wallet. But I sensed that for him the matter was largely closed. While he seemed to have some interest in local archaeology, his distrust for archaeologists was profound. He had a sense that the local folk knew the area in a way the scientists never could—that the scientists came in with their equipment and theories and book knowledge, but they nonetheless frequently did not see things in the way that people who lived there did. (This, of course, is true. The problem comes when one point of view closes itself off from the other.) Harold said that, for him, the archaeologists had really lost credibility with the dinosaur bones and canoe debacle—again, he was collapsing archaeologist, naturalist, park ranger—so that when MVAC came with this grant for the mounds, he was suspicious. The archaeologists had $150,000 to $200,000 to build this site, Harold said, and they just wanted to do it, without any questions. "Now, we're not educated people here, but you ask us to believe that without some kind of proof?" It was then that Harold put up $5,000 of his own money for the archaeologists to prove or disprove the authenticity of the mounds, he said. They didn't go for it, and as far as he was concerned, that was proof of their subterfuge.

I tried to explain that despite archaeology's use of scientific methods (which are themselves interpretive, strategic, contextualized), it's an interpretive science. None of it is built on hard facts because *there are no hard facts.* There is material evidence—bits of pottery, bones, artifacts, dirt that shows signs of having been moved. But these are not simply self-revealing; they have to be interpreted—they have to be read, in a sense. As for the platform mounds, there seems to be no indigenous record of these particular constructions, and no one who has a firsthand memory of them. "The best any archaeologist can do is put together a pretty good story," I told him. "It's more like making a court case than presenting the truth."

But Harold did not go for this academic argument. He likened the archaeologists' situation to that of salesmen. "If a vacuum salesman comes here and wants to sell me a vacuum, he has to show me that it works. He has to prove it." From Harold's point of view as one of the most successful businessmen the town has ever seen, the archaeologists had failed to make a good sales pitch. And he was suspicious about the way that the grant had been awarded to them. As he described it, they wrote their own grant and had the DNR support them—they didn't have to prove anything to anyone. He said that he had even called the Department of Transportation, which had awarded the grant, to ask: Can the archaeologists really proceed on so flimsy a basis?

As I began to see it, Harold's suspicion of this project was connected to his other dealings with archaeologists. He saw them as obstacles in the carrying out of his work. As someone who excavated land and moved lots of dirt and rock around, Harold had a lot of contact with archaeologists. If his men came across anything that looked like an artifact while they were excavating, Harold said he had to inform the state and suspend work till the find could be evaluated. For this reason, Harold told people, he had his work halted many times; he described how archaeologists came in to survey the area and sometimes to dig—slowly, slowly, a few centimeters at a time, cleaning with their hands and screens and brushes—while he had to wait. And most of the time they found nothing.

One time, he reported, a local man named Wagner found an arrowhead on the job site and Harold had to stop work for three days so the archaeologists could come in—for nothing.[149] Of course, archaeologists don't always find things by digging, as Harold himself suggested: "Couldn't an Indian boy have been riding on a horse and shot his arrow at a deer"—and have it land on the surface of the ground, an isolated artifact? But his question suggests that he imagined that archaeologists believe that wherever they find something on the surface, they expect to find something deeper. For Harold, the red tape that ties up *his* kind of digging is simply a way for archaeologists to do *their* kind of digging—a way for them to make a living, at his expense. He suspected their methods implicitly and described how one time, when he had to stop work so they could investigate, he hired two high school kids to watch them, just to make sure they weren't trying anything funny. "If they ever dig on Little Bluff, I'd do the same thing: hire a couple high school kids." But, of course, the point of the platform mound project was not to "dig." As ceremonial sites, the mounds weren't thought to be a repository for relics. They were artifacts in and of themselves. But the idea of archaeology as digging, as treasure seeking, was difficult for Harold—and many other residents, for that matter—to shake.

Harold maintained that the three terraces on Little Bluff were the result of another kind of digging. He held that instead of being constructions made by Middle Mississippians, the flat places on Little Bluff were made by horse and buggy in an effort to make the place accessible. The mounds, in effect, were created not by some long ago natives but by our grandfathers and great-uncles. For supporting evidence Harold referred to the Indian Mounds at Perrot Park, which, though long mistaken for authentic, were built by men he'd known in his lifetime. (Again, this is not strictly true; while some mounds were constructed from scratch by white workers, others were "enhanced" and rebuilt; there were originals there in the first place.) Once Harry Murray revealed that these mounds were not completely authentic, Harold took an active role in formalizing the debunking: "I made an eight-track tape of Harry Murray, and he admitted he made the Indian mounds. I sent it to [then Governor] Tommy Thompson, and the state took the signs down."

But, I persisted, even if those mounds are not strictly authentic, there *are* authentic mounds at the park. Harold was ready to acknowledge that—or, rather, he was ready to admit that there *were* mounds there, before. He described how there used to be mounds all around the shelter house and over by where the toilets now stand. But they're gone now. His parents had a farm just on the edge of the park, and he described how, when he and his brother took the cows past the shelter house and down to the river to water, his father insisted they take care not to go over the burial mounds. "But do you know that when they cleared land [to make a state campground] they just took them all out—they just bulldozed them! It makes me sick to think about it!"

In his discussion of the now destroyed burial mounds at the park, in his willingness to go look at mound sites in the region, Harold expressed a value for Native American earthworks. And, interestingly, his involvement in the platform mound project and acquaintance with Anna Funmaker enhanced this value. As he noted, "I never really thought much about burial mounds until Anna Funmaker asked: 'How would you like it if we dug up your ancestors?' And that really made an impression on me." With this change of perspective Indian mounds suddenly became for him something more than heaps of dirt; for Harold, they became analogous to the graves of loved ones, not to be disturbed.

Harold's knowledge of local archaeology centered on the low conical burial mounds, the destruction of which occurred over several decades, something he lamented. But despite this interest, he stuck to the two poles of general local understanding of native sites: Indian mounds and Trempealeau Mountain, his business's namesake. He didn't seem to know much about the effigy mounds now marked off and displayed at the park, even though they stand not fifty yards from where he claimed he once saw burial mounds. And his view of Trempealeau Mountain was restricted to simply seeing it as a sacred Indian site and not as the site of still other earthworks. When I told him that there were also effigy mounds on Trempealeau Mountain, he didn't believe me. I told him further: "There are twenty-two mounds out there."

"Laurie, I have been out there, and there are no twenty-two Indian mounds out there."

"They don't look like much now—they've all been desecrated," I went on. "I'll take you there. You'll see: each one has been dug into."

"By who?"

"People out for some Sunday treasure seeking."

"I don't believe that, Laurie. Why would people dig into those and not into other mounds? Why would they go across the bay just to do that?"

But those who had dug into the mounds hadn't confined their digging to the mountain. "They dug them up on land too," I said.

"I don't believe it. People have been going out there for a long time, and I've never heard anything about there being mounds out there."

I knew how he felt, having just seen them myself for the first time. "I didn't know there were any mounds there until I knew what to look for." I knew how that must sound to him—that because I wanted to find these mounds, I did. For him, that was no kind of proof.

Repeating something John had told me, I pushed a different vision of the landscape, saying: "There are mounds all over the place here—there are probably burial mounds on every one of those bluffs out there," I said, gesturing to the tree-covered bluffs in the distance. I was trying to express something of my own changing view of the land—how I was beginning to see it as a place full of burials and mounds, a place that has a longer history than that of white settlement. But Harold asserted the standard view of the place as a beautiful little village whose mysteries had all been revealed: "Now I don't believe that either, Laurie. Why would people put bodies on top of bluffs?" And then he took up what I found to be a troubling line of argument: "If you're my wife and you die, am I going to carry you to the top of a mountain to bury you? No! I'll put you down in the valley. And that's where we do find burials."

"But you wouldn't put just anyone up on a bluff," I protested. "It would be someone important. Just like at Nicholls Mound, the people who were buried in there probably had some kind of status. Not everybody got that kind of treatment."

But I saw that what was getting in his way was the assumption that every culture would act like his; he could not fathom that people construe and imagine the world in radically different ways. And he had never really had to fathom that. He had never lived outside the area but had thrived by staying in it, by working within the worldview of that place. On the other hand, I had left that place as soon as I could—escaped it, as I saw it—traveling to India, Tibet, Europe, China, anywhere, anywhere, anywhere.

And so I told him: "I've traveled a lot in India and among Tibetans. And one of the things I found out is that what I think is right and natural isn't really so—that it's possible for different cultures to view the world in really different ways." I suggested that just because our culture associates the highest with the best, we can't expect that all people construe things the same way. This line of argument seemed not to impress him, for the issue of height was important for his sense of the inauthenticity of the platform mounds too. As Harold said, "If they [platform mound builders] were sun worshippers [as archaeologists think], why didn't they build on the highest spot?" This had been a source of complaint for others who opposed the project. I was told that, standing outside the village hall after one town meeting about the mounds, a Ho-Chunk woman was overheard to opine, "We wouldn't build a platform mound up there," gesturing to Little Bluff. "We'd put it up there," she said, pointing to First Peak, a higher, more dramatic outcropping.

Harold felt confident in his position, supported (as he saw it) by Indians in the area. I asked him about his contacts with Anna Funmaker; he said that he had called her to ask her opinion and that she had said the mounds should not be dug. (Funmaker, you may recall, said she first heard of the mounds from an anonymous male caller.) What Harold understood from Funmaker's declarations was that the mounds were fake. And for him, that settled the question.

Despite Harold's view of things, Funmaker claims not to have disputed the *authenticity* of the mounds, as I noted earlier. Instead, she said that her resistance to the mound project came out of a general distrust of archaeologists and the wish not to have native sites disturbed. For Harold, however, the result of her position—Don't dig—intersected nicely with his own interests and the interests of other town fathers: there should be no project. Archaeologists: Go home.

When we first started to talk, Harold had made it clear: "I don't believe in the sites." Letting him know my position, I said, "I do." As the hourlong interview came to a close, however, Harold rethought his earlier position and said something I hadn't heard him say before: "I don't know if they're real or not real." I reminded him that other people perceived him as someone who denied the authenticity of the platform mounds—as someone who led the charge against the project. He said he really just wanted to ask questions. Harold noted that he had kept files on the platform mound issue so that if it ever were to come up again—even after he's gone—his kids will be able to "ask the questions." Given the kind of dichotomous thinking that pits fact against interpretation, insider against outsider, real against fake, I thought that those questions would probably just look like "No. Stop. Stay out. This is our land."

When the interview was over, we shook hands—but not in the conventional way of men clinching a business contract. Instead, he clasped the hand I offered, enclosing it in both his own. We agreed to disagree. We were relatives, after all.

Only later did I give a name to what I think I saw in Harold, what I think was at the heart of the platform mound opposition, what was at the bottom of many white relations with native people; driving away, I was struck by the benign face of violence. Harold, a hand-clasping, well-spoken, caring man had used his position and energy to stop the preservation project. He was using his considerable means to insist on only a certain kind of remembering—to insist that he lived in a certain kind of place. White settlers had been the ones who carried out the Indian removals; they were also the ones who did nothing while Indians were loaded up and shipped out; they were the ones who resisted the Ho-Chunks' return. Well-meaning people doing their jobs had destroyed mound after mound in the area as they farmed, constructed the park, built roads, made homes, remaking the place in their own image. Town fathers had erected their water tower despite what they had been told about the site's archaeological value. Friends and neighbors had banded together to oppose what they saw as the intrusion of outsiders, outsiders who might bring in tourists and travelers—more outsiders and settlers who had no history in the place, no connection at all to the story that residents had weaved together about the town, about family, about the way things are done. It was all they knew how to do.

I had told Harold that I wouldn't be able to *prove* the existence of the mounds, but I might be able to put together a decent story. He said he'd like to hear it when I do. Harold: Here it is.

Part IV
Backfill

was not the usual practice in the area, and it went against the belief that viewing the body helps one deal with grief. So we didn't have his body laid out in a coffin. At his wake we had a photo of him playing the bass guitar and singing, along with a wooden toy he had made for a grandchild, the orange slices of candy I remember him eating, and some photos of him at different stages of life. At his funeral my brother somehow summoned the courage to read a poem my dad had written called "Small Town Boy," in which my father recounted games and errands from boyhood—a wooden gun, Pom-Pom Pullaway—as well as his movement from "horse-drawn to Discovery," and his disbelief at finding himself sitting "upon a heap of sixty years and two." His jazz band played at the funeral—first a somber version of "How Great Thou Art" and then, tentatively at first, an all-out New Orleans Dixieland version of the song. "A celebration of his life," we said.

There is a headstone for my dad at Evergreen Cemetery out on the prairie. There also lie the bodies of his parents, aunts, and uncles, Jonny, and even old Thomas Hovel. We used to visit this place on Memorial Day, and as kids we put our subtraction skills to use counting up the years lived by a relative. We always stepped carefully around the new graves.

John Ebersold is fond of saying, "I wonder what your dad would have said about the platform mounds project." I always brushed John's words off, in part because I knew what Dad said the first time I mentioned them: "If there was anything up there, we would've known about it." But I have to think now that he might have listened, might have been more reasonable than some of his peers and relatives. (There is evidence to support this: My dad was not a churchgoer, though he partook of a generalized Christianity during rites of passage. Nonetheless, he came to accept my interest in Tibet and Buddhism; indeed, he began to admire what he saw of the gentle and entirely reasonable Dalai Lama presented on *60 Minutes.* Dad went so far as to claim the Tibetan lama as "the head of our church"—a "church" devoted to kindness and compassion.) Dad might not have liked to change his old memories of his hometown, he might not have liked to give up control of that piece of land, but

I've got to think he would be able to put the evidence together and come to a fair conclusion. I've got to think that he could have put the story together too.

After my dad died we had to decide what to do with the farm. My mom could rent it out to one of the big seed-corn operations in the area; we could let Pam's husband, Steve, work it; we could have him rent it; we could sell it to him. We siblings wanted to settle the question for the next growing season and assure my mother some income, but it was really too soon after Dad's death to make such decisions, and my brother-in-law could not help sometimes being cast in the role of interloper, someone who wanted to get his hands on the land. Everyone agreed, in any case, that the woods—an old oak grove—should remain untouched, that the trees and brambles should be left alone, that that acreage should not turn into housing developments or a golf course or some such. Ours were not environmental reasons, exactly. Too many memories were tied up in the woods: the games we played out there as kids, the time the children set a corner of that area on fire, the horses that used to graze out there, the deer hunting, the cross-country skiing we'd done on homemade paths, the many walks. I recall too one Christmas when I was home from college; a flock of geese settled in a field, and for some reason we all trooped out to see them, making our way through the woods. The others drove out there in trucks and cars, but I wanted to walk there and back. My dad couldn't understand that desire to make my own way in the cold, and I didn't try to hide my irritation when he tried to coax me into the cab of the truck.

The immediate family finally agreed to sell the land gradually to my brother-in-law; this would assure Mom a steady and small income for a decade. This would assure that the land would stay in the family. We drew an imaginary border around my mother's house and yard, the woods: this would remain a kind of safe haven, in her possession. What will happen to it in the future, however, no one can say.

Growing up, I had always thought my parents' farmhouse was huge. But compared to the century-old Victorian that T.S. and I make payments on, it is quite small. I don't understand how my brother ever lived in a tiny eight-by-eight bedroom; I don't see how two families could have shared the house when my parents first married. Somehow, though, our extended family still crowds in there for potlucks and Christmases, twenty or so of us crammed in together with food and kids and beer and cards and often the TV blaring too.

◆

3. Education

Six years after the archaeology center's preservation project died, and just as I was beginning to study the mounds, John told me that Rollie Rodell was again involved in a plan to try to buy the land on which the platform mounds stand. I had exchanged e-mails with Rollie some months before, so I wrote to ask him what he knew. He replied that he was trying to get the Archaeological Conservancy interested in the mounds; this national nonprofit organization buys land to preserve significant archaeological sites. I wrote back excitedly and let Rollie know that my sister Pam belongs to the church that owns the land on which the mounds stand—Mount Calvary Lutheran Church—and that she would be a good contact. He replied in some anxiety, asking me to keep the possibility quiet: "Given the reaction last time we proposed our mound preservation project my fear is that if the word spreads that some outside party is interested in purchasing the mound the reasons may become misconstrued, which could lead to a negative reaction by some members of the community."[1] Instead, Rodell hoped for the chance to explain the site's cultural and archaeological significance to the Archaeological Conservancy; only after the conservancy was convinced of its importance would the church be approached about selling it.

Although I was sworn to secrecy, I began a clandestine project to inform my sister about the platform mounds. The first time I went into detail about the mounds and my project to her, it was February and snowing, and she told me about a "squaw" buried somewhere in the valley where she lives. I told her that word is derogatory. By summer, when I was in town doing interviews and research on the platform mounds, my other sister, Debbie, was considering a lesson for her third-graders on local history that would include Nicholls Mound, the effigy mounds at the park, and the platform mounds. I volunteered to take my sisters, mother, and a vanload of our kids on an archaeological tour of the area. The irony of the former resident taking the local folks on a tour of their own place was not lost on me. In the church parking lot I showed them Lewis's and Squier's maps of the platform mounds; we hiked out to Nicholls Mound; we drove out to the park to see its displays about the 1928 excavation of Nicholls Mound. I swept my arm and pointed out the land around the shelter house; it was once full of conical mounds, I told them. Indeed, a picnic table stood on an unmarked mound below the shelter house, and we remembered picnics out here with Grandma Hovell when we were kids. We followed a path to take in the neatly groomed effigy mounds of deer and wolf; although we had been to the park many times, none of us had ever seen them before that summer—none of us had ever *heard* of them till that summer. But looking at them together then, we had little to say. What were they for? How were we supposed to feel about them? When Pam cheerfully pointed out the place near the shelter house where we used to play softball, I blurted out, "Yeah, there used to be lots of burial mounds there too."

The place to me was full of signs of a different past, but given the silence surrounding our tour, I began to doubt myself: Why *should* I care? Why do I think this stuff matters—just so I can maintain my distance from my family, from their way of seeing things, their worldview? Do I complain about their detachment from their place—the local desire to conquer and tame it—so I can simply reclaim the place for myself, transforming it to conform to my own vision?

Since my dad died, my mom is always ready to have a good time: going out to eat, out to happy hour with her male companion (my dad's sister's widower), going on trips, having a glass of wine and playing cards. She's been to the United Kingdom twice, Arizona twice, Caribbean cruises thrice, Alaska once, and to Ohio many times. Unlike my dad, who hunkered down in his later days, my mom moves lightly, without attachment or distress about changing roles and places. And, unlike my father and me, she doesn't brood or analyze.

We were going to the Ho-Chunk casino—my sisters, mother, my husband, and I—when my mom repeated something a friend had told her. He said he had gone to the casino, but "the Indians were on the warpath."

"What?" Pam asked.

"You know, they were having an uprising, and he lost his money," she said, laughing. She was repeating a story, something that was simply to be told—not analyzed or reflected on. There was no intention to hurt in her racist remarks, only tiresome habit. My mother is happy without being overly reflective, cheerful if not urbane. She is eager to be part of anything that is happening. When I asked her what she knew about George Gale, she made some calls to locate his gravestone, drove over, and shot some photographs for me. She came along to see the band Indigenous and a Ho-Chunk powwow, sat through a long video about Cahokia with me, and despite a larger indifference about Native American archaeology and history, never questioned my interests but instead clipped whatever news she read about Indian history and life and sent it to me. And one time, when members of a local amateur archaeological group showed their collections in a mall (which is, coincidentally, built over an Oneota village site), she stopped to look things over, she told me proudly.

In the summer of 2001, when I went to the public library to study the history of the Indian mascot issue in Galesville, Pam wanted to go with me. She proved to be a careful reader of images, tracing the changes in the Indian figure from the romantic chief of 1914 to the cartoon Indian of the 1950s to the headdressed warrior of today. And as she studied, the ubiquitous images of Redmen seemed to change for her—they were no longer a natural part of the landscape. "I can't believe how ridiculous some of these symbols are," she said. "It's really shocking once you start to look at them." As she looked, the images emerged as a kind of strange self-description, part of a weird phenomenon by which the mostly white folks of the town imagined themselves as Redmen, as indigenous.

Debbie teaches third grade in Trempealeau, and one of her units is about local history. She and her students had done the rounds of the old historic buildings in town, but she wanted something more. Initially, Debbie was reluctant to take on the platform mounds, given the controversy about them, but she soon developed units on all the mounds in the area, inviting local people—John, Tom Hunter, Phil Palzkill—in to speak about these places.

And people in my family opened up to different versions of history and their place in still other ways, as suggested by what happened when I returned from talking to Harold Wilber. It was my last night in town, and as usually happens when we visit, the whole extended family of twenty or so people collected in my mother's house for supper. The men and I were drinking cans of La Crosse brand beer; the other women drank sweet wine out of a box. Together with their two cousins my boys had devised a complex scenario with multiple characters and were playing it in my mom's room. So everybody was gathered at my mom's house when I returned from talking with Harold. Pam had helped me set that meeting up; my mom had been with me when I went to meet him and he wasn't there; I had complained bitterly to Debbie about his no-show; I had half-jokingly asked Bob to go with me for the interview. And now they wanted to know what he said. I told them:

He did not claim that he or his dad or brother's had built the mounds, as Clyde had said.

He deeply distrusted the archaeologists.

He didn't understand the differences among mounds—didn't realize that all mounds were not burials—and I went over the differences for them as well.

And Harold had spoken of mounds he remembered as a kid living near the park. They are all gone now. It's true, I told my family: The burial mounds at the park had been destroyed as recently as a generation ago, dug up during the road building of the 1920s and 1930s, bulldozed to make the campground, cleared to make a parking lot. This last bit horrified all of us as we sat around my mom's table. Our grandfather and great grandfather had worked on that road; this was done by guys we knew. The discussion of local archaeology continued while we ate supper. T.S., the boys, and I would return to Ohio the next day, and they would go back to work and their usual lives.

◇

4. Journeys

Now that Dad was gone I could let myself remember what had happened nearly ten years earlier, when T.S. and I had been visiting my family. We had come out for a wedding reception in our honor; the festivities were over, and we were about to return to Ohio. In the dirt driveway we said good-bye to my mom and dad, an event that was always tearful for my dad. We had driven about eight miles down the road when I remembered that I'd forgotten something—a library book, maybe, a pair of hiking boots. So we turned around and went back.

When my dad saw us, he was surprised, for in his mind's eye he had been following us, he said, and had already imagined our Jeep

Cherokee as it passed out of Trempealeau County and across the Black River.

Ever since I was a teenager, much of my effort has gone into fleeing the area I grew up in. I chose my college because it had a study-abroad program in India, and I immediately prepared to go. Just as I was about to leave for India the first time, however, I had a burning desire to get home. I was doing an India studies orientation program in Northfield, Minnesota, 120 miles away. I wouldn't ask for someone to pick me up from the bus stop or drive up to get me; I'd get home alone, without telling anyone I was coming. I got a bus as far as Winona; from there I decided to hitchhike for the first time. It was a warm spring night; two guys in a pickup stopped for me just over the bridge that crosses the Mississippi, on the Wisconsin side. They took me as far as the highway above my parents' farm; from there I didn't follow the roads but instead made a beeline across the fields. The last leg took me right through the woods; I ended up walking through the old pasture, between the old chicken coop and milk house (both now pressed into other uses) and right up to the back door. It was a Friday night; my mother was at work, and my dad had pulled some rough kind of supper together: beans, probably, a hunk of sausage and bread. He was sitting at the kitchen table. It was early evening and he'd left the lights off. He had seen me come through the barnyard as he sat with his supper and couldn't believe his eyes, he said. We hugged, he turned on the lights, and I found some supper too. We ate together.

5. Powwow

My almost-four-year-old son, Jack, and I returned to Wisconsin in August 2001 for research and a Ho-Chunk powwow, and I borrowed Pam's Lumina for the fifty-mile back-road ride to the powwow grounds in Black River Falls. While a number of relatives had expressed an interest in going to the powwow, only Jack and I made the trip that first day. The road we took to Black River Falls is County C; it took us through towns like Hegg, with its few houses and a grain elevator, and Franklin, a deserted farm town. Within the space of a few miles we passed three Lutheran churches, the result of congregational disagreements that could not be mended even among close neighbors, even among people who assert that Jesus Christ is their lord and savior. Along the way I listened to the audio version of Sarah Vowell's "Trail of Tears" (in *Take the Cannolli,* 2000), the autobiographical tale of a journey that retraces the Cherokee Trail of Tears. Part Cherokee, part Norwegian, Vowell rails against the policies of Andrew Jackson and the high-minded rhetoric that removed thousands of Cherokee, Choctaw, Chickasaw, Creek, and Seminole to Oklahoma and asserted the rights of white Americans to take the land. At the time it did not occur to me that the county through which I was driving—Jackson County—was named for President Andrew, even as my borrowed tires lapped along the blacktop, passing the road to Squaw Creek on the way.

Having never been to a powwow before, I was not sure how to act, how we'd be received. Jack and I passed the casino at high noon and the lot was full. Farther down the road other cars were collected, parked on the grass and along the gravel roads of the powwow grounds. Some attendants waved us in—there was no admission fee—and as soon as we were out of the car, we could hear the announcer, calling roll for the different drum and singing groups that would play all weekend. Thunder Bay, Spirit Island, Lake Delton, Milwaukee Bucks. Each call was answered with a drumbeat. Jack and I wandered among the vendors' stands that surrounded the arena. We saw girls in jingle dresses, kids in feathers, and men in elaborate feather bustles and headdresses standing next to minivans, chatting with nondancers in T-shirts.

"Mom, I have to get ready," Jack said.

"For what?"

"I need my costume. I'm going to dance!" he exclaimed, pulling me toward some kidsize outfits in one vendor's tent. Jack settled for a green apple sucker, we found a place in the concrete bleachers, and before we knew what was happening, a singing group was called, the drums and singing started up, and the Grand Entry had begun. It is not unlike the procession of athletes during the opening ceremonies for the Olympics. A young singer held his throat, seeking the right quality of voice. The Veterans of Foreign Wars led the procession with flags of the Ho-Chunk, the Ojibwa, the United States. And then came the dancers, stepping one by one into the arena in all their finery, and it was more than we could take in: the men in the traditional category first, feathers and leather and faces painted; then the grass dancing men in fringes of white or yellow yarn. The fancy dancers in bright colors, streamers and feathers. The traditional dancers, their heads like birds, chickens, perhaps, or pheasants, their heads jutting, alert to the movement of an insect. Then the women came in, dancing more demurely: shawl dancers, women in jingle dresses ringing loud and Ho-Chunk appliquéd dresses, the women with a single feather standing erect behind their head. The categories repeated for teen dancers, child dancers, and "tiny tots." The arena was a spiral of dancers turning in on itself. Although I attended to a single dancer for brief moments, there was not a place to look that was not whirling with color. The effect of the sound and sight is more than the still camera can capture, though I snapped away anyway, noting that some native people were taking photos too. The people in the stands—native folks, mostly—moved to the beat, standing up from their collapsible camp chairs. This was not my place, I knew, but I was reminded of places I had been, dances I had seen among Tibetans in India and in Tibet. And it struck me how very long it took me to get to this place so near my home, how strange it was that I had to go to Tibet before I could come to Black River Falls, how weird it was that the powwow is, for many white people, a million miles away from the casino down the road.

4.1. Grand Entry, Ho-Chunk Powwow, Black River Falls, September 1, 2001. Photo by author.

As far away as it was psychically from many of us, however, the powwow is not in the past. The announcer spoke into a microphone. The drums were all miked. The costumes were leather and calico and polyester, and briefly described in textiles a history of contact. Dancers chewed gum while they worked out their steps. Cell phones beeped and buzzed. Several dancers had crosses beaded on their clothes; one had a Nike swoosh painted on his hip. The drummers wore FUBU and shorts and sneakers and baseball caps. At this dry powwow we ate Indian tacos and drank Pepsi. (However, I saw one woman, apparently white, carrying a dachshund in a frontpack designed just for him and a bottle of Miller in her cool cup.) In the whirl of dancers I tried to imagine what it must feel like for the native people gathered there. As Sherman Alexie writes in "Powwow":

> today, nothing has died, nothing
> changed beyond recognition
>
> dancers still move in circles
> old women are wrapped in shawls
> children can be bilingual: yes and no[2]

They must have been thinking: this is ours; this, at least, is ours. And I knew that none of it, none of it, was meant for me.

When Jack I walked around the outer circle of the powwow ground looking for Gus Vogel, who'd said he'd meet me, I saw a young Ho-Chunk man with a Wahoo cap. Back in Oberlin I had been involved in discussions with Larry Dolan, owner of the Cleveland Indians, about getting rid of Wahoo. So I had to know what this young Indian guy thought of the buck-toothed, hook-nosed image. We tracked him down and I asked, "You like Wahoo?" He showed me his forearm; he had a tattoo there of Wahoo with the words *Cleveland Indian*—singular. "That's my name," he said. "Cleveland."

"Oh, so *you're* the Cleveland Indian," I said, laughing.

"That's my brother over there," he replied, pointing. Out here, six hundred miles from Cleveland, where Wahoo was not as ubiquitous as air, the grinning mascot didn't look the same. Cleveland had taken the image back, in a way, changing its context.

I looked for a friendly person to explain the powwow to me. A young man in a tank top behind me told me how the competition works. The announcer calls the drum/singing group—they have to be ready to play—and then he calls the category of dancers. Dancers have to be ready; usually, people will dance in competition twice a day, and there's judging going on all through that. Then there are the intertribal dances, the grand entries. Winners are announced at the end. On the first day of the powwow, he said, people hold back, dance conservatively. "Wait till the last day," more than one person told me.

We stayed for three hours. Jack was amazingly content, sucking his thumb and watching, climbing on the concrete bleachers. In our own appropriation of Native American traditions, Jack picked out a dreamcatcher for himself ("made by an Iroquois woman") so he wouldn't have to have a recurring dream about a brown snowball any more. On the way out I spotted the man I had spoken to at the French Island rendezvous, the one who had told me he didn't think much of it. His long hair was done in braids, and he was wearing cutoffs. I introduced myself, reminding him of where we had met. His name is Dale Littlejohn, he said, welcoming me, smiling, shaking my hand.

Driving out of the powwow on County Road C, past the casino, I began to imagine that there are two worlds going on in the same place—and they don't meet up much. The one world where everyone understands and celebrates the powwow and how it's done and who's who and what it means. And then there's the other part—the white world that names things Squaw Valley, that sees nothing wrong with Indian mascots, that can get only as far as the casino, and can never imagine itself at the powwow, can never think that it would have anything to learn from a powwow—that it might learn something from being *uncomfortable* at a powwow.

On the second day there was a ceremony for a little girl that allowed her to wear the eagle feather. The tribal leader called on the spirits and the community to protect her. Coupled with this was a ritual giveaway in which women distributed all manner of goods: blankets, pillows, T-shirts, candy, cigarettes, dried fruit. The family's gift to the community, in effect, ensured its support. Without ever seeming to look at my sister Debbie and me, the women avoided putting anything into our hands. It's possible that we were not even there.

Later, when I tried to conjure up the songs we had heard there, I first tripped over that terrible tomahawk chop chant sung at Atlanta Braves games and used to taunt anti-Wahoo protesters. The racism I grew up with and live in and live out is a layer in my consciousness.

On the third and last day of the powwow I watched the face of a man in purple in the traditional dance category for a time before I realized that I was looking at Dale Littlejohn. His cutoff jeans were gone, and he was in full regalia, full feather bustle, purple satin shirt, and he was dancing, dancing.

Later that night I played a cassette of the music we had heard, and Jack and I tried out the standard dance step—two steps with the right foot, "one harsh, one soft, on Mother Earth."[3] My mother danced with us, going round and round her living room.

More Mounds

In October 2001 T.S. and I, along with our sons, Liam and Jack, traveled to southern Ohio to see the famous Ohio mounds—the Hopewell mounds at Mound City, the enormous Seip Mound near Chillicothe, and the Great Serpent Mound, a magnificent Fort Ancient sculpture near the Ohio River in Peebles. My idea was to get a break from the Trempealeau research, but we kept running into familiar names: F. W. Putnam, whose work beginning in 1886 helped save Serpent Mound; another Squier, Ephraim, a journalist from Chillicothe, who, together with Edwin Davis, had in the midnineteenth century surveyed, mapped, and helped save a good number of mounds; the names Cahokia, Adena, Hopewell. When we got home, there was another familiar name on the message machine; my mom had called to say that Harold Wilber had died. While we were away, I had been thinking of a question I wanted to pose to him: Given that there was plenty of evidence that the mounds were authentic, what *really* made you oppose the platform mound project so strongly? Why did killing the project matter so much to you? And I still wanted to understand why he thought he could argue with the archaeologists about their own field of expertise. What if they had argued with him about quarries and limestone, golf courses, and business management? I recalled an interviewee's saying the summer before, "Harold's not long for this world," and indeed, he wasn't, dead of cancer at fifty-six. I thought of my dad, another youngish death in the Hovell line, and so many farmers and working people who had died of cancer, poisoned perhaps by exposure to the fertilizers and chemicals they put on the fields.

Later that same night my sister Pam called, and she was nearly giddy. Rollie Rodell had contacted the pastor of Mount Calvary Lutheran Church. The pastor had told her that the archaeologists had a million dollars, and they wanted to survey the land, ascertain property lines, and buy the land on which the mounds stand. She repeated to me what she had told her pastor: "It's a gift from God." As its treasurer, she knew the church wanted to build onto the Sunday school but had no resources. "A gift from God—that's just what I thought," the pastor had told her cheerfully. Knowing my interest in the mounds, she told me that if anyone put up opposition, she'd "make a lot of noise." Together we went through the possible disputes to authenticity, and I offered her evidence: the independent surveys from 1884, photos from 1905, and the work that the Mississippi Valley Archaeology Center had done in the 1990s. Anyway, she said, if the archaeologists want to buy the land, you have to assume they know what they are doing. And the project had the advantage of not requiring any money from the village; indeed, even if parishioners (including other members of my family) didn't want to believe the mounds were authentic, how could they oppose someone who wants to pay good money for this otherwise unusable land?

The site's inclusion on the Wisconsin list in the National Register of Historic Places does little to protect the mounds; although private owners are encouraged to preserve such places, nothing binds them to do so. Thus, if the site were ever sold, new owners could do as they please with the place. With the Archaeological Conservancy's interest, however, the mounds might be purchased by outsiders with archaeological and historical concerns at heart, by people who aimed to preserve them "forever and ever," as one spokesman said. The town fathers could believe what they wanted to believe, but my sister was ready to argue that the mounds were real, that they should be preserved, and that the conservancy should be allowed to buy them. Despite all the people, then, who had busted up the mounds—men who had built a water tower on them, driven over them, proposed to drill into them, and the people who questioned their very existence—the issue of the mounds would be revived yet again.

When Paul Gardner of the Archaeological Conservancy and Rollie Rodell of the Mississippi Valley Archaeology Center met with the church council on December 11, 2001, the council members were generally well disposed toward the project. They wanted to know whether the mounds would become part of a tourist site, if the congregation would have to worry about litter or parking for tourists. The archaeologists assured them that if parishioners preferred not to have people visit the site, they could write that into the contract. Another council member asked questions about the mounds' authenticity. He got this answer: The single auger from 1991 revealing mussel shells and fill dirt confirmed that the mounds were not a geological feature but had been built by human hands. This seemed to satisfy the questioner. Aware of the controversy that surrounded the last project, one person asked about the naysayers in the church and community who would grumble about the mounds' being fake. "Let them think you're putting something over on us," Gardner said. "Let them think you're getting a great deal." People laughed about that. My sister felt it right that the archaeologists should get the mounds—they would be owned by someone who knew what they were and who wanted to protect them. Shielded by the steep bank leading to them and sheltered by tall trees and brush, the mounds could remain as they were, though under different ownership.

◆

7. More Views

A few months after the Archaeological Conservancy approached the church and as I was researching the mounds, I asked Pam who now owned the land on which the access road was built. She didn't know but said she'd ask Clyde. "No, don't," I said, aware of his resistance to the mounds. "I'll ask John," I told her. But like me, once Pam gets an idea and wants to know something, she seeks out her answer. She went to Clyde. Again, when he heard her talk of the "platform mounds," he set his mouth and repeated the old line: "Harold Wilber built those with his brother."

Pam said quietly to her elder: "He did not." Perhaps Clyde was stunned by the blunt reply; the matter dropped. But she asked me later: "Why didn't Harold Wilber want to believe in the mounds? Why doesn't Clyde?"

"I'm still trying to figure that out," I said. "Something about people in power. Something about what you want to think about the place you live in, the place you thought you knew. If you have an idea about the place you live and who you are, and someone comes along with a new idea, one response is to hunker down, dig in your heels, close your mind."

In grappling with the mound controversy, Pam and I were able to catch glimpses of a different sense of where we came from. This new consciousness was not the right one, certainly, nor was our sense of things identical. Nonetheless, each of us began to develop a sense of place in which the town fathers were not the heroes of the story—a sense of place in which we, for moments at least, could see ourselves as part of a long line of transient dwellers on this piece of earth.

◇

8. Preservation

When I first heard that the Archaeological Conservancy might buy the land, I was excited. But as I thought more about it, what did it mean to preserve the mounds? What good was it? Of course, I was all for saving the site from development or further ignorant destruction, but if the mounds were simply owned by the Archaeological Conservancy and kept in a bell jar, as it were, did it really matter? If the mounds did not come into people's consciousness, if people were not invited to rethink their sense of where they lived, if they didn't have to change their vision of Euro-American progress, their romanticism about white settlement, the idea that Indians had been here once and then just disappeared into the mist, was the project really worthwhile?

According to its literature, the Archaeological Conservancy is interested in saving sites both because of what sites suggest about the past and what they might mean in the future. Indeed, the organization offers one of the few ways to safeguard archaeological sites. As the conservancy's website puts it:

> The ancient people of North America made no written records of their cultures. For us to gain an understanding of what happened here before Columbus, Coronado, and Raleigh, we rely on clues left behind by these early Americans in the remains of their villages, monuments, and artifacts.
>
> Over the past few decades, the knowledge and methods of modern archaeologists have advanced tremendously. Today researchers use technologies such as tree-ring dating, pollen analysis, and trace-element analysis to glean information from the archaeological record. Few of these technologies existed 50 years ago. For this reason, it's important that we keep a significant portion of raw data in the ground where future archaeologists with even more advanced knowledge and technologies will have access to it.
>
> Archaeologists still lack the clues that might someday solve the mysteries of the early Americans. By permanently preserving important cultural sites, the Conservancy makes sure they will be available for our children and grandchildren to study and enjoy.[4]

In this explanation the clues left in the ground by peoples who did not leave written records are, in effect, the property of everybody. But these raw data are to be handled only by those who have the best scientific equipment to deal with them. What's left out of this scenario, of course, are the perspectives of some native people who feel they have a more legitimate claim on these sites. "These are the things left behind," Anna Funmaker had said. " . . . I have to assume they're mine."[5]

In general, the conservancy wants to preserve sites for science and for posterity. In the case of the Trempealeau platform mounds the organization had no plans to dig, and no human remains were involved. So the conservancy's plans seemed a good way to protect the site. Without the conservancy the mounds would be in a tenuous position, as Rollie Rodell reminded me. The church owned the mounds now and members had no plans to build up there. "But there's no guarantee that that will always be the case," he said.[6] I imagined some rich man's trophy house perched on the bluff.

When I asked John Ebersold about this possibility, he assured me that—legal issues aside—it would be extremely difficult to develop the site. "It's an unbuildable outlot," he said, one on which the village won't allow development. Indeed, the village has already turned down building plans for sites that would be easier to build on, he said. Nonetheless, John wanted to see the conservancy purchase the land. "It's time," he said. "[The preservation of the mounds] is something I wanted done a long time ago. Probably it's a little grudge I've got."[7] He believes that if there is something more to be learned about the mounds, the archaeologists are the best folks to find it out, and they would do so respectfully, with a minimal amount of invasion.

Pam had the sense that preservation was a kind of protection for the mounds—a way to save them from further erosion and destruction, a way, she suggested in one church meeting, to save them from looters and vandals. Initially, Pam tended to focus on how the sale of the mounds would allow the church to build its new Sunday school—the mounds were a means to an end. But after a year of thinking about the mounds, my sister began to change her ideas. When I asked her if she thought the site of the platform mounds should be preserved, she said emphatically, "Yes. Because it's history. I think it's terrible that it's sitting there, and I didn't even know about it—lots of people don't know about it. It's part of who we are—part of where we live." Reflecting on the people who want to deny the authenticity of the mounds, she added, "It's documented. You can't argue with facts. The only danger is if too many people find out about them and think they're going to dig and find treasure."

Pam seemed to think back to a snowy trip we had made to the mounds. "It's interesting how, when you're up there, you can see why they built there. You stand up there and think and wonder what *they* were thinking when they looked at the river. It's part of history—who we are, where we came from." In this way, Pam connects native history to her own presence in the place, lamenting at the same time an intervening period of ignorance and forgetfulness. "It just kind of bothers me that I was never told anything about the mounds' being there—it's just history we should be told about. It's an important part of things—somehow the word's got to get out—without destruction."[8]

I have tended to see preservation as a way of cordoning off the mounds from the surrounding land, marking them off as special, as sacred even, as in the classic formulation of the historian of religion Mircea Eliade: if the land could be preserved, it would no longer be neutral, no longer part of homogeneous and undifferentiated space; the mounds would be marked off as a sacred center, in effect. Selling the land to the Archaeological Conservancy would reorient Trempealeau—for some people, at least—and help to found a different world in which to live.[9] That's what I hoped for, anyway, at one level. But with such hopes I verged on a romanticization of the Native American past and threatened to fossilize the mounds, cutting them off from life.

Others, I knew, had different views. For some native people, it made little difference whether the mounds resided on land owned by the Lutheran church or by the Archaeological Conservancy. Gus Vogel and Anna Funmaker were certainly not interested in preserving the mounds just so archaeologists could have access to them later. They were more concerned, as I noted earlier, with the larger fact of lost lands, lost cultures. Thus they valued preservation as a way to maintain the integrity of the works of their ancestors. They were not concerned with preserving the site for future exploration; instead, the site connected them to the past, manifested the past in the present, giving them a way to claim, We are here and we *were* here.

Instead of seeing archaeology in opposition to Native American values, the Choctaw archaeologist Joe Watkins sees archaeology as a way of opening up fruitful exchange between people. Archaeology is not all about digging up the bones of dead ancestors; he notes that "today, more tribal groups are adapting archaeological practices and methodology to protect cultural resources on their reservations."[10] In this way, techniques designed by archaeologists primarily for the purpose of preserving data for future use are adapted and transformed by Indians for other purposes: to keep them in conversation with the past, to maintain links with their history, to remind them of who they are.

I met an artist, Skip Schuckmann, whose media include earth, rocks, and water, and who has developed his own theories about the native mounds and earthworks found around the country. He does not believe that earthworks were part of an indigenous desire to represent the sacred; indeed, he questions the very category of the sacred, seeing it as a way that profane and spiritually impoverished people make sense of worldviews they don't understand. He contends that the mounds may have had a role in agriculture; they might have been a way to catch and channel water.[11] "Don't forget that the river would have flowed a lot differently back then," he said. Schuckmann placed little value on the work of archaeologists, suggesting that their science was a rigid system of error built on misconception built on prior error. And what's the good of preservation, he asked, if the land just sits there, in a vacuum? At the very least, he said, it would be better if someone tried to live with the mounds, to see what kinds of vistas they offer, to learn what there is to learn from dwelling with them, to see how they shape consciousness, to discover whether they might reveal any of their secrets.

The writer Walker Percy describes the limits of preservation this way: "The archaeologist who puts his find in a museum so that everyone can see it accomplishes the reverse of his expectations. The result of his action is that no one can see it now but the archaeologist. He would have done better to keep it in his pocket and show it now and then to strangers."[12] The platform mounds are hardly pocketsize, but if one is to see past one's own expectations, it will take effort.

9. One More Time to Trempealeau Mountain

It was midwinter 2002, and I had finished a working draft of my book, a project I had developed enough to know where the gaps were, a project that was unfinished enough that I could still expand it, change it, breathe within it. I flew home to Wisconsin in early March to attend a meeting between Paul Gardner, the regional representative of the Archaeological Conservancy, and members of Mount Calvary Lutheran Church about the fate of the platform mounds. While I was there, I wanted to see the effigy mounds on Trempealeau Mountain again; they promised to show up clearly without snow or brush to obscure them. Snow was predicted for the weekend; if I was going to see the effigy mounds, I had to go shortly after my plane landed.

I hiked out alone along the railroad tracks and remembered walking there in the heat of summer with T.S. and John. The wind was strong, and I was well bundled in a parka and a scarf I had borrowed from my mom. Once on the mountain I couldn't remember how John had led us to the mounds last time—were they on the west side or the east? And how high up? The mountain is made up of a series of ridges, and I seemed to go up and down every one. After exploring the west side to no avail (too high, as it turned out), I simply found the trail again and climbed to the top. Sometimes you can see eagles from the top of this sandstone peak. Warmed up and high on endorphins, I looked out on the half-frozen river, the bluffs with black bare trees, white shiny birches, snow patches on north sides of hills, and brown leaf-covered grass. Geese were crying like mad all over the river and bluffs; at the top of the bluff I was nearly the same height as they were in flight. If nothing else happens all weekend, this will have been enough, I thought.

But still I wanted to find the mounds. I skirted around the bluff top and down the east side, leaving the trail to go up and down ridges, up and down small hills. Finally, I saw an abutment that looked promising (though others had too). I climbed up from below, and then I was nearly on the bulky linear mound, a fat line pointing toward Chicken's Breast, and I was next to the bird mound, facing Minnesota and the river. I pressed my hands together in greeting and stayed with the bluffs for a time, catching my breath. I was glad it had been hard for me to find them.

Down below and all around I could see the vandalized burial mounds, all with gouged-out tops, some with trees growing out of them.

On the way back to the car a train clattered past, and I had to head for the ditch, but it would have been a disappointment not to have to get off the tracks at some point on the journey. The engineer spied me and waved.

Driving my mother's car, I headed for town. John and Lu were at home—their house is a gathering place on Friday evenings. Along with John's hunting dog and her three puppies, we sat on their porch, warmed by a space heater, and drank Bud Light. John and I discussed the path to the mounds in detail, the orientation of the mounds, their size and shape. I asked John how he had known about the effigy mounds when few others did; he said he first learned about them from Lewis's 1884 survey, which surfaced during the platform mound controversy. Lewis himself could have known about the mounds only if someone local had told him about them (this was barely a decade after the last Ho-Chunk removal); white residents had apparently known about the effigy mounds back then, but somehow there had been a fair amount of forgetting or not caring in between. Perhaps because of this indifference, John and I agreed: we don't want just anybody to find that bird, the linear mound. We have a feeling that they should remain hidden, that their discovery requires some effort. If people could simply follow a path to find them—if a sign were posted to tell them how important the mounds were—visitors might have a hard time seeing them.

10. To the Platform Mounds

Snow fell across the Midwest that night. Paul Gardner's plane was grounded in Ohio, and the meeting with the Archaeological Conservancy was canceled. I was in town only for the weekend, and Pam wanted me to show her the platform mounds while I was there. She wanted to see the mounds for herself. The snow was too thick to go straight up the face of the bluff, and we didn't want to stir the attention of the hotel owner who disputed the ownership of the road, so John recommended another route that would get us to the mounds from behind. Pam was still game, despite the snow, and her sister-in-law Mary wanted to come along too, and so did Bob. Despite his earlier misgivings, by that time my brother had come to see the mounds as something real, something authentic. We climbed up the back way to the mounds and followed the ridge above the church. Bob, as a public servant and son of the soil, was worried about trespassing. We teased him mercilessly about this; later, just to bug him, Mary declared that the trespassing was her favorite part of the journey. The tracks of someone who, earlier in the day, had mounted the bluff from the other direction were visible in the snow. It didn't take long to get where we were going. Soon we passed by the borrow pits and were on top of the biggest mound, the one that had been damaged by the water tower. We didn't have to debate whether the mounds were there or not. The snow blanketed them, smoothing their rough edges and making them clearly visible as three terraces. Bob quipped, almost as I had, that it was clear why people 950 years ago had chosen this spot: "A great view of the dam!" Standing knee-deep in snow, we chatted about the controversy and the dispute about the road to the mounds.

On the way down Bob talked about a local guy and his acres of junked cars; they'd been there more than thirty years, but now the village was after him to clean up his mess. As Bob saw it, this controversy was not one between newcomers and old residents but between those who had different visions of what the town should be. Should it be a bedroom community for La Crosse and Winona? Develop its

4.2. The platform mounds in snow, March 2, 2002. Photo by author.

own industry? Should it be a tourist haven for cyclists, or should it batten down the hatches against outsiders? The village, it seemed, was still being settled.

◇

11. And Home Again

After the meeting was canceled, it seemed that my trip had been for naught. But afterward I remembered the hike on Trempealeau Mountain, the visit to the platform mounds; I thought about my family's changing interest in local archaeology and the way my relatives pushed me back into the project, made me rethink my tendencies to blame them and to distance myself. Although I had long been estranged from my birthplace, doing the project opened up different ways of being home. As the Tom Waits song goes, "Never saw my hometown till I stayed away too long."[13]

We don't live in physical spaces alone; landscape is not just an objective fact. We live in places and landscapes shaped by history; our consciousness of places is shaped by the past, by the stories we tell, by the things we do, by land, trees, people, rivers, and ideas—by what we feel, by the peculiar ways we remember.

I prepared to go back home to Ohio. The winter night before I was to leave was also my uncle Clyde's seventy-sixth birthday, so Mom and I crossed the road to give him our best wishes. After we returned

255

home, the phone rang. It was Clyde. "Laurie?" he asked, sounding older and more unsteady than I imagined him. I thought he meant me, but it soon became clear he thought he had my mom, who has the same name.

"Yes," I said.

"What happened with the mounds and the church meeting?" he asked. I explained why the meeting didn't happen, how the snow had stopped it. By then he must have realized it was me on the phone.

"I just wanted to know," he said without irony.

It was July before Gardner would be able to make another appearance in Trempealeau, this time to address the entire congregation of the Lutheran church. There were the usual grumbles. My uncle Kenny repeated what he'd heard about Harold Wilber's building the mounds; others expressed the standard response, the one that cut to the heart of the matter: "I've lived here my whole life and never heard of them." In August I went with Pam to church, taking with me Squier's photos of the mounds, Lewis's and Squier's surveys. I intended for these to give the parishioners an image of the place, something they could imagine the mounds with, since Gardner had described the mounds only verbally and most churchgoers had not been up on Little Bluff since they were kids. I also brought along Pierce's massive 1917 *History of Trempealeau County;* I wanted people to know that there is evidence of the mounds in this treasured book, one that they may have used to trace their family tree but that also tells other stories. I arranged my images around the coffeepot in the fellowship room after the service. Just laying eyes on the surveys was enough for some people, it seemed. An elder of the town, a retired banker and the father of one of my childhood friends, confided to me that he thought the preservation project was a good idea. (I remembered that my dad once compared this banker to another man. This other man was nice enough, my dad said: "If he had a dollar and you needed money, he'd give you fifty cents." But of the banker, my dad said: "If he only had a dollar and you needed money, he'd give you a dollar.") The banker expressed surprise that I would return home to write about all this stuff but then admitted, "When you get older, you start looking backward. You're more interested in the past."

After remaining on the edge of the room for a time, Uncle Kenny worked his way over to the table and had a look. After a time he said, "I don't know what's the matter with Bill"—another parishioner who was vocal in his opposition to the project. Kenny said that he hoped that Bill would have a look at the mound pictures too, but he left without a glance. Despite the conservancy's offer to purchase the land, "Bill thinks the archaeologists want to get something for nothing," my uncle declared. Bill left the church without a word, without even a cup of coffee.[14]

◇

12. Finishing Up

Later that day the extended Hovell family—all my siblings and all their kids—gathered at my mother's. We had rented a twelve-cubic-yard dumpster, and the plan was to begin cleaning out the farm buildings: the barn, the machine shed, the milk house. It had been nearly eight years since my father died, and in the meantime squirrels had hidden nuts in drawers and corners, thick coats of dust and grime had settled on everything, and mice had raised entire lineages. My father was never one of those neat Scandinavian farmers; raised in the depression, he kept everything: tools, bits of metal and wood, plastic buckets, milking supplies, machine parts, nuts, bolts, nails, chains, busted engines, broken radios, batteries, bikes, seed bags, small metal signs from a city factory job in the 1950s, old furniture, rocks and a rock tumbler (another hobby), CB parts (he used to sell CBs), various types of machine oil (another sideline job), trailer hitches (from a business he had with Clyde), old glass, horse gear, dead motorcycles, a tool for castrating sheep, cattle, and pigs, and more. *This* is archaeology, we said, as we went down through the layers and years, back to a time when even Grandpa Hovell was still on the farm. Bobby worried that I would unknowingly, uncaringly throw some treasure away and checked my work. And it was true: if I had my way, we would torch the whole thing, burn it up in one cathartic blast. But, no, we went through it piece by piece, dried walnut shell by dried walnut shell, sorting through the days and years. Bob, as the oldest, exhumed from his detailed memory what he knew about our finds, about the uses of odd-shaped metal bits and farm parts, about the home businesses that Dad and Clyde made together. It was a moral imperative not to throw things out after the depression, we decided. While I insisted I would never acquire so many things—and never keep them in such total disarray—for my own kids to sort out later, Bob and Debbie vowed to have the same kind of mess—the same kind of treasures. Debbie did not participate much in the cleanup; instead, she picked through things, looking for stuff to take to her own house. A week after the cleanup I decided I wanted only one thing from the wreckage, a curry comb, a metal comb for manes and tails. My dad had it for years and used it on generations of horses.

Despite the desire to save and preserve, everyone agreed that soon the barn would have to come down; the roof had already collapsed in the hay shed as well as in the old milking parlor. My brother-in-law Steve had brought down his backhoe and prepared to dismantle a shelter attached to the barn. The whole thing had to be done delicately, as the shelter shared a wall with the barn. One bad move and the whole thing could fall. But it was a work of art, really, the way he did it: first, he dug a giant hole (mounding the dirt unceremoniously to one side) and then he started to pull off boards. T.S. and Deb's husband, Larry, tossed the wood into the hole, and when that was done, Steve stripped the corrugated tin off the roof,

4.3. Cleaning out the farm buildings, August 11, 2002. Photo by author.

sheet by sheet, almost nail by nail. Soon there was nothing left of that shelter; the job was done and done neatly. Later Steve burned the wood and covered the hole back up with dirt, flattening the mound as best he could, leaving what was left in the ground.

While the fate of the platform mounds was still pending, I imagined a dedication ceremony that would bring together a cast of characters from different times and places: representatives of the people called the Middle Mississippians; envoys from the Ioway, Ho-Chunk, and Dakota in calico and buckskin, feathers and blue jeans; Rollie Rodell and George Squier; my father and mother, my siblings, John and Lu; Gus Vogel and Anna Funmaker, Dale Little-john, Richard Grounds, and Princess Marinuka; T.S. and our children, Liam and Jack. And while we're at it, let's bring back more of the dead: my cousin Jonny, Grandpa and Grandma Hovell, my cousin Tammi, her grandpa Kenny Drugan, Antoine Grignon and James Reed, Mary Jane Farnham, and Eben Pierce. Let's all stand on the highest platform and pray and sing and smoke a pipe. Let's bow our heads and raise our arms and keen and meditate on what has been lost.

But this image was too full of Hollywood imaginings, too full of utopic Thanksgiving stories, too full of romance. I put us all back in our respective times and places, and we returned as well to our particular ways of relating to and being with the mounds. Some of us worshipped the sun from atop them, perhaps, while others grazed cattle, built fires, erected water towers, and cleared brush. Some of us stared at the river and dreamed of the past. Some of us remained below the mounds, intent on something else.

Instead of this imagined celebration, we went to a family party. It was my sister Debbie's fiftieth birthday, and she was hosting a bash with food and drinks and music. The place was thick with the past. Jim Bee and his band were there; though he hadn't seen me in years, he called me a ham, remembering the old family joke. So many relatives gathered there—aunts, cousins, uncles, friends—that there was not enough time to talk to them all. We met each other with the memory of who we used to be; we carried our pasts along with us but lightly, for the band was playing "Cab Driver" and "Blue Spanish Eyes," all the songs my dad used to play. Brothers stood belly by belly; children took the dance floor or lurked in the corners playing their own games. Everybody seemed to be wearing red. We saw the faces of the generations—our own faces—in the visages of others around us. This dance recalled wedding dances and parties past; I met up with kids I went to kindergarten with, my first-grade teacher. My dad was there, we know, and the cousins and grandparents we remember. The people in that place are tied together so tight that there's nowhere to turn to escape memories and stories. It was this knitted-togetherness that scared me so as a teenager. I had to propel myself far to escape, I thought, but here I was, back in the middle of it, relishing it. Though I wasn't even born when it happened, it seemed like yesterday that Debbie turned five and my dad brought our pony into the house for her. That gesture was there too, and for those moments it was good to be there, good to be so enmeshed. We had a place to be.

In 2002 the Archaeological Conservancy secured the support of Mount Calvary Lutheran Church to pursue purchasing the land on which the platform mound complex sits. A snag interrupted the proceedings, however, when land titles showed that the village retained ownership of part of the land, in particular, a V-shaped piece on the northern platform. The Archaeological Conservancy decided to try to buy this bit of land from the village. In May 2004, when Paul Gardner presented the Archaeological Conservancy's proposal to the village, the village board summarily dismissed the request to acquire and preserve the mound complex. The board apparently did not want to reconsider the issue, given the outrage generated by the preservation project a decade earlier; indeed, some board members had lost their seats over this issue, the current members noted. They also stated that they believed the mounds were adequately preserved by the village, though they did not say how they reconciled that belief with the huge hole that the village had put in one mound or the garbage pile that workers left in it.

For now the mounds—however damaged—still stand on a small bluff, facing the river.

Notes

Introduction

1. Although Trempealeau is officially a village, many local people refer to it in conversation as a town.

2. Josef Breuer and Sigmund Freud, *Studies on Hysteria, Standard Edition of the Complete Psychological Works of Sigmund Freud* (1893–95; repr., London: Hogarth, 1955), 2:139. Freud used the metaphor of archaeology many times in his work. For example, in conversations with his patient the Rat Man, Freud "likened the preservation of things unconscious to that of objects in a tomb." See Edward R. Wallace, *Freud and Anthropology: A History and Reappraisal* (New York: International Universities Press, 1983), 7.

3. Ashis Nandy, *The Intimate Enemy: Loss and Recovery of Self under Colonialism* (New Delhi: Oxford University Press, 1983), xv.

4. Ibid., 71.

Part I. The Surface

1. Mark Twain, *Life on the Mississippi* (1883; repr., New York: Penguin, 1986), 402.

2. Recently, Peter Straub, a visitor to and relative of residents of Tamarack Valley, ten miles away, has set a mystery novel in a town that much resembles Trempealeau; he wrote the novel in collaboration with Stephen King. See *Black House,* by Stephen King and Peter Straub (New York: Ballantine, 2002).

3. The term *coulee* has a regional usage that means valley and comes from the French *coulée,* meaning flow.

4. Robert Hovell Sr., "Getting around in the Good Old Days," 1988, unpublished manuscript.

5. Eben Douglas Pierce, "Biography," in *History of Trempealeau County,* compiled by Franklyn Curtiss-Wedge and edited by Eben Douglas Pierce (Chicago: H.C. Cooper, 1917), 282.

6. Ibid.

7. I am following Katherine Fitzgerald's use of the term *Yankee* here.

Most settlers in the midnineteenth century came from Vermont, New York, and parts of New England; later they would come from England and Scotland. See Fitzgerald, "The Platteville Papers: Inscribing Frontier Ideology and Culture in a Nineteenth-Century Writing Assignment," *College English* 64, no. 3 (January 2002): 273–301.

8. Pierce, "Locality Settlements," in *History of Trempealeau County* (see note 5), 97.

9. The phrase is Eric Wolf's. See Wolf, *Europe and the People without History* (Berkeley: University of California Press, 1982). Wolf argues against developmental and teleological views of history that give the West and the United States the starring role and neglect histories of interconnection and interaction in which other players have had an active part.

10. Grignon's recollections are printed in abbreviated form in Pierce, "Historical Papers," in *History of Trempealeau County* (see note 5), 129–36. A longer version of these, also edited by Pierce, appears as "Recollections of Antoine Grignon," in *Proceedings of the State Historical Society of Wisconsin for 1913* (Madison: The Society, 1914), 110–36.

11. Pierce, "Biography" (see note 5), 397.

12. Janyce Y. Anderson, letter to the editor, *Galesville (Wisc.) Republican*, 14 September 2000, p. 2.

13. The name Winnebago is said to derive from the Algonquin word *Ouinipigou* from *ouinipig,* meaning saltwater sea or bad-smelling water, which led the French to refer to them as *Puans,* or "stinkards" (Claude Charles Le Roy Bacqueville de la Potherie, *History of the Savage Peoples Who Are Allies of New France,* in Emma Helen Blair, ed. and trans., *The Indian Tribes of the Upper Mississippi Valley and Region of the Great Lakes* [1911; repr., Lincoln: University of Nebraska Press, 1996], 1:289).

14. The others are in Baraboo, Nekoosa, and Wisconsin Dells.

15. Roland L. Rodell, "A Middle Mississippian Presence in the Upper Mississippi Valley: Investigations at Trempealeau, Wisconsin," *Reports of Investigations of the Mississippi Valley Archaeology Center at the University of Wisconsin–La Crosse,* no. 136 (1991): 68 (a report submitted to the Historic Preservation Division, State Historical Society of Wisconsin).

16. Ibid., 68–69.

17. Ibid., 69.

18. Minutes of the Village of Trempealeau Planning Committee meeting, 15 October 1991, office of the Village of Trempealeau.

19. Ibid., 10 June 1992.

20. Rob Dreislein, "Mounds of Controversy," *Winona Daily News,* 19 October 1993.

21. Ibid.

22. Jason Abraham, "Controversy of the Mounds," *Winona Daily News,* 7 August 1994, p. 2D.

23. Ibid., pp. 1D–2D.

24. Philip Deloria has explored many ways in which non-Indian Americans have played out fantasies about Indians. See *Playing Indian* (New Haven, Conn.: Yale University Press, 1998).

25. This area of southwest Wisconsin was not covered by glaciers; geologists thus refer to it as the Driftless Area.

26. I am grateful to Robert Boszhardt of Mississippi Valley Archaeology Center for showing this image to me. See Robert F. Boszhardt, *Deep Cave Rock Art in the Mississippi Valley* (St. Paul, Minn.: Prairie Smoke Press, 2003), 38.

27. J. C. H. King, *First People, First Contacts* (Cambridge, Mass.: Harvard University Press, 1999), 18.

28. Although earlier archaeologists posited the notion that the Hopewell and Adena—named for a farmer and a plantation in Ohio, respectively—were different human groups, new evidence has undermined this distinction. The Adena and Hopewell, many now contend, were distinct neither physiologically nor in their periods of activity. See Roger G. Kennedy, *Hidden Cities: The Discovery and Loss of Ancient North American Civilization* (New York: Free Press, 1994), 17.

29. Ibid.

30. In an extended burial a skeleton is laid out, as in a coffin burial. Sometimes, though, skeletons were disarticulated, and only some bones were buried, as in partial burials, or were bundled together (perhaps in a sack or other such container) and then buried, as in bundle burials.

31. See William Green, "Changing Interpretations of Effigy Mound Ages, Origins, and Cultural Affiliations," *Effigy Mounds National Monument Cultural Affiliation Report,* Office of the State Archaeologist, *Research Papers* 26, no. 3 (2001): 85–114.

32. George H. Squier, "Archaeological Resources of Western Wisconsin," *Wisconsin Archaeologist* 13, no. 3 (October 1914): 123–34.

33. Ibid. Interestingly, though Squier was aware of the many conical mounds on Trempealeau Mountain, he does not mention the bird and linear mounds there.

34. Archaeologists debate the exact manner in which Middle Mississippian culture arrived in the area. I discuss this issue, and Mississippian culture in general, in greater depth in part II.

35. Lance Michael Foster, "The Ioway and the Landscape of Southeast Iowa," *Journal of the Iowa Archaeological Society* 43 (1996): 2.

36. For information on the Oneota I am indebted to the Mississippi Valley Archaeology Center, "Past Cultures," http://perth.uwlax.edu/mvac (11 July 2005).

37. Robert F. Boszhardt, "Oneota Group Continuity at La Crosse: The Brice Prairie, Pammel Creek, and Valley View Phases," *Wisconsin Archaeologist* 75, nos. 3–4 (September–December, 1994): 214. Boszhardt suggests several possible reasons for the Oneotas' departure from the area: the negative pressures of "critical resource depletion, climatic degradation, epidemic disease, and pressures from the east, as well as the more positive appeal of bison hunting further west" (214). Evidence of contact between Europeans and Oneota in northeast Iowa and southeast Minnesota was discovered in the early twentieth century. See Mildred Mott, "The Relation of Historic Indian Tribes to Archaeological Manifestations in Iowa," *Iowa Journal of History and Politics* 36 (1938): 227–314.

38. Kennedy, *Hidden Cities,* 21.

39. Ibid., 20.

40. There is much debate about the population numbers of Native Americans before European contact. In 1966 the anthropologist Henry F. Dobyns estimated that about 95 percent of the aboriginal population died within the first 130 years of contact. See "Estimating Aboriginal American Population: An Appraisal of Techniques with a New Hemispheric Estimate," *Current Anthropology* 7, no. 4 (October 1966): 395–416. Other scholars dismiss Dobyns's numbers as politically motivated. For discussions of this issue see Shepard Krech III, *The Ecological Indian* (New York: W. W. Norton, 1999), 73–99, and Charles C. Mann, "1491," *Atlantic Monthly,* March 2002, pp. 41–53.

41. Krech, *The Ecological Indian,* 93.

42. Bacqueville de la Potherie, *History of the Savage Peoples* (see note 13), 1:293.

43. Gary Clayton Anderson, *Kinsmen of Another Kind: Dakota-White Relations in the Upper Mississippi Valley, 1650–1862* (St. Paul: Minnesota Historical Society Press, 1997), 19. Anderson's figures here are for the larger Sioux nation (including Dakota, Lakota, and Nakota), not only the Dakota; nonetheless, the Dakota were the Sioux people most in contact with

Europeans. Anderson points out that Sioux population declines were not as great as those experienced by Indians in New England, whose populations fell from about ninety thousand people to ten thousand from 1600 to 1674. *Sioux,* I should note, is a pejorative derived through French from the Ojibwa term *Nadowe-isi-w,* meaning "little snake." The terms *Dakota, Lakota,* and *Nakota* are dialectical variations for a term meaning "an alliance of friends." Today many people from these groups prefer Dakota, Lakota, or Nakota. Nonetheless, although some consider *Sioux* to be pejorative, it is still widely used as a self-definition and has the advantage of encompassing allied peoples who shared a varied and connected culture. I thus maintain its use when no other more specific designation seems appropriate.

44. This is a controversial subject among scholars. For one view see William Green's "Examining Protohistoric Depopulation in the Upper Midwest," *Wisconsin Archaeologist* 74, nos. 1–4 (1993): 284–317.

45. The editor was Emma Helen Blair, "Biographical Sketch of Nicolas Perrot; condensed from the notes of Father Tailhan," in *The Indian Tribes of the Upper Mississippi Valley* (see note 13), 2:250.

46. Bacqueville de la Potherie, *History of the Savage Peoples* (see note 13), 1:367.

47. See "Remains of a French Post Near Trempealeau," with articles by Eben Douglas Pierce, George H. Squier, and Louise Phelps Kellogg in *Proceedings of the . . . Annual Meeting of the State Historical Society of Wisconsin* (Madison: The Society, 1915), 111–23. I have also benefited from reading Roland Rodell's unpublished manuscript on the ostensible Perrot Post.

48. Nancy Lurie, "An Aztalan-Winnebago Hypothesis," 1973, unpublished manuscript.

49. J. O. Dorsey and Cyrus Thomas, in *Handbook of American Indians,* quoted in Blair, *The Indian Tribes of the Upper Mississippi Valley* (see this part's note 13), 1:367n239.

50. Foster, "*Tanji na Che:* Recovering the Landscape of the Ioway," in Robert F. Sayre, ed., *Recovering the Prairie* (Madison: University of Wisconsin Press, 1999), 179.

51. Lurie, "An Aztalan-Winnebago Hypothesis."

52. Bacqueville de la Potherie, *History of the Savage Peoples* (see note 13), 1:367.

53. Dorsey and Thomas, *Handbook of American Indians,* in Blair, *The Indian Tribes of the Upper Mississippi Valley,* 1:367–68n239.

54. David Lee Smith, "Winnebago," in Frederick E. Hoxie, ed., *Encyclopedia of North American Indians* (Boston: Houghton Mifflin, 1996), 682.

55. Lurie, "An Aztalan-Winnebago Hypothesis."

56. Smith, "Winnebago," 682.

57. Ibid.

58. Ibid.

59. Mark Wyman, *The Wisconsin Frontier* (Bloomington: University of Indiana Press, 1998), 156.

60. Pierce, "Reign of the Indians," in *History of Trempealeau County* (see note 5), 41.

61. An unsigned Ho-Chunk history of this era is offered in "The Ho-Chunk Nation—A Brief History," *Ho-Chunk Nation,* www.ho-chunk nation.com/History.htm (5 July 2005).

62. Andrew Jackson, "Indians Should Be Removed to the West" (1829), in Bruno Leone, ed., *Native Americans: Opposing Viewpoints* (San Diego: Greenhaven, 1998), 95.

63. Susan Lampert Smith, "Ho-Chunk Stubbornness—They Survived Because of It," *Wisconsin State Journal,* 15 March 1998, p. 1A.

64. "The Ho-Chunk Nation—A Brief History."

65. Karen D. Lone Hill, "Sioux," in Hoxie, *Encyclopedia of North American Indians* (see note 54), 591.

66. For more on the Sioux Nation see Lone Hill, "Sioux," 590, and J. C. H. King, *First People, First Contacts: Native Peoples of North America* (Cambridge, Mass.: Harvard University Press, 1999), 254.

67. Lone Hill, "Sioux," 591.

68. King, *First People,* 254.

69. Pierce, "Reign of the Indians" (see note 5), 43.

70. Anderson, *Kinsmen of Another Kind,* xxv.

71. Ibid., 38.

72. See Anderson, *Kinsmen of Another Kind,* for an extensive discussion of these ties and the history of the Dakota.

73. Perrot, *Memoir,* 1:245.

74. Pierce, "Reign of the Indians" (see note 5), 41.

75. Ibid., 43.

76. Ibid.

77. Angie Debo, *A History of the Indians of the United States* (Norman: University of Oklahoma Press, 1970), 184–88.

78. As Roland Rodell pointed out to me, Hennepin and two other Frenchmen passed through the Trempealeau area as captives of the Sioux in 1680. See Pierce, introduction to *History of Trempealeau County* (see note 5), xi.

79. Merle Curti, *The Making of an American Community: A Case Study of Democracy in a Frontier County* (Stanford, Calif.: Stanford University Press, 1959), 12.

80. Ibid., 12–13.

81. Ibid., 13.

82. Ibid., 14.

83. Anderson, *Kinsmen of Another Kind*, 68.

84. One of these settlers was Charles H. Perkins, who married Reed's stepdaughter, Mary Ann Farnham, and who was a great grandfather of my brother-in-law, Steve Grover.

85. Curti, *The Making of an American Community*, 16.

86. Ibid., 18–19, 22.

87. Ibid., 20.

88. Ibid., 20–21. In Curti's account their name is spelled with one "l"; in later years it would be "Nicholls."

89. Ibid., 31.

Part II. What's under the Surface

1. William Green to author, 27 October 2003.

2. George Squier did his own excavations in the 1880s and also worked with local men on the excavation of Perrot Post. Officially, the Antiquities Act of 1906 permitted only professional archaeologists to remove antiquities from federal lands, but since these sites were not on federal land, they were not covered by this act.

3. See W. C. McKern, "New Excavations in Wisconsin Hopewell Mounds," in S. A. Barrett, ed., *Year Book of the Public Museum of the City of Milwaukee* (Milwaukee: Public Museum of Milwaukee, 1930), 21–22.

4. Ibid., 17.

5. The Shrake mounds were located in what is now the campground of Perrot State Park.

6. Robert Ray Hovell Sr., "Getting around in the Good Old Days," 1988, unpublished manuscript.

7. Both William Green and Roland Rodell informed me of Stull's interest; he donated his artifacts and notes to the Mississippi Valley Archaeology Center in 2003.

8. George Gale, *Upper Mississippi: or, Historical Sketches of the Mound-Builders, the Indian Tribes, and the Progress of Civilization in the North-West; from A. D. 1600 to the Present Time* (1867; repr., Chicago: Clarke, 1975), 26.

9. My sister Pam Grover tells me that I am conflating two incidents here.

10. According to the University of Minnesota Extension Service's website, a tipboard is a "form of charitable gambling in which tickets are sold off a board and then a seal is broken to reveal the winner." See Shirley J. Anderson, Roselyn A. Biermaier, and Sandra K. Syverson, "Gambling: A Challenge for Youth," *1992 Southwest Minnesota Gambling Survey,* http://www.extension.umn.edu/distribution/youthdevelopment/DA6291.html (11 July 2005).

11. David Lowenthal, *The Past Is a Foreign Country* (New York: Cambridge University Press, 1985), 50–51.

12. Hamlin Garland, *A Son of the Middle Border* (New York: Macmillan, 1917), 364, 365, 366.

13. This idea was suggested to me by Sandra Zagarell, Oberlin College.

14. Jensen is quoted in Lowenthal, *The Past Is a Foreign Country,* 50–51. For the original see Jensen, *America's Yesterdays: Images of Our Lost Past Discovered in the Photographic Archives of the Library of Congress* (New York: American Heritage, 1978), 11.

15. George Squier appears not to have been related to Ephraim George Squier, the newspaper editor who, along with Edwin H. Davis, documented the impressive effigy mounds of southern Ohio in 1848. See Squier and Davis, *Ancient Monuments of the Mississippi Valley* (1848; repr., Washington, D.C.: Smithsonian Institution Press, 1998).

16. George H. Squier, "Archaeology," in *History of Trempealeau County,* compiled by Franklyn Curtiss-Wedge and edited by Eben Douglas Pierce (Chicago: H.C. Cooper, 1917), 26.

17. Harold Wilber, interview by author, 30 July 2001.

18. Putnam was also crucial to the preservation of the Great Serpent Mound in Peebles, Ohio, which dates to about 1200 CE.

19. Squier, from correspondence dated 22 July 1884, quoted in Roland L. Rodell, "A Middle Mississippian Presence in the Upper Mississippi Valley: Investigations at Trempealeau, Wisconsin," *Reports of Investigations of the Mississippi Valley Archaeology Center at the University of Wisconsin–La Crosse,* no. 136 (1991): 15 (a report submitted to the Historic Preservation Division, State Historical Society of Wisconsin).

20. William Green and Roland Rodell, "The Mississippian Presence and Cahokia Interaction at Trempealeau, Wisconsin," *American Antiquity* 59, no. 2 (1994): 337. The Northwestern Archaeological Survey was funded by Minnesotan Alfred T. Hill. Whether Squier and Lewis ever met is

unclear, though Lewis probably would have secured the permission of George Squier's father to survey his land.

21. My discussion is indebted to Green and Rodell, "The Mississippian Presence," and Rodell, "A Middle Mississippian Presence."

22. Green and Rodell, "The Mississippian Presence," 338.

23. Ibid., 339, from G. H. Squier to C. E. Brown, 13 December 1915, Charles E. Brown Collection, Wisconsin Historical Society.

24. Ibid., 339, from a document dated 11 November 1921, Charles E. Brown Collection, Wisconsin Historical Society.

25. Green and Rodell, "The Mississippian Presence," 341.

26. William Green, "Middle Mississippian Peoples," *Wisconsin Archaeologist* 78, nos. 1–2 (1997): 208. W. H. Holmes's influential classifications are found in *Aboriginal Pottery of the Eastern United States,* 1903.

27. Squier, "Archaeology," 32.

28. Green and Rodell, "The Mississippian Presence," 350.

29. Ibid.

30. Squier, "Archaeology," 32.

31. Ibid.

32. Ibid.

33. Wilber interview.

34. For more on this see "Remains of a French Post near Trempealeau," with articles by Eben Douglas Pierce, George H. Squier, and Louise Phelps Kellogg in *Proceedings of the . . . Annual Meeting of the State Historical Society of Wisconsin* (Madison: The Society, 1915), 111–23.

35. George H. Squier, "Archaeological Resources of Western Wisconsin," *Wisconsin Archaeologist* 13, no. 3 (October 1914): 134.

36. Ibid., 127.

37. Ibid., 132, 134.

38. The two larger structures are the Temple of the Sun at Teotihuacan and the Temple of Quetzalcoatl at Cholula, both in Mexico. The site near Collinsville, Illinois, was named for the Cahokia Indians who lived in the region in the eighteenth century (Lynda Norene Shaffer, *Native Americans before 1492: The Moundbuilding Centers of the Eastern Woodlands* [New York: M. E. Sharpe, 1992], 51).

39. Maureen Korp, *The Sacred Geography of the American Mound Builders* (Lewiston, N.Y.: E. Mellen, 1990), 8–9.

40. Shaffer, *Native Americans before 1492,* 52.

41. Ibid., 65.

42. For this description I am indebted to Timothy Pauketat and

Thomas E. Emerson, eds., introduction to *Cahokia: Domination and Ideology in the Mississippian World* (Lincoln: University of Nebraska Press, 1997), 11.

43. George Milner, *The Cahokia Chiefdom: The Archaeology of a Mississippian Society* (Washington, D.C.: Smithsonian Institution Press, 1998), 113.

44. Shaffer, *Native Americans before 1492,* 51.

45. Quoted in Pauketat and Emerson, *Cahokia,* 11.

46. By this time bow-and-arrow technology had been around for several centuries.

47. Korp, *Sacred Geography,* 8.

48. Milner, *The Cahokia Chiefdom,* 123–24.

49. Ibid., 124.

50. Rinita A. Dalan, "The Construction of Mississippian Cahokia," in Pauketat and Emerson, *Cahokia* (see note 42), 99–100.

51. Milner, *The Cahokia Chiefdom,* 13.

52. Ibid., 14.

53. Archaeologists refer to this period as the Stirling-Moorehead period. The standard dates for the various phases in this period are Lohmann, 1050–1100; Stirling, 1050–1200, and Moorehead and Sand Prairie phases, 1200–1350.

54. Korp, *Sacred Geography,* 52.

55. Ibid., 32. Korp also argues that the origin myths of these Native American tribes connect them to the Mississippians.

56. Green and Rodell, "The Mississippian Presence," 335.

57. Green, "Middle Mississippian Peoples," 206.

58. This is what Lynne Goldstein suggests in the case of Aztalan in "The Implications of Aztalan's Location," in James B. Stoltman, ed., *New Perspectives on Cahokia: Views from the Periphery* (Madison, Wisc.: Prehistory Press, 1991), 220.

59. Green and Rodell, "The Mississippian Presence," 337.

60. Ibid., 352.

61. Ibid., 335–36.

62. Ibid., 352.

63. Ibid.

64. Ibid., 353.

65. Roger G. Kennedy, *Hidden Cities: The Discovery and Loss of Ancient North American Civilization* (New York: Free Press, 1994), 20.

66. Roland Rodell, interview by author, 23 July 2001.

67. Lurie makes this suggestion in an unpublished paper (of which Rodell was aware) titled "An Aztalan-Winnebago Hypothesis," 1973. Lurie bases her argument on a rereading of the writings of archaeologists McKern and Mott as well as the accounts of Perrot, which suggest that the Ioway were just leaving the Trempealeau region when Perrot arrived.

68. William Green to author, e-mail, 20 May 2002.

69. Lance Michael Foster to author, e-mail, 17 May 2002.

70. Lance Michael Foster, "*Tanji na Che:* Recovering the Landscape of the Ioway," in Robert F. Sayre, ed., *Recovering the Prairie* (Madison: University of Wisconsin Press, 1999), 179.

71. McKern published an article on the Oneota material in the region. See W. C. McKern, "Preliminary Report on the Upper Mississippi Phase in Wisconsin," *Bulletin of the Public Museum of the City of Milwaukee* 16 (1945): 109–285.

72. S. A. Barrett to E. M. Malles, April 22, 1938, on file in the Trempealeau village records.

73. G. O. Leavitt to S. A. Barrett, 22 April 1938, village records. Why these letters have the same dates is not clear.

74. See John Hildebrand, "The Appraisal," *Harper's Magazine,* November 2001, pp. 56–63.

75. I explore the dynamics of this attraction as it plays out personally and historically in *English in Tibet, Tibet in English: Self-Presentation in Tibet and the Diaspora* (New York: Palgrave, 2001).

76. Garland, *Son of the Middle Border,* 376.

77. Jim is the father of Russ Stull, who, as mentioned earlier, took an early interest in local archaeology.

78. "Owner of Motel Near Mound Site Left 'Out in Cold,'" *Galesville (Wisc.) Republican,* 10 February 1994, p. 16.

79. Ibid.

80. James Gallagher, interview by author, 4 September 2001.

81. This and "Gus Vogel" are pseudonyms.

82. Jason Abraham, "Controversy of the Mounds," *Winona Daily News,* 7 August 1994, p. 2D.

83. Ibid., 1D–2D.

84. Kennedy, *Hidden Cities,* vii.

85. Robert "Ernie" Boszhardt, interview by author, 4 September 2001.

86. Katherine Fitzgerald, "The Platteville Papers: Inscribing Frontier Ideology and Culture in a Nineteenth-Century Writing Assignment," *College English* 64, no. 3 (January 2002): 288.

87. Pierce, introduction to *History of Trempealeau County* (see note 16), xi.

88. Mark Twain, *Life on the Mississippi* (1883; repr., New York: Penguin, 1986), 402.

89. See Mircea Eliade's *The Sacred and the Profane: The Nature of Religion* (New York: Harcourt, Brace, 1957).

90. Trempealeau County Tourism Council, "Trempealeau County, Wisconsin, the Official Guide," 2001, p. 2.

91. See Philip Deloria, *Playing Indian* (New Haven, Conn.: Yale University Press, 1998).

92. *The Arrowhead*, Galesville (Wisc.) High School, Galesville, 1914, Galesville Public Library.

93. As a graduating senior, I received a scholarship named in his honor.

94. Alanson Skinner, quoted in Paul Radin, *The Winnebago Tribe* (1923; repr., Lincoln: University of Nebraska, 1990), 61.

95. This section is based on interviews I conducted with this informant in August and September 2001.

96. Vine Deloria Jr., *Custer Died for Your Sins* (New York: Macmillan, 1969), 80.

97. Vine Deloria Jr., *God Is Red: A Native View of Religion* (Golden, Colo.: North American Press, 1992), 14.

98. This section is based on an interview I conducted with Anna Funmaker on 4 September 2001.

99. Larry J. Zimmerman, "Remythologizing the Relationship between Indians and Archaeologists," in Nina Swidler et al., eds., *Native Americans and Archaeologists: Stepping Stones to Common Ground* (Walnut Creek, Calif.: Altamira, 1997), 54.

100. Radin, *The Winnebago Tribe,* 28. Roland Rodell also pointed out to me that Radin's view may have influenced Ho-Chunk self-perception.

101. For more on this issue see William Green, "Changing Interpretations of Effigy Mound Ages, Origins, and Cultural Affiliations," *Effigy Mounds National Monument Cultural Affiliation Report* 26, no. 3 (2001): 85–109.

102. MVAC employs one Ho-Chunk archaeologist, for example.

103. David Hurst Thomas, *Skull Wars: Kennewick Man, Archaeology, and the Battle for Native American Identity* (New York: Basic Books, 2000), 142.

Part III. What's at the Bottom

1. George Gale, *Upper Mississippi: or, Historical Sketches of the Mound-Builders, the Indian Tribes, and the Progress of Civilization in the North-West; from A. D. 1600 to the Present Time* (1975; repr., Chicago: Clarke, 1975), 11.

2. Merle Curti, *The Making of an American Community: A Case Study of Democracy in a Frontier County* (Stanford, Calif.: Stanford University Press, 1959), 22.

3. Ibid., 23.

4. Gale, *Upper Mississippi*, 11–12. Gale uses the term *Mound-Builder* with capitalization and hyphenation, a pejorative form.

5. Alan S. Downer, "Archaeologists-Native American Relations," in Nina Swindler et al., eds., *Native Americans and Archaeologists: Stepping Stones to Common Ground* (Walnut Creek, Calif.: AltaMira, 1997), 26.

6. Gallatin, quoted in Gale, *Upper Mississippi*, 18.

7. David Hurst Thomas, *Skull Wars: Kennewick Man, Archaeology, and the Battle for Native American Identity* (New York: Basic Books, 2000), 46.

8. Gale, *Upper Mississippi*, 13–14, emphasis in original.

9. Ibid., 41.

10. Ibid.

11. Ibid., 40.

12. George H. Squier, "Archaeology," in *History of Trempealeau County*, compiled by Frederick Curtiss-Wedge and edited by Eben Douglas Pierce (Chicago: H.C. Cooper, 1917), 27.

13. Ibid.

14. George H. Squier, "Certain Archaeological Features of Western Wisconsin," *Wisconsin Archaeologist* 4, no. 2 (January 1905): 27–28.

15. Squier, "Archaeology," 26–29.

16. Gale, *Upper Mississippi*, 11.

17. Ibid., 14.

18. Squier, "Certain Archaeological Features," 30–31.

19. Thomas Biolsi and Larry Zimmerman, eds., introduction to *Indians and Anthropologists: Vine Deloria Jr. and the Critique of Anthropology* (Tucson: University of Arizona Press, 1997), 11.

20. Vine Deloria Jr., *God Is Red: A Native View of Religion* (1973; repr., Golden, Colo.: Fulcrum, 1992), 13.

21. Squier, "Archaeology," 26.

22. Squier is referring here to the Natchez in particular.

23. Squier requested that if other of his relatives were not buried in this plot, it should be used for paupers. Only his wife was buried with him.

24. William Green informs me that he suggested adding "Scholar," a response to having seen the poorly tended grave in the 1980s (Green to author, 27 October 2003).

25. George H. Squier, "Archaeological Resources of Western Wisconsin," *Wisconsin Archaeologist* 13, no. 3 (October 1914): 128.

26. This is a St. Paul company that does engineering and various kinds of testing for clients in industry and government.

27. Although the site has been on the Wisconsin list of the National Register of Historic Places since 1991, it does not protect them in any way.

28. Norma Van Vleet, village clerk, minutes of regular board meeting, 4 October 1993, office of the Village of Trempealeau.

29. William Green and Roland Rodell, "The Mississippian Presence and Cahokia Interaction at Trempealeau, Wisconsin," *American Antiquity* 59, no. 2 (1994): 341.

30. Jim Gallagher, interview by author, 4 September 2001.

31. Jim Stull, interview by author, telephone, 25 July 2001.

32. Minutes of the Platform Mound Committee, 30 June 1994, office of the Village of Trempealeau.

33. Harold Wilber, interview by author, 30 July 2001.

34. Ibid.

35. Roland Rodell, interview by author, 4 September 2001.

36. Others recall that she was adamant in her opposition to the platform project, though in her conversations with me Funmaker tended to play down her role and her concern.

37. Roland Rodell to author, 14 January 2003.

38. Suzan Shown Harjo, "Fighting Name-Calling: Challenging 'Redskins' in Court," in *Team Spirits: The Native American Mascots Controversy* (Lincoln: University of Nebraska Press, 2001), 190. *The Oxford English Dictionary* does not mention this specific use of the term *redskin*. The *OED* defines the term as "Native American" more generally and lists the first usage as 1699 by S. Smith: "Ye first Meetings House was solid mayde to withstande ye wicked onsaults of ye Red Skins."

39. C. Richard King and Charles Fruehling Springwood, eds., "Imagined Indians, Social Identities, and Activism," in *Team Spirits: The Native American Mascots Controversy* (Lincoln: University of Nebraska Press, 2001), 4–5.

40. The district stopped using the Indian profile on its stationery in 2002.

41. Phil Lamke, letter to the editor, *Galesville (Wisc.) Republican,* 20 July 2000, p. 2.

42. Roy Suttie, letter to the editor, *Galesville (Wisc.) Republican,* 16 November 2000, p. 2.

43. George Christiansen, letter to the editor, *Galesville (Wisc.) Republican,* 24 August 2000, p. 2.

44. Suzy Fonfara, letter to the editor, *Galesville (Wisc.) Republican,* 10 August 2000, p. 3.

45. Christiansen, letter to the editor, 2.

46. Decorah was a Ho-Chunk leader of French background; I discuss him further in chapter 8 of part III. His name is spelled variously; I preserve the variant spellings used by my sources.

47. Fonfara, letter to the editor, 3.

48. Ibid.

49. Ibid.

50. Ibid.

51. "Logo, Grad Test Dominate Board Meeting," *Galesville (Wisc.) Republican,* 17 August 2000, p. 1.

52. Jay Rosenstein, *In Whose Honor? American Indian Mascots in Sports,* VHS, 46 min., New Day Films: Ho-Ho-kus, N. J., 1996. It was shown on PBS's news show *P.O.V.* in 1997 and circulates widely on video. For more on this documentary and the debate at the University of Illinois, see Carol Spindel, *Dancing at Halftime: Sports and the Controversy over American Indian Mascots* (New York: New York University Press, 2000).

53. Lofgren, letter to the editor, *Galesville (Wisc.) Republican,* 3 August 2000, p. 2.

54. Ibid.

55. Fonfara, letter to the editor, 3.

56. Lofgren, letter to the editor.

57. Bruce Lehman, letter to the editor, *Galesville (Wisc.) Republican,* 14 September 2000, p. 3.

58. Ibid., 3, 12.

59. For more on the Ojibwa/Chippewa fight for fishing rights, see Donald L. Fixico, "Chippewa Fishing and Hunting Rights in the Great Lakes," in *The Invasion of Indian Country in the Twentieth Century: American Capitalism and Tribal Natural Resources* (Niwot: University Press

of Colorado, 1998), 103–22, and Rick Waley, *Walleye Warriors: An Effective Alliance against Racism and for the Earth* (Philadelphia: New Society, 1994).

60. These bumper stickers are cited in Fixico, "Chippewa Fishing and Hunting Rights," 117.

61. Lehman, letter to the editor, 12.

62. Ibid., 3.

63. Christiansen, letter to the editor, 2.

64. In particular, the Trademark Trial and Appeal Board of the U.S. Patent Office found that the name Redskins is offensive and thus not protected by federal trademark laws. For an account of this case, see Harjo, "Fighting Name-Calling," 189–207. Similarly, in 1972 Russell Means initiated a lawsuit against the Cleveland Indians alleging slander, libel, and defamation. See Ellen J. Staurowsky, "Sockalexis and the Making of the Myth at the Core of Cleveland's 'Indian' Image," in King and Springwood, *Team Spirits*, 83.

65. Of course, Kansas is the name of a Native American tribe. The Chiefs have maintained the arrowhead as part of their logo.

66. Howard Hare, letter to the editor, *Galesville (Wisc.) Republican*, 24 August 2000, p. 3.

67. Ibid.

68. William Crogan, letter to the editor, *Galesville (Wisc.) Republican*, 20 July 2000, p. 3.

69. Hare, letter to the editor.

70. Suttie, letter to the editor.

71. Penny Bonnar, "Logo/nickname Debate Continues," *Galesville (Wisc.) Republican*, September 14, 2000, p. 1.

72. Lofgren, letter to the editor.

73. U.S. Commission on Civil Rights, "Statement . . . on the Use of Native American Images and Nicknames as Sports Symbols," 13 April 2001, available at http://aistm.org/2001usccr.htm (July 7, 2005).

74. This story was told to me by Karen and Gus Vogel.

75. W. G. Sebald, "A Natural History of Destruction," trans. Anthea Bell, *New Yorker*, 4 November 2002, pp. 68–69.

76. La Crosse is, of course, a French name for an Indian game.

77. The name is cited in Pierce, "Explorers at Trempealeau Mountain," in *History of Trempealeau County* (see note 12), 52.

78. Richard A. Grounds, "Tallahassee, Osceola, and the Hermeneutics of American Place-Names," *Journal of the American Academy of Religion* 69, no. 2 (June 2001): 297.

79. This 1856 version of the poem enjoyed popularity throughout the nineteenth century; Richard Grounds also reprints parts of it in his essay.

80. Katherine Fitzgerald, "The Platteville Papers: Inscribing Frontier Ideology and Culture in a Nineteenth-Century Writing Assignment," *College English* 64, no. 3 (January 2002): 282.

81. Grounds, "Tallahassee, Osceola," 302.

82. Grounds also discusses the "redundant use" of American heroes' names for places in "Tallahassee, Osceola," 293.

83. Ibid., 299.

84. This is from Gale's unpublished papers at the Wisconsin Historical Society and is cited in Edwin C. Bailey, *The Past and Present of Winneshiek County: A Record of Settlement, Organization, Progress and Achievement* (Chicago: S.J. Clarke, 1913), 24.

85. Vine Deloria Jr., "Indians Today, the Real and the Unreal," *Custer Died for Your Sins* (Norman: University of Oklahoma Press, 1988), 3.

86. *Arrowhead,* 1916, p. 43. Emmons is listed as "a Massachusetts schoolgirl," though there are Emmons living in the area now.

87. Grounds, "Tallahassee, Osceola," 299.

88. *Arrowhead,* 1916, p. 44.

89. Ibid., 1928, p. 74.

90. Ibid.

91. Grounds, "Tallahassee, Osceola," 302.

92. Bert Gipple, "The Burial of Maninuka 42 Years Ago," *Galesville (Wisc.) Republican,* dated by hand as 1926, in an archive on local history, Galesville Public Library.

93. Ibid.

94. This seems to have been written in 1911, reprinted in 1941 in the *Galesville (Wisc.) Republican,* and reproduced in "The Midnight Burial of Princess Marinuka," *(Melrose, Wisc.) Chronicle,* 5 September 2001, p. 19.

95. "The Midnight Burial."

96. From a newspaper article titled "Lake Marinuka," undated but probably 1926, in the *Galesville (Wisc.) Republican,* archived in a file at the Galesville Library.

97. "The Midnight Burial."

98. Michael Lesy's *Wisconsin Death Trip* (New York: Pantheon, 1973) suggests how very present death and dead bodies were for Wisconsin's citizens in the 1890s. Lesy excerpts newspaper accounts from around Wisconsin in the 1890s that suggest the familiarity citizens had with death, murder, violence, suicide, and arson. Included in the volume are photographs

of the dead dressed for their own funerals taken by a photographer working in Black River Falls.

99. "The Midnight Burial."

100. Reprinted in "The Midnight Burial."

101. "Princess Marinuka Now Rests in a Tomb of Concrete on the Original Burial Spot at Arctic Springs," undated clipping, probably from the *Galesville (Wisc.) Republican* in 1926. I found the clipping in an archive on local history at the Galesville Public Library.

102. Reprinted in "The Midnight Burial."

103. Charles Freeman writes: "Years afterward [after Freeman's childhood encounter with Chief Decorah himself, that is], on motion of Captain Arnold, the village board confirmed the name "Marinuka", which I gave the lake we rowed across that October night, so many years ago." This is quoted in "The Midnight Burial." It is not clear when this was written.

104. This fraternal organization was originally known as the Sons of Liberty; they were the men who dressed up as Mohawk Indians for the Boston Tea Party. Founded in 1765, the Order of Redmen (now the Improved Order of Red Men) claims to have fashioned itself after the Iroquois Nation and, according to its website, is presently "devoted to inspiring a greater love for the United States of America and the principles of American Liberty" (www.redmen.org).

105. Earl Chapin, "The Princess of the Lake," *Sunday, Roto Magazine* of the *St. Paul Pioneer Press*, 17 July 1957, n.p.

106. See also Grounds's discussion of Osceola's skull, "Tallahassee, Osceola," 313–16. After his capture and death in Florida in 1838, Osceola's head was removed by Dr. Frederick Weedon. The decapitating physician displayed the head and even used it to punish his children by hanging it on a bedpost in the room where they slept (314).

107. Henry David Thoreau, *A Week on the Concord and Merrimack Rivers*, ed. Carl Hovde, William L. Howarth, and Elizabeth Hall Witherell (Princeton, N.J.: Princeton University Press, 1980), p. 53.

108. Ibid., 316–17.

109. "The Midnight Burial."

110. *Galesville (Wisc.) Republican,* 1 November 1956, p. 1. This is the first use that I can find of the nickname Redmen in the *Republican.* The Galesville and Ettrick school districts consolidated during this period.

111. Years later, my friend's father donated the artifacts to Carson-Newman College. An attempt was recently made to repatriate the bones, but the college could not locate them.

112. "The Ho-Chunk Nation—A Brief History," *Ho-Chunk Nation,* http://ho-chunknation.com/History.htm (5 July 2005).

113. For a more complete account of the movements in this period, see Gary Clayton Anderson's *Kinsmen of Another Kind: Dakota-White Relations in the Upper Mississippi Valley, 1650–1862* (St. Paul: Minnesota Historical Society Press, 1984).

114. Perrot's account appears in Emma Blair, ed. and trans., *The Indian Tribes of the Upper Mississippi Valley and Region of the Great Lakes* (1911; repr., Lincoln: University of Nebraska Press, 1996), James Clifford has argued for thinking of cultures not as fixed to places but as sites traversed, sites of traveling-in-dwelling and dwelling-in-traveling. See Clifford, "Traveling Cultures," in Lawrence Grossberg et al., eds., *Cultural Studies* (New York: Routledge, 1992), 108.

115. These categories are described by Philip Weeks, *Farewell My Nation: The American Indian and the United States, 1820–1890* (Arlington Heights, Ill.: H. Davidson, 1990), 10–11. In the 1930s the policy of assimilation was abandoned into favor of a policy of self-determination under John Collier, commissioner of Indian Affairs.

116. Brenda J. Child, "Boarding Schools," in Frederick E. Hoxie, ed., *Encyclopedia of North American Indians* (Boston: Houghton Mifflin, 1996), 78.

117. J. O. Dorsey and Cyrus Thomas, *Handbook of American Indians,* cited in Blair, *The Indian Tribes of the Upper Mississippi Valley,* 1:367n239.

118. Marlita A. Reddy, ed., *Statistical Record of Native North Americans* (Detroit: Gale Research, 1993), cited by Lance Foster, "Some Twentieth-century Tribal Statistics," *Baxoje, the Ioway Nation,* http://ioway.nativeweb .org/history/20thcstats.htm (7 July 2005).

119. Kelly, "1990 Census Breakdown of Ioway Tribal Members per State," *Baxoje, the Ioway Nation,* http://ioway.nativeweb.org/history/1990 perstate.htm (12 July 2005).

120. Mark Wyman, *The Wisconsin Frontier* (Bloomington: Indiana University Press, 1998), 160.

121. Quoted in Susan Lampert Smith, "Ho-Chunk Stubbornness—They Survived Because of It," *Wisconsin State Journal,* 15 March 1998, p. 1A.

122. Wyman, *The Wisconsin Frontier,* 170.

123. Ibid., 161.

124. Quoted in Smith, "Ho-Chunk Stubbornness."

125. John T. DeLaRonde, "Personal Narrative," in State Historical Society of Wisconsin, *Annual Report and Collections of the State Historical Society of Wisconsin for the Year 1876* (Madison: The Society, 1876), 7:345–65.

I am indebted to Susan Lampert Smith's article for pointing out this account.

126. Ibid., 363.

127. Ibid.

128. Ibid.

129. Pierce, "Reign of the Indians," in *History of Trempealeau County* (see note 12), 41–42.

130. In 1912 Grignon and Squier did some excavations on the presumed site of Perrot Post. See George H. Squier's "Archaeological Sketch," in "Remains of a French Post near Trempealeau," in *Proceedings of the . . . Annual Meeting of the State Historical Society of Wisconsin* (Madison: The Society, 1915), 113.

131. Eben Douglas Pierce, ed., "Recollections of Antoine Grignon," in *Proceedings of the . . . Annual Meeting of the State Historical Society of Wisconsin* (Madison: The Society, 1914), 110–36.

132. Ibid., 119.

133. Smith, "Ho-Chunk Stubbornness."

134. Blair, appendix C, *The Indian Tribes of the Upper Mississippi*, 2:289.

135. See "The Ho-Chunk Nation—A Brief History."

136. Smith, "Ho-Chunk Stubbornness."

137. Ibid.

138. Pierce, "Reign of the Indians" (see note 12), 42.

139. Andrew Jackson, "Indians Should be Removed to the West" (1829), in Bruno Leone, ed., *Native Americans: Opposing Viewpoints* (San Diego: Greenhaven, 1998), 95.

140. Pierce, "Reign of the Indians" (see note 12), 42–43.

141. Blair notes that the number of enrolled Winnebago in Wisconsin was 1,500 in 1887 and 1,180 in 1907, while in Nebraska in 1907 the population was 2,613 (*The Indian Tribes of the Upper Mississippi Valley*, 1:289n299).

142. Smith, "Ho-Chunk Stubbornness."

143. Anna Funmaker, interview by author, 4 September 2001.

144. Cynthya Porter, "Fountain City—part 2," *Winona (Minn.) Post*, 11 August 2002.

145. According to my uncle Clyde, wheeled scrapers are shovel-like tools for digging up dirt; they are pulled by horses and steered by a driver. Putting wheels on these contraptions made them easier for the driver to handle.

146. Wilber interview. The rest of the section is also based on the Wilber interview.

147. William Green informs me that the editor may indeed have a point. Eighteenth-century manuscripts were generally low-acid rag paper while early twentieth-century newspapers used high-acid pulp and thus tended to disintegrate more quickly (Green to author).

148. Quoted in Green and Rodell, "The Mississippian Presence," 338.

149. When I related this story to William Green, a former archaeologist for the historic preservation division of the Wisconsin State Historical Society, he said that he doubted that finding an arrowhead would cause any job to stop for three days.

Part IV. Backfill

1. Roland Rodell to author, e-mail, 6 February 2001.

2. Sherman Alexie, "Powwow," *The Business of Fancydancing: Stories and Poems* (New York: Hanging Loose Press, 1992), 52.

3. Robert DesJarlait, "The Contest Powwow Versus the Traditional Powwow and the Role of the Native American Community," *Wicazo Sa Review,* Spring 1997, p. 117.

4. Archaeological Conservancy, "Why Save Archaeological Sites?" http://www.americanarchaeology.com/aaabout.html#anchor893832 (July 2002).

5. Anna Funmaker, interview by author, 4 September 2001.

6. Roland Rodell, interview by author, telephone, 23 May 2003.

7. John Ebersold, interview by author, telephone, 26 May 2003.

8. Pam Grover, interview by author, telephone, 2 June 2003.

9. See Mircea Eliade, "Sacred Space and Making the World Sacred," in *The Sacred and the Profane: The Nature of Religion* (New York: Harcourt, Brace, 1957).

10. Joe Watkins, *Indigenous Archaeology: American Indian Values and Scientific Practice* (Walnut Creek, Calif.: AltaMira Press, 2000), 10.

11. Such a practice is not without corollaries. In ancient times the Dutch built mounds to escape high water.

12. Walker Percy, "The Loss of the Creature," *The Message in the Bottle: How Queer Man Is, How Queer Language Is, and What One Has to Do with the Other* (New York: Farrar, Straus and Giroux, 1975), 62.

13. Tom Waits, "San Diego Serenade," *Heart of Saturday Night,* Asylum, 7E-1015, 1974.

14. "Bill" is a pseudonym.

Wisconsin Land and Life

A Thousand Pieces of Paradise: Landscape and Property in the Kickapoo Valley
Lynne Heasley

A Mind of Her Own: Helen Connor Laird and Family, 1888–1982
Helen L. Laird

Buried Indians: Digging Up the Past in a Midwestern Town
Laurie Hovell McMillin

Wisconsin Land and Life: A Portrait of the State
Edited by Robert C. Ostergren and Thomas R. Vale

DATE DUE

JA 17 0		
MY 05		
SE 03		
SE 24		
OC 01		